THE GLORIOUS NEW-C(

In 2 Corinthian 3:7-18, Paul argues that covenant, having fulfilled and abolis... ... ..., ... believers, having glory now, increasing glory and, in eternity, absolute glory, are ministers of this glorious new covenant. In 2 Corinthians 4:1-6, the apostle sets this out: by means of this ministry, God saves sinners from their sin, their Satanic blindness and their bondage, and brings them into the glorious liberty of the sons of God, justifying, sanctifying and glorifying them.

By expounding 2 Corinthians 3:7 – 4:6, David Gay works all this out in detail, making constant application to *every* believer today.

All books
by David H.J.Gay
are available on
Amazon Books and Kindle

Free Mobi and Epub downloads
are available in 'Links' at
David H J Gay Ministry (sermonaudio.com)

Free pdf downloads
are available on
archive.org and openlibrary.org

The
Glorious
New-Covenant
Ministry

Its Basis and Practice

David H.J.Gay

BRACHUS

BRACHUS 2014
davidhjgay@googlemail.com

Scripture quotations, unless otherwise stated,
are from the New International Version

Contents

Introduction

Are you a Christian? That is, has God's Spirit brought you to repent of your sin, and to rest in Christ, trusting him, and him only, relying upon his precious blood, shed upon the cross, to cleanse you from your sin and to present you faultless before God his Father? Are you submitting to Christ as Lord? You are a Christian – in these terms? Excellent! It is with you in mind that I have written this book.

Let me tell you what you will find in the following pages. I have taken 2 Corinthians 3:1 – 4:6, expounding and applying it to us as believers today. A question at once suggests itself: Why did Paul, when writing to the Corinthians – who, almost certainly, were mostly Gentiles – say so much about the law of God, given to Israel through Moses on Sinai? A most interesting question! The answer is more than interesting. It is highly significant!

As with the author of any book, Paul had a background and an agenda, the two being intimately connected. He wrote for a reason. Once we have determined both the background and the agenda which drove the apostle to write as he did, we shall then be able to apply his teaching to ourselves.

The Corinthian church – in common with many other New Testament churches – was being attacked by false teachers, men who are usually called 'Judaisers'. Their virulent attack, which was widespread in those early days of the gospel, centred on the law. Paul wrote to the Corinthians in order to confront the Judaisers and their teaching, to challenge their ministry and thwart their aim. Indeed, that is why he wrote to so many New Testament churches on the law. Furthermore, he did this because he wanted to instruct believers in order to protect them from error, and to bring them into the fullest possible enjoyment of all their privileges in Christ. He wanted them to enjoy Christ. Paul was adamant: believers, having been redeemed by the Lord Jesus Christ from bondage, should not allow themselves to be taken under the law, and so be enslaved all over again. Moreover, he wanted to put backbone into them, nerving them for the task which Christ had given them along with all other believers; namely, that of preaching the gospel to all mankind, seeking their everlasting salvation.

That was the apostle's agenda.

What about me and this book? Do I have a background? Do I have an agenda? If not, then it can only be that I am writing as a detached academic (which I am far from being), or else an antiquarian, entirely taken up with events that took place 2000 years ago, events which have no practical relevance to us and the situation in which we find ourselves today.

Nothing could be further from my mind! The very point of Scripture is that while it certainly deals with specific issues relevant to the age in which it was written, the principles it sets out are relevant for all time and all circumstances. Moreover, it is the job of every believer to find that relevance and drive it home – to himself first of all, and then to others. And as a preacher and teacher among God's people, what other purpose should I have than to expound Scripture and apply it to us today? I am most decidedly of William Perkins' mind – Perkins was an early English Puritan – when he asked of the preaching of Scripture: 'What's the use of it?' Perkins, I hasten to add, was not questioning the value of expounding Scripture. No! What he was after was this: when you have expounded the text of Scripture, then you must apply it. If you don't, it's a waste of time – expounding Scripture as some kind of algebraic exercise for its own sake, rather like code-breaking or solving a crossword puzzle for the fun of it – detached and distant, virtually unrelated to daily life and experience. I know of no more pertinent comment that could be made about a great deal of contemporary preaching – but, in this book, I must not let myself be drawn down that road!

So who are the 'Judaisers' today? Well, there's no shortage of them, I assure you.

First of all, there are those who argue we must go back to the law, full stop – feasts, sabbath... the lot! If we don't – no salvation! That's one sort of contemporary Judaiser; virtually a direct copy of the very thing Paul confronted. But it doesn't stop there. While the following are not, strictly speaking, Judaisers, nevertheless, the principles Paul sets out certainly apply to them.

So who am I talking about? The Reformed, I am sorry to say, following John Calvin, are heavy on the law, arguing that we must preach the law in order to 'prepare' sinners for Christ, to get them 'fit' to repent and believe.[1] And they then go on to claim that when sinners have been made 'fit' and brought to faith, in order to get them sanctified – which sanctification, undeniably, is a biblical requirement for believers – they must have the law preached to them all over again. On both counts, the Reformed are quite wrong. The New Testament does not support either 'preparationism' or 'sanctification by the law'. Such preachers are, in my terms, 'legal preachers', and they certainly form part of the background to what I say here. Indeed, this more 'subdued' law preaching can be even more dangerous than the overt variety.

Moreover, Rome continues to advocate the law – in the sense of works and sacraments[2] – for justification and sanctification (which it wrongly conflates). Since all roads lead to Rome, it seems to me that it is hardly possible to write any book for contemporary believers without making reference to the ever-present threat posed by Romanising doctrine and practice. Rome certainly forms part of the background to what I say here. Often hidden and subtle this Romeward trend might be, but it's there, all the same, just below the surface.

And then there are those evangelicals who, without formulating any system, have, all too often, fallen into some sort of 'legal preaching'. Whatever am I talking about? Take the number of men and women who can best be described as mere attenders at preaching services – men and women who have been attending in this way for years, and who have conformed to certain specified evangelical rules and norms, but who as yet are unconverted – who, even so, are made to feel perfectly at home![3] What is more, alongside this, I fear that many saints simply do not realise that they

---

[1] See my *Christ* as to why Gal. 3:24 does *not* support this idea.
[2] I let the objectionable (completely unscriptural) word stand throughout this book.
[3] Solomon Stoddard, grandfather of Jonathan Edwards, pushed this inclusivism so far as to call the Lord's supper 'a converting ordinance', thus building a bridge with another aspect of the background to my book – the elevation of baptism and the Lord's supper to an unscriptural position.

are being fed this diet of 'legal preaching' which looks for nothing more than outward conformity, often to man-made rules, as the touchstone of all sanctification, and the sure definition and guarantee of it. 'Recipe preaching' I call it: 'do this; don't do that; tick the boxes; keep attending; behold: sanctification'! In other words, preaching and practicing religion and morality – rather than the law of Christ. All this, too, plays its part in the background to this volume.

Then, of course, we have those who overtly preach salvation by works. (I include those who preach salvation by sacraments). Now don't run away with the idea that I'm talking about Rome again. I am. But, sad to say, sacramentalism and sacerdotalism have spread their tentacles far wider than Rome. *Sacramentalists* believe that spiritual grace is conveyed (or made effective) by an outward act. For instance, they believe that when water is applied to someone, something spiritual and inward happens to that person; that person receives grace, is regenerated, or whatever. Again, sacramentalists believe that by eating bread and drinking wine they receive the actual body and blood of Christ. And so on. *Sacerdotalists* believe that certain men have the ability, the gift, the power and the right to carry out the actions in question, and thereby convey the grace, the gift, or whatever, inherent in those actions. Naturally, therefore, sacerdotalists happily delegate vital parts of their religion – even their spiritual life (and their eternity?) – into the hands of these men, who, they believe, because they have been consecrated or ordained, are better able, more qualified, to carry it out for them. In such a system, worship and spiritual service is a specialised task best left to a special class – priests – who do it on behalf of the rest. Hence arose (1800 years ago) the unbiblical notion of the clergy and the laity – with all its attendant and well-documented curses of priestcraft. And all this, like law preaching, can be incipient as much as overt. Again, as before, in their more 'subdued' forms, they are even more dangerous than in their overt. And there is no shortage of either!

The Church of England Prayer Book is explicit: when the priest sprinkles the child he declares: 'Seeing now that this child is regenerate...'.[4] But it doesn't stop there! Not a few Presbyterians are consistent, and go the whole hog and hold to baptismal regeneration, cogently arguing that they can cite Calvin and the Westminster Confession in support. Among the Baptists, too, regeneration by immersion is making its presence increasingly felt.[5] Moreover, in addition to the notion of infant baptism, sacramentalism and sacerdotalism are never far away from (they are intrinsic to) the concepts of church hierarchy and clergy. All such thinking is maintained by a heavy dependence on the old covenant, the law,[6] and are demolished by a clear understanding of the teaching of the principles of the new covenant.

One good test of all this lies ready at hand. Answer this question: You are sure you are right with God? On what grounds? Does Jesus figure in your answer? No? Then you are caught in my net. Does Jesus feature in your answer, but with an 'and'? Is it 'Jesus and...'? I don't care what comes after the 'and'; you too are caught in the net. There is no 'and' – not baptism,[7] the Lord's supper, prayers, tears, feelings, rites, laws, observances, works, merits, traditions, parental connections, chapel going, attendance at services... It is Jesus and Jesus only; Jesus crucified; Jesus raised; Jesus coming again; Jesus only!

I would not be misunderstood: I am not for a moment suggesting that by parroting the words, 'Jesus... Jesus... Jesus', all is well. Far from it. The words are only vehicles: Jesus must be all in the mind and heart and will and life. If he is not, if we rely on slogans, this declaration by Christ will come to haunt us: 'Not everyone who says to me: "Lord, Lord", will enter the kingdom of

---

[4] The 1979 version has: 'We thank you, Father, for the water of baptism. In it we are buried with Christ in his death. By it we share in his resurrection. Through it we are reborn by the Holy Spirit' (bookofcommonprayer.net).

[5] To save repeating what I have said elsewhere on the arguments that undergird this book, please see my previous works. The titles should tell you which one to refer to at any particular point.

[6] Not only do Romanists, Anglicans and Presbyterians overtly go to the old covenant for their doctrine and practice: Charismatics do. Many others do it unknowingly.

[7] As for Mark 16:15-16, read both clauses together. Immersion is not essential to salvation, but it is essential for all believers, in obedience to Christ. The rest of the New Testament puts this beyond all doubt.

heaven, but only he who does the will of my Father who is in heaven' (Matt. 7:21).

All systems – law, works, rites, ceremonies, sacraments – anything and everything but 'Jesus only' – come under my definition of 'legal preaching', and form the background to what I say here. Such systems are, as I see it, the proper equivalent of that which drove Paul to write to Corinth – and Galatia, Rome, Philippi, Colosse, and so on – and moved the writer of Hebrews to set out his treatise. I believe the regimes I have just spelled out are rightly covered and dealt with by the apostolic declaration on Christ's redemption of his people from the law.[8]

With this in mind, I am convinced, therefore, that 2 Corinthians 3:1 – 4:6 has a great deal to say to today's churches, and what it has to say is of vital importance. We desperately need to recover the culture, the outlook, the ethos that Paul set out so powerfully in these verses; namely, the 'ministry' of the new covenant.

So while I want to be positive in this work, that's the background to it. The agenda? Well, do I need to spell it out? If I do I must have failed even before I start. But just in case it needs spelling out, let me say what I am looking for.

In writing this book, I want to do what I can to set out biblical instruction to us as believers, not only in order to protect us from error, but to bring us into the fullest possible enjoyment of all our privileges in Christ in the gospel. I fear that too many of us live at a level far below the spirituality of the New Testament. I want to obey Peter's injunction, and 'grow in the grace and knowledge of our Lord and Saviour Jesus Christ', and so bring 'him [Christ]... glory both now and for ever!' (2 Pet. 3:18). I want that for myself. I want to enjoy Christ, and I want my fellow-believers to enjoy him too. I want us all to exult in the liberty that Christ has wrought for us, the sheer joy of being members of the new covenant. I want us to magnify Christ. I see these things written large across the New Testament: the early believers suffered grievously for their faith,

---

[8] I challenge all law preachers to tackle chapters such as Rom. 6 – 8; Gal. 2 – 6; Phil. 3; Heb. 7 – 10 – not proof-texts – and establish their case without recourse to medieval glosses (moral, ceremonial and judicial law); in other words, to establish their case by material available to the apostles, *and used by them, and set out by them*.

and yet they enjoyed a sense of exuberant assurance, liberty and confidence, and a level of spirituality, that is all too evident by its absence today.

In short, I want to play my part to the fullest possible extent in the new-covenant priesthood of all believers, and I hope the same for you, reader. For this 'priesthood' truly is a glorious ministry, and I want us all, as believers, to play our full part in it. That is why I have written this book.

Let me pause for a moment to say a little more about this 'ministry'. And it is necessary.

First, although 'ministry' has come to mean the occupation of certain believers, and what these believers do, especially in a pulpit, or elsewhere, in carrying out their duties as church officers, this is a gross imposition on Scripture, and one of the dire consequences of 1800 years of Christendom. 'Ministry', of course, can mean 'preaching' and 'teaching' in the usual understanding of those words, but it also includes 'preaching' and 'teaching' in a much wider sense – in conversation, in writing, and more. What is more, 'ministry' goes far wider than preaching; it includes worship (and this includes far, far more than 'meetings' in a meeting house), service, self-denial, and so on. Having said that, in this book, I concentrate mostly on the 'preaching' (not excluding 'teaching') aspect – not that the others are unimportant – but because 'preaching' clearly is the thrust of the passage we are looking at.

Secondly, I must emphasise that 'ministry', in New Testament terms, is not confined to a few believers. *Every* believer (including every believing *woman*) is a minister of the new covenant.

Both these points are vital, and I will return to them. Many preachers and commentators – as far as I can judge, the overwhelming majority of them – simply assume that Paul was speaking solely about 'pulpit work', and that confined to a few select individuals. This is quite wrong. It puts an unbiblical weight on a few men, gives them an unbearable burden, grants them an unwarranted kudos, cuts off the overwhelming majority of believers from their rightful ministry, and so deprives them, the church at large, and unbelievers into the bargain, of untold blessing. As a matter of urgency, we need to return to New Testament thinking on this 'new-covenant ministry of all believers'.

Let me start with assurance. How urgently we need to get back to the New Testament in this area! What a difference there is between the average believer today, and the believers of the New Testament, when it comes to assurance. Take sanctification. How urgently we need to get back to the New Testament in *this* area. Speaking for myself, I have had more than enough of bondage in my Christian experience: bondage to mere conformity, and sanctification based on fear. I want to be sanctified – Robert Murray M'Cheyne prayed that God would make him as holy as a pardoned sinner can be made – but I want to be truly sanctified, sanctified as defined by the New Testament, and in the way set out in the New Testament; that is, out of love: God's love to me – the sense of it – moving me to serve and obey him in his commands under the law of Christ out of love in return. I want my spiritual life to be a matter of the heart. And in writing this book, I want this for as many believers as possible. I want us to get back to the new covenant! John Colwell:

The promise of the gospel is that, through the sheer grace of God, we [believers] are now included in the sonship of the Son before the Father; we are defined unequivocally by mercy, unequivocally by love. But the promise of the gospel is also that, in anticipation of the final resurrection... we can live here and now in the power of the Spirit. The Spirit who indwelt and empowered Jesus is the same Spirit who is promised, here and now, to the Christian. According to... Romans, it is this promise of the Spirit, which itself is a consequence of all that has been achieved in the humanity of Christ, that distinguishes the Christian from those who... sought to obey the law... in the Old Testament. God has now achieved that which 'the law was powerless to do'; the 'righteous requirements of the law' can now be 'fully met' in those who live 'according to the Spirit'... (Rom. 8). The command of the gospel, then, does not come to us without, at the same time, promising the impartation of the ability to fulfil it: the command of the gospel is simultaneously the promise of the Spirit... Through the Spirit's indwelling, our lives can become an echo of the perfect obedience of Christ.[9]

Furthermore, I am convinced that 2 Corinthians 3:1 – 4:6 has a great deal to say about the way we should approach sinners, unbelievers, with the gospel. Naturally! If I'm right, and if this

---

[9] John Colwell: *Living the Christian Story...*, T. & T.Clark Ltd., Edinburgh, 2001 pp133-134 (Google Books).

passage talks about the glorious ministry of the new covenant, it must have an enormous bearing on the way we address unbelievers. I am convinced that this is another area that needs radical reformation today. We need to return to the biblical *freeness* of the preaching of the gospel. Too often sinners have been approached with 'legal preaching'. I hope that what I write here will do something to encourage real 'gospel preaching'. Sinners need it! And so do saints. For the same gospel which is saving to sinners is edifying to saints. This is one of the glories of the new-covenant ministry.

Reader, we stand desperately in need of recovering this new-covenant ministry. Too often we find a potent mixture: legal gospel, legal assurance, legal sanctification and lax discipline. I hope I have said enough already to encourage you to read on. I believe this passage raises several vital matters to which we need to give serious thought in these trying days.

Furthermore, I believe that we in the west are in a time of judgement. I recognise, of course, that some – perhaps many – will disagree with me about this. From where they are sitting, nothing could be further from the truth: spiritually speaking, they are in a thriving time, with conversions among sinners and spiritual growth among believers. If so, it can only be that they are enjoying all that is set out by Paul in my chosen passage, and although I will be telling them nothing that they do not know, I hope they will feel further encouraged by what I say. I also hope that they are not so occupied with their own success, and, maybe, a triumphalist prophetic view, that they are beginning to forget that there is a vast number of sinners who are yet to be reached with the gospel. And in that regard, they must keep in mind the power of those bent on stopping us in that task. I further hope that they will pray that their blessing might reach the rest of us who – for whatever reason – feel at times as though we are left forlorn, lying like Thames barges on the mud flats beyond the reach of the tide. For we need reviving!

I am of this hymn writer's mind:

Saviour, visit thy plantation,
Grant us, Lord, a gracious rain!
All will come to desolation,
Unless thou return again.
Lord, revive us,
All our help must come from thee!

Surely, once thy garden flourished,
Every part looked bright and green;
Then thy word our spirits nourished,
Happy seasons we have seen.
Lord, revive us,
All our help must come from thee!

But a drought has since succeeded,
And a sad decline we see;
Lord, thy help is greatly needed,
Help can only come from thee.
Lord, revive us,
All our help must come from thee!

Dearest Saviour, hasten thither,
Thou canst make us bloom again;
Oh, permit us not to wither,
None can hope in thee in vain.
Lord, revive us,
All our help must come from thee!

Break the tempter's fatal power,
Turn each stony heart to flesh;
And begin, from this good hour,
To revive thy work afresh.
Lord, revive us,
All our help must come from thee![10]

But it is not enough to pray for revival – and stop there. Sadly, faced, as we are, by a two-pronged opposition – the one, apathetic; the other, growing confident in outright hostility and attack – the majority of evangelical (I include Reformed) churches seem to adopt one of two basic courses.

---

[10] The hymn was written by John Newton but I think this version has been altered by John Ryland.

One course is that taken by those churches which think they should take both the method of approach and the substance of the 'message' – and adapt them to the culture of the age, and, thereby, enjoy huge 'success'. Rather like the Labour party in the UK in the 1990s, which, desperate for power, instigated a series of 'ask the people' meetings, presumably willing, if they found a consensus of popular measures, to adopt them in hope of winning the election, such churches are prepared to give the people what they want (as opposed to what they need), adulterating, diluting, watering down the 'message', or disguising it, in an effort to make the gospel palatable to fallen man and his culture. By appeasing the opposition, they hope to 'win' them.

The other approach seems to be that adopted by churches which hunker down, retreat into a ghetto – a 'being faithful' mentality – to await the return of Christ. Meanwhile, they peter out of existence: 'Where there is no vision, the people perish' (Prov. 29:18, AV).[11] A non-growing church is a dying church. And growth needs to be in the spirituality of the members before, and then alongside, growth in numbers *through conversions*. Sadly, some churches seem to feel this is beyond them, and the best they can do is to maintain the faith until they die. While maintaining the faith is commendable (2 Tim. 4:6-8), we must see conversions. Surely Rachel's *angst* must be ours, spiritually speaking: 'Give me children, or I'll die!' (Gen. 30:1).

Both approaches – compromise and retreat – are wrong. As to the latter course, for a start, we must not – as Paul put it – 'lose heart' (2 Cor. 4:1). May I say how this thought has helped me, even as I am writing this? Truth to tell, I was feeling a little down and low about my lack of success, and then it dawned on me – the very piece I was writing, the very scripture I was working on, was rebuking my loss of heart! This encourages me to think that others might be helped. But it is not only a question of losing heart. We must make sure that we really are engaging in 'the new-covenant ministry', and, having got that right, not lose heart in carrying out *this* ministry.

---

[11] There are, I admit, various interpretations of this text.

As to the former course – 'adapting' the 'message' – while I stand by what I said, I nevertheless hasten to add that I fully recognise – indeed, I can do nothing but advocate – that we must be culturally aware, and we must use all legitimate means to make sure we really do 'reach' people, that we really do communicate with them. I take Paul as my example here. I note the way he adapted himself to reach the different congregations throughout Acts. But it all depends on the meaning of 'adapt'. When addressing Jews in the synagogue, or crude pagans, or academic Greek philosophers, or magistrates and kings, large groups or small, he always preached Christ – but he found a way of reaching each different class of hearer. *So must we.*[12] Having said that, however, we must never – never – allow the world, the culture with which we are faced, to call the shots. There's all the difference between being aware of the condition of the people we are dealing with, and allowing our hearers to dominate the method and the 'message'; there's all the difference between the boat being in the water, and the water being in the boat.

As I said, both responses to the culture of the age – compromise and retreat (and retrench) – are wrong. In this book, I appeal for something far more radical; that is, biblical. We need to go back to the old paths, the good way, the way spelled out by Paul in 2 Corinthians 3:1 – 4:6.

This is no new suggestion. God, through Jeremiah, addressed the people of Judah thus:

This is what the LORD says: 'Stand at the crossroads and look; ask for the ancient paths, ask where the good way is, and walk in it, and you will find rest for your souls'.

Our response must not be that of Jeremiah's hearers:

But you said: 'We will not walk in it'. I appointed watchmen over you and said: 'Listen to the sound of the trumpet!' But you said: 'We will not listen'.

If that is our response, we might well have to hear something similar to this from God:

---

[12] See Simon Gay: 'Preaching Christ to a Godless Generation' (*Evangelical Times* July 2013).

'Therefore hear, O nations; observe, O witnesses, what will happen to them. Hear, O earth: I am bringing disaster on this people, the fruit of their schemes, because they have not listened to my words and have rejected my law. What do I care about incense from Sheba or sweet calamus from a distant land? Your burnt offerings are not acceptable; your sacrifices do not please me' (Jer. 6:16-20).

Speaking of us and our time, I am convinced that the old paths, 'the good way' of reaching sinners and edifying saints, is the way marked out by Paul in my chosen passage; namely, the glorious ministry of the new covenant. Paul was faced with a hostile culture; indeed, he was faced with hostile cultures, plural – Jewish and Greek (including Roman), let alone rank pagan. To the Jews, that which the apostle preached was monstrous, a scandal; to the Greeks, it was nonsense, utter madness.[13] But Paul certainly did not allow those cultures either to dampen his spirit or adulterate his approach. You can say that again! Did he complain? Did he apologise? Did he aim to be liked? Did he water down his message? Quite the opposite! In a very real sense, the opposition made him all the bolder. This he made abundantly plain to all. He did not cower and seek a compromise; he showed confidence and offered a challenge. Remember how the apostle opened his first letter to the Corinthians. He certainly came out of his corner fighting:

Christ... [sent] me to preach the gospel – not with words of human wisdom, lest the cross of Christ be emptied of its power. For the message of the cross is foolishness to those who are perishing, but to us who are being saved it is the power of God.

Paul immediately took the fight to the hostile cultures:

---

[13] Anticipating the application to come, the Jewish culture Paul faced is not so very different to the Christendom we face today. I am thinking of the religiosity of many who attend those churches which are caught up in Christendom, churches, to my mind, that are increasingly moving away from the gospel; indeed, I confidently expect their increasing hatred of it. And the Greeks? How about the rise of the atheistic and intellectual constituency in our day? – not forgetting the devotion to the gods of sex and sport.

Introduction

For it is written: 'I will destroy the wisdom of the wise; the intelligence of the intelligent I will frustrate'. Where is the wise man? Where is the scholar? Where is the philosopher of this age?[14]

The apostle moved on at once to God's answer to those cultures:

Has not God made foolish the wisdom of the world? For since in the wisdom of God the world through its wisdom did not know him, God was pleased through the foolishness of what was preached to save those who believe.

The cultures did not like it. Nevertheless, Paul was not in the least repentant:

Jews demand miraculous signs and Greeks look for wisdom, but we preach Christ crucified: a stumbling-block to Jews and foolishness to Gentiles, but to those whom God has called, both Jews and Greeks, Christ the power of God and the wisdom of God. For the foolishness of God is wiser than man's wisdom, and the weakness of God is stronger than man's strength.

The apostle reminded the Corinthians of their experience:

Brothers, think of what you were when you were called. Not many of you were wise by human standards; not many were influential; not many were of noble birth. But God chose the foolish things of the world to shame the wise; God chose the weak things of the world to shame the strong. He chose the lowly things of this world and the despised things – and the things that are not – to nullify the things that are, so that no one may boast before him. It is because of him that you are in Christ Jesus, who has become for us wisdom from God – that is, our righteousness, holiness and redemption. Therefore, as it is written: 'Let him who boasts boast in the Lord'.

Paul then referred to his attitude in coming to Corinth with the gospel:

When I came to you, brothers, I did not come with eloquence or superior wisdom as I proclaimed to you the testimony about God. For I resolved to know nothing while I was with you except Jesus Christ and him crucified. I came to you in weakness and fear, and with much trembling. My message and my preaching were not with wise and

---

[14] Compare the way Christ deliberately provoked the Jews over the sabbath (Luke 6:1-5,6-11; 13:10-17; 14:1-5; John 5:9-10; 7:19-24; 16-18; 9:13-16, for instance).

20

persuasive words, but with a demonstration of the Spirit's power, so that your faith might not rest on men's wisdom, but on God's power.

Yet again, Paul squared up to the hostile culture he had to face:

We do, however, speak a message of wisdom among the mature, but not the wisdom of this age or of the rulers of this age, who are coming to nothing. No, we speak of God's secret wisdom, a wisdom that has been hidden and that God destined for our glory before time began. None of the rulers of this age understood it, for if they had, they would not have crucified the Lord of glory. However, as it is written: 'No eye has seen, no ear has heard, no mind has conceived what God has prepared for those who love him' – but God has revealed it to us by his Spirit. The Spirit searches all things, even the deep things of God. For who among men knows the thoughts of a man except the man's spirit within him? In the same way no one knows the thoughts of God except the Spirit of God. We have not received the spirit of the world but the Spirit who is from God, that we may understand what God has freely given us. This is what we speak, not in words taught us by human wisdom but in words taught by the Spirit, expressing spiritual truths in spiritual words. The man without the Spirit does not accept the things that come from the Spirit of God, for they are foolishness to him, and he cannot understand them, because they are spiritually discerned. The spiritual man makes judgements about all things, but he himself is not subject to any man's judgement: 'For who has known the mind of the Lord that he may instruct him?' But we have the mind of Christ (1 Cor. 1:17 – 2:16).

It's all here: cultural opposition to the gospel, and the demands that culture makes upon the gospel and the preacher; Paul's dismissive attitude towards that culture – he ridicules it, he treats it with contempt; his resolution, determination, not to compromise God's revealed word – he will preach Christ, the crucified Christ, despite the culture; he will not be diverted; indeed, he will confront the culture head-on with the gospel; and so on. And all this, despite the fierce opposition it raised, and worse – the suffering and pain it brought.[15] In short, as everywhere throughout the New Testament, the apostle firmly takes his stance, feet well apart, within the new-covenant ministry. Do not miss his repeated emphasis upon God, his Spirit, his power. Do not miss Paul's conviction that Christ *is*

---

[15] I fail to see how Paul would comprehend – let alone commend – the spirit of the churches today: user-friendly, inclusive, and all that.

all: 'We have the mind of Christ'! The apostle obviously took the medicine he ladled out to the Ephesians:

Be strong in the Lord and in his mighty power. Put on the full armour of God so that you can take your stand against the devil's schemes. For our struggle is not against flesh and blood, but against the rulers, against the authorities, against the powers of this dark world and against the spiritual forces of evil in the heavenly realms. Therefore put on the full armour of God, so that when the day of evil comes, you may be able *to stand* your ground, and after you have done everything, to *stand*. *Stand firm* then, with the belt of truth buckled round your waist, with the breastplate of righteousness in place, and with your feet fitted with the readiness that comes from the gospel of peace. In addition to all this, take up the shield of faith, with which you can extinguish all the flaming arrows of the evil one. Take the helmet of salvation and the sword of the Spirit, which is the word of God. And pray in the Spirit on all occasions with all kinds of prayers and requests. With this in mind, be alert and always keep on praying for all the saints. Pray also for me, that whenever I open my mouth, words may be given me so that I will fearlessly make known the mystery of the gospel, for which I am an ambassador in chains. Pray that I may declare it fearlessly, as I should (Eph. 6:10-20).

Clearly, he wanted to be assertive, confident, not in the least apologetic for the gospel. In fact, I'm sure that assurance and nerve marked his ministry. All this, I am convinced, could not be more relevant to us in our day. I will not stop to press the point further, except to point out than when the early church met persecution, right from the start, they responded by seeking God for increased boldness, and God gave them the boldness as they got on with exercising their ministry (Acts 4:18-31; 5:17-21,27-42; 6:8 – 7:60; 8:1-4, *etc.*). They certainly didn't sit around, bemoaning their lot, navel-gazing and talking about the 'good old days'.[16]

And there is one further point. It is not really a point at all. It is *the* point. I did not use the word 'glorious' in the title of my book for

---

[16] I don't want to be triumphalistic about this; 'bragging' about confidence can be just a step away from disaster! I remember a conversation with a headmistress who was my boss. She reminded me that it was a dangerous thing to ask God for patience. He does not supply it as a gift off the shelf; rather, he gives us circumstances which tend to make us impatient!

nothing. As I will show, 'the ministry' I am talking about is 'glorious' – glorious in all the ends I have delineated: it is saving for sinners, and sanctifying for saints. There's glory for you! It is a glory to every child of God. Above all, it is God's own designed way of bringing glory to himself. As Paul states, the new-covenant ministry is 'glorious' because it is the ministry of the Spirit, and as such it brings glory. As he asks, comparing the new covenant with the law: 'How much more *glorious* is the ministry that brings righteousness! For what was *glorious* has no glory now in comparison with the surpassing *glory*. And if what was fading away came with *glory*, how much greater is the *glory* of that which lasts!... Now the Lord is the Spirit, and where the Spirit of the Lord is, there is freedom. And we, who with unveiled faces all reflect the Lord's *glory*, are being transformed into his likeness with ever-increasing *glory*, which comes from the Lord, who is the Spirit.' What is more, 'this ministry' brings to sinners 'the light of the knowledge of the *glory* of God in the face of Christ' – and in bringing that 'light' to sinners it brings *glory* to God (2 Cor. 3: 9 – 4:6). I'm sure the same goes for the saints also: God is *glorified* by the fruits of the gospel made evident in the lives of his people.

How necessary this is today. The glory that the worldling has is an earthly glory at best. If I may adapt John Newton's words: 'Fading is the worldling's glory'. What else can it be? But the believer has glory now – a spiritual glory. This glory is growing throughout his pilgrimage here. And it will culminate in the eternal glory. Now what will that be? It will be a glory that is at present incomprehensible and indescribable – rather like the apostle's experience (2 Cor. 12:1-6). If the believer's present joy is 'inexpressible' while he is 'receiving the goal of [his] faith' (1 Pet. 1:8), what will it be when he finally gets it? Should not the poverty-ridden sinners (spiritually speaking) not be granted the proper preaching of all this?

Philip Doddridge:

> *Awake, my soul, stretch every nerve,*
> *And press with vigour on!*
> *A heavenly race demands thy zeal,*
> *And an immortal crown.*

Introduction

A cloud of witnesses around
Hold thee in full survey;
Forget the steps already trod,
And onward urge thy way.

'Tis God's all-animating voice
That calls thee from on high;
'Tis his own hand presents the prize
To thine aspiring eye.

That prize with peerless glories bright,
Which shall new lustre boast,
When victors' wreaths and monarchs' gems
Shall blend in common dust.

Blest Saviour, introduced by thee,
Have I my race begun;
And, crowned with victory, at thy feet
I'll lay my honours down.

As I have already said, I intend to be positive in this book. I have been pleased to note how frequently I have used the word 'glory' (or its derivatives) in this small volume. You can't get much more positive than 'glory' and 'glorious'.

But, as is my wont, I am also out for application. So, reader, I respectfully ask that as you now come to the body of this book, you will make a resolution. What's that? Just this: 'I resolve that if I come across any cap in these pages which fits me, I'll take it off its biblical peg and start wearing it'. For my part, reader, I promise to do what I can to describe the various caps – sizes and all – as set out in 2 Corinthians 3:1 – 4:6, and do all I can to help you in the fitting process. But, of course, I have to be the first in the fitting room, and be the first to start wearing the appropriate headgear.

The New-Covenant Ministry Stated

When it's all boiled down, there are two sorts of 'ministry', and only two: legal and gospel. As I have explained, although by 'ministry' the New Testament includes so much more than preaching, in this book I concentrate mostly on the 'preaching' aspect – not that the others are unimportant, but 'preaching' clearly is the thrust of the passage we are looking at. We are thinking, therefore, about 'legal preaching 'and 'gospel preaching'.

As I have explained, in the apostle's day the legal preachers were Judaisers who wanted to take believers under the law of Moses. Paul would have none of it. So much so, he stood against it at Antioch, then purposely travelled from Antioch to Jerusalem with Barnabas to attend a very important meeting called within the Jerusalem church to deal with the issue. Then, accompanied by Judas and Silas, he and Barnabas returned to Antioch with the decision of that meeting (Acts 13 – 15). In addition, Paul wrote at length to many New Testament churches to put a stop to the drive back to the law.[1] These facts, on their own, tell us how important this matter was to the apostle.

The particular passage which forms the basis of this book comes from Paul's second letter to the church at Corinth. Let this stand as the epigraph – and the basis – of all I say here. As I have made clear, I will apply all this to the legal preaching so common today. Paul declared:

Are we beginning to commend ourselves again? Or do we need, like some people, letters of recommendation to you or from you? You yourselves are our letter, written on our hearts, known and read by everybody. You show that you are a letter from Christ, the result of our ministry, written not with ink but with the Spirit of the living God, not on tablets of stone but on tablets of human hearts. Such confidence as this is ours through Christ before God. Not that we are competent in ourselves to claim anything for ourselves, but our competence comes from God. He has made us competent as ministers of a new covenant – not of the letter but of the Spirit; for the letter kills, but the Spirit gives

---

[1] It was a 'drive' on the part of the Judaisers, and (probably) a 'drift' on the part of the believers.

life. Now if the ministry that brought death, which was engraved in letters on stone, came with glory, so that the Israelites could not look steadily at the face of Moses because of its glory, fading though it was, will not the ministry of the Spirit be even more glorious? If the ministry that condemns men is glorious, how much more glorious is the ministry that brings righteousness! For what was glorious has no glory now in comparison with the surpassing glory. And if what was fading away came with glory, how much greater is the glory of that which lasts! Therefore, since we have such a hope, we are very bold. We are not like Moses, who would put a veil over his face to keep the Israelites from gazing at it while the radiance was fading away. But their minds were made dull, for to this day the same veil remains when the old covenant is read. It has not been removed, because only in Christ is it taken away. Even to this day when Moses is read, a veil covers their hearts. But whenever anyone turns to the Lord, the veil is taken away. Now the Lord is the Spirit, and where the Spirit of the Lord is, there is freedom. And we, who with unveiled faces all reflect the Lord's glory, are being transformed into his likeness with ever-increasing glory, which comes from the Lord, who is the Spirit. Therefore, since through God's mercy we have this ministry, we do not lose heart. Rather, we have renounced secret and shameful ways; we do not use deception, nor do we distort the word of God. On the contrary, by setting forth the truth plainly we commend ourselves to every man's conscience in the sight of God. And even if our gospel is veiled, it is veiled to those who are perishing. The god of this age has blinded the minds of unbelievers, so that they cannot see the light of the gospel of the glory of Christ, who is the image of God. For we do not preach ourselves, but Jesus Christ as Lord, and ourselves as your servants for Jesus' sake. For God, who said: 'Let light shine out of darkness', made his light shine in our hearts to give us the light of the knowledge of the glory of God in the face of Christ (2 Cor. 3:1 – 4:6).

I will divide this passage into two.

First, 2 Corinthians 3. In this section, Paul sets out the contrast between the old and new covenants, arguing that the old covenant, having reached its God-ordained end with the coming of Christ, is now obsolete, having been replaced by the new covenant. In stating this, the apostle lays the foundation for what follows; hence I call this section 'The New-Covenant Ministry: Its Basis'.

Secondly, 2 Corinthians 4:1-6. In this section, Paul sets out the consequences of what he has said in chapter 3; hence I call this 'The New-Covenant Ministry: Its Practice'.

And, as you can see, there is one word, one concept, which dominates the whole: 'glory'. Hence the title I have chosen for this book:

The Glorious New-Covenant Ministry: Its Basis and Practice.

The New-Covenant Ministry: Its Basis

As so often in New Testament times, Judaisers were, once again, on the attack; this time at Corinth. We may summarise their erroneous argument thus: the Abrahamic and Mosaic covenants were one, and if Gentiles want to become children of Abraham they must be circumcised. This, of course, was only the tip of the iceberg. Paul: 'I declare to every man who lets himself be circumcised that he is obligated to obey the whole law' (Gal. 5:3; see also Rom. 2:25). The Judaisers were arguing that in order to be saved, all – including Gentiles – must come under the law. As Luke recorded:

Some men came down from Judea to Antioch and were teaching the brothers: 'Unless you are circumcised, according to the custom taught by Moses, you cannot be saved'... Some of the believers who belonged to the party of the Pharisees... said: 'The Gentiles must be circumcised and required to obey the law of Moses' (Acts 15:1,5).

This is commonly – but mistakenly – limited to justification. Not at all! Justification is involved, certainly, but, as I have shown elsewhere, salvation here includes justification, sanctification and glorification. The Judaisers were not going around addressing unbelievers; they had infiltrated the churches and were addressing believers, seeking to destroy their liberty and enslave them all over again (Acts 15:1; Gal. 2:4; Jude 4). Paul would not tolerate it for a moment. He could not have put it more strongly than he did to the Galatians (you should read the entire letter, reader, and do so aloud, and in more than one version):

We who are Jews by birth and not 'Gentile sinners' know that a man is not justified by observing the law, but by faith in Jesus Christ. So we, too, have put our faith in Christ Jesus that we may be justified by faith in Christ and not by observing the law, because by observing the law no one will be justified... Through the law I died to the law so that I might live for God. I have been crucified with Christ and I no longer live, but Christ lives in me. The life I live in the body, I live by faith in the Son of God, who loved me and gave himself for me. I do not set aside the grace of God, for if righteousness could be gained through the law, Christ died for nothing! You foolish Galatians! Who has bewitched you? Before your very eyes Jesus Christ was clearly portrayed as crucified. I would like to learn just one thing from you: Did you receive the Spirit by observing the law, or by believing what you heard? Are you so foolish? After beginning with the Spirit, are you now trying to attain your goal by human effort?... All who rely on observing the law are under a curse, for it is written: 'Cursed is everyone who does not continue to do everything written in the book of the law'. Clearly no one is justified before God by the law, because, 'The righteous will live by faith'. The law is not based on faith; on the contrary: 'The man who does these things will live by them'. Christ redeemed us from the curse of the law by becoming a curse for us, for it is written: 'Cursed is everyone who is hung on a tree'. He redeemed us in order that the blessing given to Abraham might come to the Gentiles through Christ Jesus, so that by faith we might receive the promise of the Spirit...

The law, introduced 430 years later, does not set aside the covenant previously established by God and thus do away with the promise... What, then, was the purpose of the law? It was added because of transgressions until the Seed to whom the promise referred had come... Is the law, therefore, opposed to the promises of God? Absolutely not! For if a law had been given that could impart life, then righteousness would certainly have come by the law. But the Scripture declares that the whole world is a prisoner of sin, so that what was promised, being given through faith in Jesus Christ, might be given to those who believe. Before this faith came, we were held prisoners by the law, locked up until faith should be revealed. So the law was put in charge until Christ came that we might be justified by faith. Now that faith has come, we are no longer under the supervision of the law. You are all sons of God through faith in Christ Jesus...

Tell me, you who want to be under the law, are you not aware of what the law says? For it is written that Abraham had two sons, one by the slave woman and the other by the free woman. His son by the slave woman was born in the ordinary way; but his son by the free woman was born as the result of a promise. These things may be taken figuratively, for the women represent two covenants. One covenant is from Mount Sinai and bears children who are to be slaves: This is Hagar. Now Hagar stands for Mount Sinai in Arabia and corresponds to the present city of Jerusalem, because she is in slavery with her children. But the Jerusalem that is above is free, and she is our mother... Now you, brothers, like Isaac, are children of promise. At that time the son born in the ordinary way persecuted the son born by the power of the Spirit. It is the same now. But what does the Scripture say? 'Get rid of the slave woman and her son, for the slave woman's son will never share in the inheritance with the free woman's son'.

Therefore, brothers, we are not children of the slave woman, but of the free woman.

It is for freedom that Christ has set us free. Stand firm, then, and do not let yourselves be burdened again by a yoke of slavery. Mark my words! I, Paul, tell you that if you let yourselves be circumcised, Christ will be of no value to you at all. Again I declare to every man who lets himself be circumcised that he is obligated to obey the whole law. You who are trying to be justified by law have been alienated from Christ; you have fallen away from grace. But by faith we eagerly await through the Spirit the righteousness for which we hope. For in Christ Jesus neither circumcision nor uncircumcision has any value. The only thing that counts is faith expressing itself through love...

So I say, live by the Spirit, and you will not gratify the desires of the flesh. For the flesh desires what is contrary to the Spirit, and the Spirit what is contrary to the flesh. They are in conflict with each other, so that you do not do what you want. But if you are led by the Spirit, you are not under law...

Those who want to make a good impression outwardly are trying to compel you to be circumcised. The only reason they do this is to avoid being persecuted for the cross of Christ. Not even those who are circumcised obey the law, yet they want you to be circumcised that they may boast about your flesh. May I never boast except in the cross of our Lord Jesus Christ, through which the world has been crucified to me, and I to the world. Neither circumcision nor uncircumcision means anything; what counts is a new creation (Gal. 2:15 – 3:26; 4:21 – 5:6,16-18; 6:12-15).

As the apostle warned the Philippians:

Watch out for those dogs, those men who do evil, those mutilators of the flesh. For it is we who are the circumcision, we who worship by the Spirit of God, who glory in Christ Jesus, and who put no confidence in the flesh – though I myself have reasons for such confidence. If anyone else thinks he has reasons to put confidence in the flesh, I have more: circumcised on the eighth day, of the people of Israel, of the tribe of Benjamin, a Hebrew of Hebrews; in regard to the law, a Pharisee; as for zeal, persecuting the church; as for legalistic righteousness, faultless. But whatever was to my profit I now consider loss for the sake of Christ. What is more, I consider everything a loss compared to the surpassing greatness of knowing Christ Jesus my Lord, for whose sake I have lost all things. I consider them rubbish, that I may gain Christ and be found in him, not having a righteousness of my own that comes from the law, but that which is through faith in Christ – the righteousness that comes from God and is by faith. I want to know

Christ and the power of his resurrection and the fellowship of sharing in his sufferings, becoming like him in his death, and so, somehow, to attain to the resurrection from the dead. Not that I have already obtained all this, or have already been made perfect, but I press on to take hold of that for which Christ Jesus took hold of me. Brothers, I do not consider myself yet to have taken hold of it. But one thing I do: Forgetting what is behind and straining towards what is ahead, I press on towards the goal to win the prize for which God has called me heavenward in Christ Jesus. All of us who are mature should take such a view of things (Phil. 3:2-15).

It's all here. The law mongers wanted believers under the law for justification, sanctification and glorification. Paul would not concede an inch. As can be seen, he says so, and in no uncertain terms. I make no apology for having quoted at length: I want to let the apostle speak for himself. As I have hinted, an even fuller reading (and reading aloud) will make his argument all the more clear.

Coming closer to our passage, listen to the apostle addressing the Corinthians. Yet again, he does not mince his words. He leaves nobody in any doubt:

For such men are false apostles, deceitful workmen, masquerading as apostles of Christ. And no wonder, for Satan himself masquerades as an angel of light. It is not surprising, then, if his servants masquerade as servants of righteousness. Their end will be what their actions deserve. I repeat: Let no one take me for a fool. But if you do, then receive me just as you would a fool, so that I may do a little boasting. In this self-confident boasting I am not talking as the Lord would, but as a fool. Since many are boasting in the way the world does, I too will boast. You gladly put up with fools since you are so wise! In fact, you even put up with anyone who enslaves you or exploits you or takes advantage of you or pushes himself forward or slaps you in the face. To my shame I admit that we were too weak for that! What anyone else dares to boast about – I am speaking as a fool – I also dare to boast about. Are they Hebrews? So am I. Are they Israelites? So am I. Are they Abraham's descendants? So am I (2 Cor. 11:13-22).
Examine yourselves to see whether you are in the faith; test yourselves. Do you not realise that Christ Jesus is in you – unless, of course, you

fail the test? And I trust that you will discover that we have not failed the test (2 Cor. 13:5-6).[1]

Do not miss the apostle's emphasis upon boasting and boldness in 2 Corinthians. Broadening this, note the word 'glory', 'glorious' or 'glorify', appearing, on my count, twenty-three times in the letter, mostly in the third chapter; 'glory' is the theme of the entire letter; 'glory' is certainly the theme of 2 Corinthians 3. In particular, the apostle glories and boasts in connection with what he calls his 'ministry'. *This* is the issue he focuses on when confronting the false teachers, the legal teachers, at Corinth, with their boasting and self-exaltation. See, in particular, 2 Corinthians 10 – 12.[2]

And that leads us towards the central aspect of Paul's argument, the crux of his case against the Judaisers. His ministry is more powerful and more glorious than theirs. That is his claim. They boast. Very well! He, too, can boast. What is more, he will boast! Further, he can outdo them in their boasting. And he does! How? Is it because he is a better preacher, and all the rest of it, than they? No! In some senses, on his own admission, he might be regarded as a poorer preacher (1 Cor. 1:17; 2:1,3-4,13; 2 Cor. 10:10; 11:6), though, in these letters to Corinth[3] (see for instance, 1 Cor. 4:10; 2 Cor. 11:19,21), it must not be forgotten, irony is never far below the surface with the apostle. No! What makes the difference between him and the law mongers is 'commendation', that pet theme of the Judaisers. They are forever on about it! They demand letters of commendation. That is why Paul speaks of commendation so frequently in this letter (2 Cor. 3:1; 4:2; 5:12; 6:4; 10:12,18), and stands up to his detractors on the issue: 'Letters of commendation? Well, I've got them!' Really? 'Oh yes!' He addresses the Corinthians plainly: 'You are my letters! You believers! Every one of you at Corinth! Bits of paper? I don't need bits of paper! My

---

[1] There are hints of it in his first letter also (1 Cor. 4:14-21; 5:6-8). See immediately below. See also Phil. 3:2-11. My justification for this reading of 2 Cor. 13:5-6 will, I'm afraid, have to await the publication of my work on assurance – which, I hope, will be soon. To develop the argument here would lengthen this volume too much.

[2] On my count, the words 'boast' or 'boasting' come 28 times in the letter, 18 of which occur in these three chapters.

[3] And elsewhere.

gospel success, my spiritual power, my sufferings, and God's evident approval of my ministry, as revealed in the lives of others, you Corinthians in particular – there's my "commendation"' (2 Cor. 3:1-3; 4:2; 5:11 – 6:4; 10:13-18; 12:11-12; see also 1 Cor. 3:6; 9:1-2). (Compare Christ in John 5:36-39, especially verse 36; see also John 10:25,38). 'Now then, the Judaisers – what's theirs? Let's hear it!' (2 Cor. 10:12-18).[4]

As he had already told the Corinthians in his first letter:

I am not writing this to shame you, but to warn you, as my dear children. Even though you have ten thousand guardians in Christ, you do not have many fathers, for in Christ Jesus I became your father through the gospel. Therefore I urge you to imitate me. For this reason I am sending to you Timothy, my son whom I love, who is faithful in the Lord. He will remind you of my way of life in Christ Jesus, which agrees with what I teach everywhere in every church. Some of you have become arrogant, as if I were not coming to you. But I will come to you very soon, if the Lord is willing, and then I will find out not only how these arrogant people are talking, but what power they have. For the kingdom of God is not a matter of talk but of power. What do you prefer? Shall I come to you with a whip, or in love and with a gentle spirit?' (1 Cor. 4:14-21).[5]

We have not yet reached the core of the apostle's argument. The fundamental difference between his ministry and that of the Judaisers lies in something much more radical than its evident power, as compared to theirs.

The truth is, the Judaisers' ministry is in a totally different realm, a different age, a different system, to the apostle's. They are – obviously so – living and working in the age and ambience of the law, and their ministry shows it. Theirs is an old-covenant ministry,

---

[4] Did the Judaisers boast about their 'converts'? The evidence seems to suggest that they boasted about their letters of commendation – the praise of men. And, of course, there was always the boasting about having the law, and all that went with it – a feature all too common among the Jews (John 5:45; 9:28; Rom. 2:17-20; see also Mic. 3:11). But converts? Converts to what? Converts to the flesh! 'They want you to be circumcised that they may boast about your flesh' (Gal. 6:13; see also Phil. 3:3).

[5] He is not contradicting 1 Cor. 4:1-5. Remember, he calls himself 'a fool' for boasting, explaining that he was forced into it (2 Cor. 11:16-23; 12:6,11).

a ministry of law. Paul, however, lives in the realm of the Spirit, and his ministry is that of the new covenant. *This* is what makes all the difference. His boasting, power and commendation come from his being in the realm of the Spirit, and not in the realm of the law. Paul's power does not come from himself (2 Cor. 2:16; 3:5; 4:7-12,16-18; 6:3-10). Not at all! He can boast, yes, but only because God in Christ has made him 'competent' as a minister of the new covenant (1 Cor. 15:10; 2 Cor. 3:5-6). And this competence derives directly and inevitably from his being in the new covenant, his labouring in the realm of the Spirit, and his use of spiritual weapons appropriate to that covenant (2 Cor. 6:7; 10:3-5):

Are we beginning to commend ourselves again? Or do we need, like some people, letters of recommendation to you or from you? You yourselves are our letter, written on our hearts, known and read by everybody. You show that you are a letter from Christ, the result of our ministry, written not with ink but with the Spirit of the living God, not on tablets of stone but on tablets of human hearts. Such confidence as this is ours through Christ before God. Not that we are competent in ourselves to claim anything for ourselves, but our competence comes from God. He has made us competent as ministers of a new covenant – not of the letter but of the Spirit; for the letter kills, but the Spirit gives life... For though we live in the world, we do not wage war as the world does. The weapons we fight with are not the weapons of the world. On the contrary, they have divine power to demolish strongholds. We demolish arguments and every pretension that sets itself up against the knowledge of God, and we take captive every thought to make it obedient to Christ (2 Cor. 3:1-6; 10:3-5).

And *this* is the heart of the matter – the new covenant. *This* is what makes the difference between the Judaisers and the apostle. They labour in the letter, the law, the old covenant; he labours in the Spirit, in the gospel, the new covenant. And it is not only, as it were, the message that is different. The power, the boasting, the glory of the apostolic ministry, its very ethos, lies in that it is a ministry of the new covenant, not the old. With the change of covenant, the entire ministry has changed.

Let me stress this. Remember the chicken and the egg? Apply it here. Which comes first – the change of covenant, or the evident power? There is no doubt about it; it is as plain as a pikestaff. Paul does *not* argue that since he possesses power and glory, there must have been a change of covenant. No! What he says is, the old covenant has gone, being fulfilled in Christ; the new has come. And since the old covenant had a glory, the new covenant must have even greater glory – which it has – and, as a consequence, he has that power and glory, and the Judaisers do not. It's all a result of the change of covenant. He is in the new covenant; they are in the old. And it shows. It's as simple as that! It's all a question of covenant!

The Judaisers, locked in the old covenant, preaching the law, are using thrash and slap to enforce their doctrine, hitting the Corinthians into line. So much so, the apostle can rebuke the Corinthians: 'In fact, you even put up with anyone who enslaves you or exploits you or takes advantage of you or pushes himself forward or slaps you in the face'. Paul will have none of it: 'To my shame I admit that we were too weak for that!' (2 Cor. 11:20-21). Taking this line, Paul, of course, is being ironical. It's not a question of weakness. He's not weak! No: at all! He's in a different covenant to the Judaisers. He has no intention whatsoever of hitting the Corinthians. Severity might be required, as a last resort. If so, he will not shirk it: 'And we will be ready', he says, 'to punish every act of disobedience, once your obedience is complete' (2 Cor. 10:6). But that is not his forte: 'This is why I write these things when I am absent, that when I come I may not have to be harsh in my use of authority – the authority the Lord gave me for building you up, not for tearing you down' (2 Cor. 13:10). Read again the above extract from 1 Corinthians 4:14-21.

Moreover – and it is important to keep it in mind – in the matter of discipline, the apostle would never have aimed for mere outward conformity – a common failure of a law-approach. Paul would not have been interested in mere rule-keeping. The discipline would have begun at the heart and worked to the experience. Take 1 Corinthians 5. Yes, he insists that the church should expel the offender, but notice how Paul makes the Corinthians think about their lack of grief over the affair: 'Shouldn't you rather have been filled with grief and have put out of your fellowship the man who did this?'. Note the spiritual tone: 'The name of our Lord Jesus... spirit, and the power of our Lord Jesus... hand this man over to Satan, so that [his] flesh may be destroyed and his spirit saved... not with... malice and wickedness, but with... sincerity and truth'.

So, in 2 Corinthians 3, having made his point about the two covenants, in order to make sure that the Corinthians really do take it on board – since it is so easily and so often forgotten or whittled away (it was in the apostle's day, and it is so today – never more so than today) – the apostle then launches into a comparison of the two. A comparison? He *contrasts* them, irrefutably spelling out that contrast in a series of devastating terms, deliberately polarising the two covenants as starkly as he can.

I must underline this. The apostle deliberately polarises the issue, and he does it for *us*. He demands that we choose between two mutually exclusive systems. He simply will not allow us to make a mongrel system out of the two; it is either/or. In reality, of course, there is no choice: it has to be the new covenant – every time!

Before we move on to these contrasts, however, let me point out the excellence of the NIV here; I refer to its use of 'the old covenant', a literal translation of Paul's *tēs palaias diathēkēs*, literally ' of the old covenant' (verse 14). And when he speaks of 'tablets of stone... the letter... the letter... the ministry that brought death, which was engraved in letters on stone... the ministry that condemns men' (verses 3,6,7,9) and speaks of Moses (verses 13,15), there is no question whatsoever but that the apostle is speaking of the old covenant, the entire Mosaic economy, the law, including the ten commandments, which he contrasts with 'the new covenant' (verse 6), the work and realm and ministry of 'the Spirit' (verses 6,8,17-18).

I say it again, there can be no doubt. Paul *is* contrasting the old and new covenants, and he is contrasting the two covenants in their entirety. He is not contrasting certain aspects of the two covenants, certain man-made and artificial segments of the covenants (none of which exist in Scripture, though they are ubiquitous in theological literature).[6] No! He is, root and branch, contrasting the old and new covenants.

And what a devastating series of contrasts he draws between the two. But, yet again, even that is not quite right. Although I will now

---

[6] Such as moral, ceremonial and judicial law; law as a covenant and law as a rule; law as a/the covenant of works and law as a/the covenant of grace; different administrations of the same covenant; and so on.

list these contrasts, they do not actually form a list; they make one continuous line of reasoning. Do not miss the apostle's use of 'but... for... but... now if... so that... if... for... and if... therefore...' (verses 6-12) – all of which, I grant, are small Greek words in themselves, yet all of them are mighty words of reasoned argument. And when they follow hard, one after another, what an argument it is! What reasoning! So let's get away from a proof-text and bullet-point mentality, let's get away from a 'list-driven' Christianity, and let's get a firm grip on the apostle's argument. Indeed, let his argument grip us.

Nevertheless, in contradiction of what I have just said, in order to make things as clear as I can, I will now list the various contrasts the apostle draws.

Each of these, on its own, would constitute a powerful enough statement of contrast between the old and new covenants, showing the undoubted superiority of the new covenant over the old. Gathered together, in one small section of Scripture, they form an invincible catalogue, demonstrating beyond all fear of contradiction that the old and new covenants, far from being one covenant, are chalk and cheese. Not only that: as these statements make plain, the old covenant was, in comparison with the new, outward, weak, fading, useless, and is now, with the completion of the redeeming work of Christ, and his resurrection, obsolete.

And that's not all:

The old covenant was to do with the flesh; the new covenant is the covenant of the Holy Spirit (verses 3,6,8).

The old covenant was an outward covenant, written on stone; the new covenant is an inward covenant, written on the heart (verses 2-3,7).

The old covenant killed; it spelled death; the new covenant is life (verses 3,6-7).

The old covenant was deliberately temporary, designed by God to be so; the new covenant is permanent; it remains, it lasts (verses 11,13).

The old covenant had glory, but its glory was lesser and fading; the new covenant has a glory which exceeds, excels, being so much greater than the glory of the old covenant (verses 7-11).[7]

The old covenant condemned; the new covenant is saving (verse 9).[8]

The old covenant spelled bondage; the new covenant brings liberty (verses 12,17).

What a phenomenal series of statements. Breathtaking! And all of a piece with this:

If perfection could have been attained through the Levitical priesthood (for on the basis of it the law was given to the people), why was there still need for another priest to come – one in the order of Melchizedek, not in the order of Aaron? For when there is a change of the priesthood, there must also be a change of the law... The former regulation is set aside because it was weak and useless (for the law made nothing perfect), and a better hope is introduced, by which we draw near to God...

The ministry Jesus has received is as superior to theirs as the covenant of which he is mediator is superior to the old one, and it is founded on better promises. For if there had been nothing wrong with that first covenant, no place would have been sought for another. But God found fault with the people and said: 'The time is coming, declares the Lord, when I will make a new covenant with the house of Israel and with the house of Judah. It will not be like the covenant I made with their forefathers when I took them by the hand to lead them out of Egypt, because they did not remain faithful to my covenant, and I turned away from them, declares the Lord. This is the covenant I will make with the house of Israel after that time, declares the Lord. I will put my laws in their minds and write them on their hearts. I will be their God, and they will be my people. No longer will a man teach his neighbour, or a man his brother, saying: "Know the Lord", because they will all know me, from the least of them to the greatest. For I will forgive their wickedness and will remember their sins no more'. By calling this

---

[7] Note the apostle's 'deliberate tautology' – without redundancy, of course.
[8] 'Righteousness', *dikaiosunē*, 'justification'. But this does not mean that the apostle is speaking only about the law for justification. 'Righteousness' here includes the whole of salvation, not excluding sanctification. The context proves it.

covenant 'new', he has made the first one obsolete; and what is obsolete and ageing will soon disappear...

He sets aside the first to establish the second... The Holy Spirit also testifies to us about this. First he says: 'This is the covenant I will make with them after that time, says the Lord. I will put my laws in their hearts, and I will write them on their minds'. Then he adds: 'Their sins and lawless acts I will remember no more' (Heb. 7:11-19; 8:6-13; 10:9-17).

I fail to see how the New Testament could be clearer.[9] The old covenant had a glory, but, having fulfilled its God-appointed purpose, it is finished; the new has come. The old covenant still stands, of course, as a piece of writing, writing to which Paul can refer – as he does when using the law as a paradigm,[10] or model, or illustration (Rom. 13:8-10; Gal. 5:14-15; Eph. 6:1-4). But by no stretch of the imagination (at least, an imagination ruled by Scripture) can this be used to turn the ten commandments into the believer's perfect rule of life. Take 1 Corinthians 9:19-23, for example.

But even so, we still have not reached the apostle's ultimate concern. No! We have not yet got to the fundamental conclusion and application of his words in 2 Corinthians 3. We shall soon come to that. But let me end this chapter in the same way as the apostle does when writing this passage. As we draw near to the conclusion of this chapter 3 of Corinthians, what do we read? How does the apostle produce a climax to his argument? Like this: when a sinner is converted, 'whenever anyone turns to the Lord' (verse 16), all is changed (2 Cor. 5:17). Do not miss the 'anyone'; Paul *is* speaking of each and every believer. From that moment of turning to the Lord, he (or she) has the Spirit of God, and now lives under the new covenant, in the realm of the Spirit – with all that this entails in terms of life and liberty and glory:

In Christ... whenever anyone turns to the Lord, the veil is taken away. Now the Lord is the Spirit, and where the Spirit of the Lord is, there is freedom. And we, who with unveiled faces all reflect the Lord's glory,

---

[9] Though, amazingly, the majority of believers fail to see it, and their teachers tell them that those who can see it, and argue for it and its consequences, are to be dismissed as antinomians!

[10] See my *Christ* p289.

are being transformed into his likeness with ever-increasing glory, which comes from the Lord, who is the Spirit (2 Cor. 3:14-18).

Some climax, isn't it? In the new covenant, in the gospel, God takes sinners, ruined sinners, dead sinners, and transforms them into saints. He makes them new creatures in Christ. They live a new life: 'If anyone is in Christ, he is a new creation; the old has gone, the new has come! All this is from God, who reconciled us to himself through Christ... God made him who had no sin to be sin for us, so that in him we might become the righteousness of God' (2 Cor. 5:17-21). And in this have a present glory. Not only so: this glory is increasing. It is 'ever-increasing glory'! And, in the ultimate, it will be absolute and total glory:

How great is the love the Father has lavished on us, that we should be called children of God! And that is what we are! The reason the world does not know us is that it did not know him. Dear friends, now we are children of God, and what we will be has not yet been made known. But we know that when he appears, we shall be like him, for we shall see him as he is (1 John 3:1-2).

Do not miss the reference to the love of God in all this – a general love to all men (John 3:16; 2 Pet. 3:9), and a special love for his elect (Rom. 8:39; Gal. 2:20; Eph. 5:25; Tit. 3:3-7). Well might Samuel Medley sing:

> *Awake, my soul, in joyful lays*
> *And sing thy great Redeemer's praise.*
> *He justly claims a song from thee –*
> *His **loving-kindness**, oh, how free!*

> *He saw me ruined in the fall,*
> ***Yet loved me notwithstanding all.***
> *He saved me from my lost estate –*
> *His **loving-kindness**, oh, how great!*

> *When I was Satan's easy prey*
> *And deep in debt and bondage lay,*
> *He paid his life for my discharge –*
> *His **loving-kindness**, oh, how large!*

Robert Hawker:

Reader, let you and I, learn to rightly value our privileges! Blessed be God, we are not come to the mount, that might be touched, and that burned with fire, and blackness, and darkness, and tempest! Oh, what an awful dispensation, to shadow forth the terror, and dread, with which the broken law of God stood over the alarmed conscience of the trembling, guilty soul! Well might it be called, the ministration of death. For it denounced everlasting indignation and wrath, tribulation and anguish, to every soul of man that does evil. Reader, what a mercy is it, that the poor sinner is come not to mount Sinai, but mount Zion; not to the law to condemn, but to the Gospel to save; even to Jesus the mediator of the new covenant; and to the blood of sprinkling, that speaks better things than that of Abel. Lord, take away every remaining veil, of darkness and unbelief. Cause my soul, with open face, to behold as in a glass, the glory of the Lord! Cause my soul to be changed into the same image, from glory to glory, even as by the Spirit of the Lord. And... almighty Spirit, grant me freedom of access to the mercy seat of my God, in Christ. For where you, Lord, are, there is liberty. Oh, for liberty to pray, to plead, to wrestle with my God in prayer, in the blood, obedience, and death, of our Lord Jesus Christ. Give me, Lord, that sweet spirit of adoption, that I may be no longer under a spirit of bondage, but cry, Abba Father! And, oh,... be an unceasing witness to my spirit, that I am a child of God![11]

And the upshot of all this?[12] Since we, as believers, are members of the new covenant, and since we have, therefore, this 'liberty' and 'ever-increasing glory', how can we think of going back to the old covenant? In light of 2 Corinthians 3, it ought to be utterly out of

---

[11] Robert Hawker: *Commentary* (2 Cor. 3).

[12] Do not forget how John goes on: 'Everyone who has this hope in him purifies himself, just as he is pure. Everyone who sins breaks the law; in fact, sin is lawlessness. But you know that he appeared so that he might take away our sins. And in him is no sin. No one who lives in him keeps on sinning. No one who continues to sin has either seen him or known him. Dear children, do not let anyone lead you astray. He who does what is right is righteous, just as he is righteous. He who does what is sinful is of the devil, because the devil has been sinning from the beginning. The reason the Son of God appeared was to destroy the devil's work. No one who is born of God will continue to sin, because God's seed remains in him; he cannot go on sinning, because he has been born of God. This is how we know who the children of God are and who the children of the devil are: Anyone who does not do what is right is not a child of God; nor is anyone who does not love his brother' (1 John 3:3-10). Ultimate glory is the end, but progressive sanctification – in the new-covenant way, of course – is the way we get to it.

the question. But, returning to the Corinthians for a moment, this is precisely what the Judaisers wanted. If men – unbelievers and believers – would not submit to the law, no salvation! In this spirit, they were teaching the Corinthians to submit to the law, and the Corinthians (in common with several other churches) were buying into it. Paul could not let it go unchallenged. So much was – and is – at stake. *Is* at stake, I say. It applies to legal preaching today. The gospel is at stake. The eternal welfare of sinners is at stake. The sanctification and glorification of believers is at stake – not merely their happiness, and certainly not their amusement! And in facing the hostile world – which, according to Christ's command (Matt. 28:18-20; Mark 16:15-16) believers have to evangelise – the old covenant is useless. To go back to the law is not only foolish; it is utterly wrong; it is disastrous.

If I may use an illustration. Reader, what would you think of a man who insisted on lighting a candle for illumination when he was sitting in the glare of the full mid-day sun at the height of summer? What would you think of him putting on his thermals at such a time? You would think him mad or, at the very least, ill.

But even this illustration is too weak. It is not only daft to go back to the law; it is wrong! This is the age of the Spirit. Believer, you have the Spirit. In Christ you have liberty and ever-surpassing, increasing, glory – now! Do not desert the Spirit, and go back to the flesh. Do not leave the gospel, and go back to the law. *Keep to the gospel.* Do not allow yourself to be taken back to the law. The law is the flickering candle; the gospel is the meridian sun. In fact, the candle has been extinguished. The law is obsolete, having finished its God-appointed task, having been fulfilled by Christ. This is what the apostle is pressing upon the Corinthians, and doing it with all the power he can muster.

Can this be right? Is this really what the apostle is saying? We have a way of finding out. Bearing in mind what we have seen so far, along with material I have not dealt with – that is, Moses' veil, the blindness of the natural man's heart, the removal of the veil in Christ – all of which leads up to the triumphant conclusion of the chapter with its exuberant declaration of life, liberty and joy of believers, we only have to go on into 2 Corinthians 4. Chapter divisions, remember, are entirely artificial, and an imposition on the original text. Too often they hinder us in trying to grasp the full force and flow of the scriptural argument. We must not let it happen here.

But before we go on, let me summarise where we have got to: the believer is in the new covenant; every believer (whether man or woman) is a minister of the new covenant. The new covenant is the air that we as believers breathe, the kingdom in which we live (Luke 22:29), the governance under which we thrive, the realm of which we are citizens. The notion that we – the children of the new covenant – should mix law and gospel, old covenant and new, let alone elevate law over gospel, ought to be utterly out of the question. After all, as Paul told the Romans – and told them in some detail: 'For what the law was powerless to do', God has accomplished 'through Christ Jesus' by 'the law of the Spirit of life'. As the apostle said of himself and every believer: God in this way 'has set [us] free from the law of sin and death' (Rom. 8:2-3). Consequently, there can be no question of going back to the temporary (by God's appointment), and now completed, obsolete system. The law will not justify a sinner nor sanctify a saint.

Nevertheless, the Judaisers of Paul's day wanted to take men under the law; their contemporary counterparts still do. Sad to say, old error constantly rears its head, clothing itself in new garb. Legal preaching is happening today, now.[13] Old error never seems to die. And there's a very good reason for its constant resurgence – as Paul makes clear in what he goes on to say.

Paul resisted the error in his day, and did so with all the power at his disposal. How thankful we should be that he stood up to the Judaisers and won the battle in his day. Thank God, too, that we have the record of it in Scripture, to guide and nerve us in our battle. Thank God for what Paul goes on to set out here. And taking a good long look at that will form the substance of the next extended section of my book.

---

[13] Just one example: baby-sprinkling is utterly dependent on the old covenant. It hasn't a shred of New Testament for it. See my *Infant*.

The New-Covenant Ministry: Its Practice

Let me quote the relevant passage once again. Do not miss the opening 'therefore': all that now follows, does so directly as a consequence of Paul's argument in the previous chapter. In other words, having made his case – that Christ has fulfilled the old covenant, and has established the glorious new covenant – the apostle now presses home his application:

Therefore, since through God's mercy we have this ministry, we do not lose heart. Rather, we have renounced secret and shameful ways; we do not use deception, nor do we distort the word of God. On the contrary, by setting forth the truth plainly we commend ourselves to every man's conscience in the sight of God. And even if our gospel is veiled, it is veiled to those who are perishing. The god of this age has blinded the minds of unbelievers, so that they cannot see the light of the gospel of the glory of Christ, who is the image of God. For we do not preach ourselves, but Jesus Christ as Lord, and ourselves as your servants for Jesus' sake. For God, who said: 'Let light shine out of darkness', made his light shine in our hearts to give us the light of the knowledge of the glory of God in the face of Christ (2 Cor. 4:1-6).

In addition to the 'therefore', do not miss the apostle's reference to what he calls 'this ministry', clearly drawing on the verses which went before. In those verses, Paul had set out the contrast between the old covenant – the law of God given to Moses on Sinai – and the new covenant brought in by Jesus Christ. He had done this in face of the Judaisers who were trying to take the believers at Corinth under the law. He would have none of it. Defying the men of the law, Paul made sure the Corinthians got the point, as he, using all his power as an apostle, spelled out the stark contrast between the old and new covenants, the completion and end of the old covenant, and the full glory of the abiding new covenant.

And what a phenomenal series of statements he made in doing it! The argument is unassailable. The crescendo is magnificent, breathtaking.

Even so, we still have not reached the apostle's ultimate goal. No! We have not yet got to the fundamental conclusion and application which Paul is about to make in 2 Corinthians 4; namely the *practice* of 'the glorious new-covenant ministry'. We come to it now.

Before I start, let me remind you of those 'vital points' to which I said I would return. 'Ministry' goes far wider than 'pulpit work'; we must not read the word through glasses which have been prescribed for us by 1800 years of Christendom, and thus grievously restrict what the New Testament means by 'ministry'. What is more, we must not confine the 'ministry' to that of the apostle. In 2 Corinthians chapters 2 to 4, without question Paul *is* speaking of his own ministry, and that of his fellow-apostles and fellow-workers, yes, but notice how the apostle uses 'we' in these three chapters. Sometimes by 'we' he does mean, perhaps, just himself, maybe with other apostles and fellow-workers in mind (2 Cor. 2:17; 3:1; 4:7-15), although it's not absolutely certain in all these passages. In any case, notice how he quickly moves into 'you' (2 Cor. 3:1-3). So what should we make of the 'we' and 'ours' in the next verse, leading on to the words I quoted above? And it is, I think, unlikely that the 'we' in 2 Corinthians 3:12-18; 4:16-18; leave alone 5:1 and on, should be limited to Paul himself, or to Paul and his fellow-apostles. It is as plain as plain can be that he is speaking of *all* believers. If not, then we have to accept that Paul was saying all this about himself and his fellow-apostles, treating the Corinthians as mere interested bystanders. They might pray for him, of course; they might attend his meetings, yes; they might gaze at him, open-mouthed; but that's as far as it goes! Does anybody seriously think this is what Paul was wanting here?

Yet, looking at much contemporary church life, one could so easily get the impression that for the majority of believers, Christianity – at least, as far as its public face is concerned – is, very largely, a spectator sport. As such, it is tragic, a travesty of what the New Testament sets out so clearly. Not only in passages like 1 Corinthians 12-14 and Ephesians 4:1-16, but throughout the New Testament, in countless commands and exhortations, all believers are expected and encouraged to be active in 'the ministry'. I fear, however, the subtitle – *Slogan Or Substance?* – of my *The Priesthood Of All Believers* too often has the answer:

'Little or nothing more than a slogan'. Too often, I'm afraid, the fact is: 'The pastors and the people love to have it so' (see Jer. 5:31). How much we have lost by this unspeakably sad contraction of the New Testament pattern.

Let me now expand on these matters by exploring the way in which the apostle sets out the glories of the new-covenant ministry of believers in 2 Corinthians 4:1-6. I will do so under nine main headings:

1. To whom does the new-covenant ministry belong?

2. What is the problem that confronts humanity, which problem the new-covenant ministry, and only the new-covenant ministry, is designed to deal with?

3. Despite impossible odds, what is the only attitude for the new-covenant minister?

4. What is it in particular about the new-covenant ministry that proves it to be the only way a sinner can be saved?

5. How does God, by the new-covenant ministry, bring sinners to everlasting glory?

6. When God works savingly in a sinner, where does he work?

7. What constitutes the privilege and duty of the new-covenant minister?

8. What things have no part in the new-covenant ministry?

9. What is God's overall end in the new-covenant ministry?

1. New-Covenant Ministers

The new-covenant ministry belongs to all God's people, without exception. I say it again, with proper emphasis: the new-covenant ministry belongs to *all* God's people, *without exception*.

Without question, in 2 Corinthians 4 Paul *is* speaking of his own ministry, and that of his fellow-apostles and fellow-workers. And the specially endowed apostles were – and their writings and works remain – absolutely essential and fundamental to the gospel and the church, yes. Coming down the scale of authority, there is a vital role in the church of God for able teachers and preachers – and these are not ten a penny. Only God can make them 'competent'.

All that is perfectly true. But, as I have explained, we must not limit the 'we' in this argument to Paul himself, or to Paul and his fellow-apostles. All believers have a 'ministering' gift and ability. All of them. And this 'ministry' is a vital aspect of their priestly status within the new covenant. This ministry needs emphasising – and exercising! When a sinner is converted, 'whenever anyone turns to the Lord' (verse 16), all is changed (2 Cor. 5:17). From that moment, he or she has the Spirit of God, the Spirit of adoption, the Spirit of sonship, the witness, the seal and the anointing of the Spirit (Rom. 8:14-17; 2 Cor. 1:21-22; Gal. 4:5-7; Eph. 1:13-14; 4:30; 1 John 2:20-27; 4:13; 5:6,9-11). Every believer lives under the new covenant, in the realm of the Spirit – with all that that entails in terms of life and liberty and glory. Every believer, each believer, is, in biblical terms, a minister of the new covenant. Every believer, without exception, from the moment of conversion, is a royal priest invested and endowed with all the panoply of grace needed to enable him or her to exercise his or her spiritual ministry.[1] And that means every believer has a ministry to both *unbelievers and believers*. Malachi surely hit the right note:

---

[1] I am not saying that believers are immediately endowed with all the experience required for the full and most profitable exercise of their ministry – experience comes only by experience! Believers have to grow (2 Pet. 3:18) until they die. But, even so, all believers, at conversion, are priests, kings and ministers.

Those who feared the LORD talked with each other, and the LORD listened and heard. A scroll of remembrance was written in his presence concerning those who feared the LORD and honoured his name. 'They will be mine', says the LORD Almighty, 'in the day when I make up my treasured possession. I will spare them, just as in compassion a man spares his son who serves him. And you will again see the distinction between the righteous and the wicked, between those who serve God and those who do not' (Mal. 3:16-18).

Those who 'feared the LORD' – not just the priests and prophets. The same goes for the new covenant. When the apostle says: 'We do not lose heart' (2 Cor. 4:1), therefore, he doesn't mean that it was only the apostles who didn't lose heart; or that the general run of believers should not lose heart in their ministers. He surely means that believers as believers should not – do not – lose heart in *their* own ministry. *All* Christ's people are kings, priests and prophets by reason of their union with Christ, and *all* have a ministry. The prophets foretold it, and Christ established it; not literally, of course, but in a spiritual sense. Believers, therefore, are ministers. They are 'competent' – all of them are 'competent as ministers'; and each believer has God's Spirit and can, in a measure, teach other believers, and preach the gospel to unbelievers. The point can be broadened: God equips all his people to fulfil that particular ministry which he has for each of them. To deny it is to fly in the face of the provisions of the new covenant (Isa. 54:13; 61:6; Jer. 31:31-34; 33:14-22; Zeph. 3:9-10; John 6:45; 1 Thess. 4:9; 5:11; Heb. 8:8-12; 10:15-18; 1 Pet. 4:10-11; 1 John 5:20).

All this hinges on the believer's union with Christ. Let me quote from my *The Priesthood Of All Believers*:

Union with Christ! 'In Christ'. This is a huge theme, of immense importance, which I have explored a little more fully in other works. For now, I simply note that believers are 'in Christ', and Christ is in them (John 17:21,23; Rom. 8:10; Gal. 2:20; Eph. 3:17; Col. 1:27). God regards believers as he does Christ. They are one with him. Indeed, in eternity God will conform them to the likeness of his Son, even in the body (Rom. 8:29; 1 Cor. 15:49; Phil. 3:21; 1 John 3:2). But even now, all believers are spiritually 'in Christ', united to him, and, being united to Christ, they receive as their own all that Christ is and has done for them. In short, they died with him, they were buried with him, they rose with him, they ascended with him, they are seated in heaven with him (Rom. 5:12 – 8:39; Eph. 1:1 – 2:22). They are 'in Christ'. And that is why the children of God are called Christians; they are CHRISTians (Acts 11:26), 'in Christ' and Christ in them. They partake of him. They participate in the divine nature (2 Pet. 1:4). They are members of Christ, even of his body (1 Cor. 6:15; 12:27; Eph. 5:30), Christ being the head (Eph. 1:22-23; Col. 1:18,24; 2:19). And just as in a well-ordered man, the head governs, the members submit; the head commands, the members obey – so with Christ. All depends on him, the head. It used to be thought that a man died when his heart stopped. For many years now, 'brain-dead' has been the more reliable term. A man can be kept alive without his heart – but not without his head. We now know that the head is the most vital organ of them all. Further, Christ is the vine; believers are the branches (John 15:1-10); they draw all their life from and in him. Again, as he is anointed of God ('Christ' means 'anointed'), so are they anointed in him (2 Cor. 1:21; 1 John 2:20,27). In all these biblical metaphors which describe the union of Christ and his people, there is an emphasis upon life, 'oneness' and 'likeness'. Christ and his people are one.[2]

As for the union of Christ with all his people, we have the climax of his great prayer just before his crucifixion. Having prayed for his immediate disciples (the apostles), Jesus went on:

My prayer is not for them alone. I pray also for those who will believe in me through their message, that all of them may be one, Father, just as you are in me and I am in you. May they also be in us so that the world may believe that you have sent me. I have given them the glory that you gave me, that they may be one as we are one: I in them and you in me. May they be brought to complete unity to let the world know that you sent me and have loved them even as you have loved me. Father, I want those you have given me to be with me where I am, and to see my glory, the glory you have given me because you loved me before the creation of the world. Righteous Father, though the world does not know you, I know you, and they know that you have sent me. I have made you known to them, and will continue to make you known in order that the love you have for me may be in them and that I myself may be in them (John 17:20-26).

Note the link between the union of Christ and all his people, and the union that exists between and in all the children of God. Do not miss the repeated reference to 'glory'. All this is fundamental to the new covenant, as is the doctrine and practice of the priesthood of all

---

[2] My *Priesthood* p100; see also my *Particular* (second edition) p78.

believers. In union with Christ, all believers have received this 'common' ('same') ministry.

Furthermore, we need to stress the 'this' in 'this ministry'. Paul is still contrasting the old and new covenants, and building on that contrast. Let me remind you of two contrasts between the old and new covenants in the matter of ministry and priesthood. While in the old covenant, there were many priests and high priests, in the new covenant there is only one great high priest: Christ. That's the first contrast. Then again, in the old covenant, the ministry was confined to the special few – priests, levites and prophets. Sadly, this old covenant principle still holds sway over many believers; they think that 'ministry' is for the favoured few, a special, favoured class – the ordained, the inducted or whatever, the Lord's 'anointed'. This is a grievous mistake, and spells a sad loss, both to the individual believer and the church. In the new covenant, each believer, every believer, man or woman, is as much a minister as any other believer. All are anointed (1 John 2:20-27). *'This ministry', therefore, is every believer's spiritual birthright.* Believer, do not lose it; do not neglect it; do not let yourself be cheated of it by a professional 'one-man-band' mentality; above all, do not get anywhere near copying Esau who despised his birthright (Gen. 25:29-34; Heb. 12:16-17). 'This ministry', I stress it yet again, is every believer's prerogative. This is his or her life.

Consequently, although in our passage the apostle is dealing primarily with *his* ministry as opposed to the ministry of the Judaisers, the principles he sets out apply to all believers. All believers are, from the moment of their conversion, in the new covenant; they are full members (there is no other sort) of the new-covenant fraternity; indeed, all of them, without exception, and at once, both men and women, are ministers or priests of the new covenant. So what Paul says about himself in this passage, he really does say about all believers without exception. And that which lies behind *his* power and glory, and brings power and glory to him and his ministry, lies behind every believer, and produces that same power and glory in us as believers, and in and through our ministry. Yes, I know it sounds staggering, but it is the truth. 'Ministry' is something every believer engages in; all believers, therefore, are ministers. In Paul's words, all of them are 'competent as ministers', and have 'this ministry'. Each believer has God's Spirit and can, in a measure, teach others, and address sinners with the gospel.

I stress this so heavily because I most definitely am not writing solely for that band of men known as 'ministers', engaged in 'pulpit work'. Far too often this is how this passage has been read, expounded and preached. And it is quite wrong. I am writing for what the New Testament calls 'ministers'; in this context, that is, believers – all believers, every believer without exception. *And in doing this I am doing nothing different to what Paul himself did in this very passage!*

On Patmos, John 'saw under the altar the souls of those who had been slain because of the word of God and the testimony they had maintained' (Rev. 6:9). Are we to assume that he had a vision of the souls of 'pastors', or did he see the souls of many men and women, all of whom had testified of Jesus – surely by life (and death) and lip?

In this book, I am concentrating – as Paul did in my chosen passage – on the preaching aspect of 'this ministry'; that is 'preaching Christ' as the work of every believer. While A.W.Tozer rightly applied this to the entire range of 'the ministry', his comments certainly include this 'preaching ministry'. Do not miss his interjected note of dignity:

Is this for ministers? This is for ministers, certainly. Is it for housewives? Yes, housewives, and clerks and milkmen and students [as long as they are believers]. If you will thus see it and thus believe it and thus surrender to it, there won't be a secular stone in the pavement. There won't be a common, profane deed that you will ever do. The most menial task can become a priestly ministration when the Holy Ghost takes over and Christ becomes your all in all.[3]

Nevertheless, because all believers are 'ministers', it does not mean there is no need for recognised and stated able preachers who are to edify the church by their teaching. The very suggestion shows a lack of understanding of what the New Testament means by the many different words it uses for 'preach' and 'teach'. Obviously, the promise that no member of the new covenant will need a human

---

[3] A.W.Tozer: *How to be Filled with the Holy Spirit*, Martino Publishing, Mansfield Centre, 2010, p30.

teacher (Heb. 8:11; 1 John 2:20-21,27) cannot possibly mean what it appears to be saying at first glance. After all, both John and the writer to the Hebrews were teaching as they were saying it. Of course we need teachers and preachers, ministers.

But my point here is that all believers are competent ministers, gifted by God. And that includes the ability, using the Scriptures (2 Tim. 3:14-17) for one of the great purposes God gave them to us, to instruct (yes!), strengthen, encourage, reprove (yes!), comfort, and confirm fellow-believers. Moses' wish (Num. 11:29) has been more than amply fulfilled. In addition, believers, all believers, are fully competent to address sinners with the gospel.

I realise that I am touching a very sensitive point, saying something contrary to common practice in many churches, and one which, perhaps, will disturb some readers. Some might go as far as to think – and accuse me of it – that I am subverting the preaching and teaching ministry. So let me try, yet again, to set any anxious heart at rest. *I am, myself, anxious – anxious **not** to give the impression that I am dismissing the need for stated, and recognised, gifted teachers.* I'm not! Let me give a couple of examples to prove it. From Acts 8:4; 11:19-20, we can see how 'ordinary' (I detest the word in this context) believers 'preached' the gospel; by God's grace, they were 'competent': 'The Lord's hand was with them, and a great number of people believed and turned to the Lord' (Acts 11:21). But go on to Acts 11:22-26. Barnabas recognised that these 'established' believers, along with the new converts, needed solid teaching. The 'ordinary' believers were 'ministers', yes, all of them, but none of them were gifted sufficiently to sustain an edifying ministry to the church – which the church was crying out for.[4] Barnabas rose to the occasion. He brought Paul to Antioch, and the pair of them, both gifted teachers, 'for a whole year... met with the church and taught great numbers of people'. And they were successful, for it wasn't long before the Antioch church had three more capable 'prophets and teachers' listed alongside Barnabas and Paul (Saul), who was listed last! (Acts 13:1; see also 15:35).

---

[4] The church always is. It is today! I certainly hope churches are praying for, and on the look-out for, able teachers. I hope they are preparing the next generation, and the next generation is eager for it (2 Tim. 2:2).

I think that all this speaks for itself, and should calm the fears of any who think I might not hold to a stated, gifted ministry. I certainly hope so. I could not be more emphatic on the need, and the biblical warrant, for an able, stated preaching and teaching ministry. Please see the Appendix for more on this matter.

My point here, however, must not be lost. All believers have a 'ministering' gift and ability. All of them. All of them without exception. And this is an aspect of their priestly ministry under the new covenant. This ministry needs emphasising – and exercising!

Granted then that this 'glorious new-covenant ministry' is the ministry which belongs to every believer, let me show how the apostle takes us further into the glories of this ministry.

2. *The Problem Confronting Humanity*

The heading of this section could be more fully expressed thus: What is the problem that confronts humanity, which problem the new-covenant ministry, and only the new-covenant ministry, is designed to deal with?

Problem? Well, 'problem' is hardly an adequate word for what I am talking about; namely, what's wrong with the world, with humanity, with society, with men. And there is something wrong with the world, isn't there?[1] Would anybody disagree? But 'problem' is too weak; how about 'disaster' or 'catastrophe' or 'plight'? What am I talking about – this 'problem'? And what is the answer to it? Is there an answer?

Before I get to that, let me point out that it is no part of the new covenant to run away from facts, even awkward facts. Notice how Paul does not run away from the problem we face in seeking to advance the gospel in the world. We dare not bury our heads in the sand. Sadly, as I know by experience, this is done. I recall, about 35 years ago, an evangelical 'pastor' came to our house to take a Bible study. He was accompanied by his wife. Having been alarmed by an *avant-garde* report about incest on the radio that evening, I mentioned it to the 'pastor's' wife. 'It doesn't happen, David, it doesn't happen', was her staggering ostrich-like response. Imagine a doctor who refused to admit, let alone face, disease, its causes as well as its symptoms!

And that's the word – 'symptoms'. Let us start by looking at the symptoms of the problem we have to face. I do so by quoting the apostle once more:

And even if our gospel is veiled, it is veiled to those who are perishing. The god of this age [Satan] has blinded the minds of unbelievers, so

---

[1] I can hear many saying: 'Yes! And it's all because of the Church, Christianity'. They've put the wrong body in the dock! Christendom – 'the Church' – I agree, has wrought havoc in the world. Christendom is one of Satan's greatest engines for the ruination of souls. But Christendom has nothing to do with the new covenant!

that they cannot see the light of the gospel of the glory of Christ, who is the image of God' (2 Cor. 4:3-5).

There's a world of misery, ignorance, blindness, ruin, shame, guilt, grief, malignity and helplessness bound up in those words.

Let me explain.

Man's misery

Problem? Let's think about it for a moment or two. Think about the misery in the world. And what untold misery there is. Think of the misery going on, even as you read this. Although I'm no prophet, let me make a prediction: some time in the next few days we shall get news of some war or another, news which speaks of the wanton maiming, violation and slaughter of men, women and children. As I write, it's Egypt. A few days ago, it was Syria, but now Egypt has pushed that country off centre-stage. Having said that, on re-reading the manuscript, even as I read, Syria with the gas attack in Damascus has come to the top of the political agenda yet again. On and on it goes, remorselessly. If I had been writing in the late 1930s and early 40s, it would have been Europe, Africa, Japan, Asia – well, the world, really. War – and all the displacement, the suffering, the death of millions which it drags in its wake – is that not a problem? How ironic that H.G.Wells and Woodrow Wilson might pronounce that the world war that started in 1914 was the war that ended all wars, yet just over twenty years later the Second World War erupted! Something is wrong! How ugly it all is.

Wells himself came to admit it:

In spite of all my disposition to a brave-looking optimism, I perceive that now the universe is bored with [man], is turning a hard face to him, and I see him being carried less and less intelligently, and more and more rapidly... along the stream of fate to degradation, suffering and death.[2]

Again, as I write, I have to confess that I, for one, have grown weary of politician after politician informing me that yet another conference has been proposed to deal with the problem of Syria; I'm fed up with hearing politicians interminably telling the Syrian

---

[2] Stuart Barton Babbage: *The Mark of Cain*, The Paternoster Press, Exeter, 1966, pp21-22.

authorities that they must be nice people and stop bombing and gassing innocents. And all the rest of it. Is that not a 'problem'?

Let me make another prophetic suggestion. It won't be many days before we shall be having news of yet another paedophile doing abominable things to some 5- or 6-year old. A few weeks ago – I am writing this in the UK in the summer of 2013 – the talk was all of Mark Bridger and the dreadful things he did. In the early 1960s, I was living in north Manchester when the topic of the day was the dreadful cruelties and perversions of Ian Brady and Myra Hindley – the repercussions (what a word!) of which are still being played out, even as I write. No problem?

'Ah! But these are extreme cases'. Of course! Of course they are. Nobody pretends otherwise. But they are only the open flowering of what is endemic, but largely hidden (we vainly hope!), in all our experience. Reader, do you shudder with offence at that? Let me say two things:

First: 'Man is born to trouble as surely as sparks fly upward' (Job 5:7); *man*, please note; all men, mankind! Do you disagree with that? If so, do you ever sing 'Abide with me'? In the UK, at every F.A. Cup and Rugby League finals thousands do. I wonder if the fans realise what they are singing:

> *Swift to its close ebbs out life's little day;*
> *Earth's joys grow dim; its glories pass away;*
> *Change and decay in all around I see.*

Well? Change and decay in all around I see? Can you still deny the misery of the world?

And, reader, do you know who said this?

I am now the most miserable man living. If what I feel were equally distributed to the whole human family, there would not be one cheerful face on the earth. Whether I shall ever be better I cannot tell; I awfully [fear] I shall not. To remain as I am is impossible; I must die or be better, it appears to me.

Pretty dismal, isn't it? Well, it was Abraham Lincoln in 1841. In short, as Lincoln proved – and admitted for himself – natural man is lost, ruined, wretched!

Secondly, I am merely repeating what Jesus told us – and told us as bluntly as any man could wish. Let me explain.

Man's corruption

I start by listing some of the things which blight our lives – yes, all of us – in one way or another. Are you repelled by the thought? Do you deny that your life is blighted? Well then, how about malice, bitterness, evil thoughts, anger, the bearing of grudges, jealousy, pride, the telling of lies, greed, lusting, spite, and so on, and on? Do you know anything of them – in your own heart, I mean? Take greed: is it not a fact that on one page of the magazine we can read an article tempting us to some dietary indulgence, while on the next we read of a new-fangled diet to help us lose weight? Do I detect a wry smile? Well, that's a mere symptom of what I am talking about. Why are there so many food programmes on TV? Why is obesity a massive problem in the UK, even as I write? While I recognise that a certain – small – percentage of the population have a medical problem, there is no baulking the fact that overwhelmingly the 'problem' is simply one of greed, lack of self-control, the inability to say 'no'.

As I said, Christ spelled it all out 2000 years ago. Quoting a law which had been written 1500 years before his time, he demanded absolute love to God and neighbour *and enemy* (Lev. 19:18; Matt. 5:43-44; 19:19; 22:39; Rom. 13:9; Gal. 5:14; Jas. 2:8), did he not? Now who can live with that? And this is precisely where 'sin' comes into the picture: the root sin is failing to live according to these demands. And we are all sinners (Rom. 3:23). As Jesus put it:

For from within, out of men's hearts, come evil thoughts, sexual immorality, theft, murder, adultery, greed, malice, deceit, lewdness, envy, slander, arrogance and folly (Mark 7:21-22).

May I underline something of the utmost importance in Christ's words? Notice how he clearly spelled out the symptoms of the problem. *But he did not start there.* He opened by driving us to the source of the trouble – our heart! It is 'out of men's hearts' that sins come. And Jesus certainly pulled no punches in letting us know what he had in mind. What is more, the things he listed are within us all, reader. Make no mistake about it: these things are within us all. '*Men's* hearts', said Christ – of us all. We are all sinners, as I have just reminded you (Rom. 3:23). I am; you are.

Following his Master, Paul did not mince his words:

The wrath of God is being revealed from heaven against all the godlessness and wickedness of men who suppress the truth by their wickedness, since what may be known about God is plain to them, because God has made it plain to them. For since the creation of the world God's invisible qualities – his eternal power and divine nature – have been clearly seen, being understood from what has been made, so that men are without excuse. For although they knew God, they neither glorified him as God nor gave thanks to him, but their thinking became futile and their foolish hearts were darkened. Although they claimed to be wise, they became fools and exchanged the glory of the immortal God for images made to look like mortal man and birds and animals and reptiles. Therefore God gave them over in the sinful desires of their hearts to sexual impurity for the degrading of their bodies with one another. They exchanged the truth of God for a lie, and worshipped and served created things rather than the Creator – who is forever praised. Amen. Because of this, God gave them over to shameful lusts. Even their women exchanged natural relations for unnatural ones. In the same way the men also abandoned natural relations with women and were inflamed with lust for one another. Men committed indecent acts with other men, and received in themselves the due penalty for their perversion. Furthermore, since they did not think it worthwhile to retain the knowledge of God, he gave them over to a depraved mind, to do what ought not to be done. They have become filled with every kind of wickedness, evil, greed and depravity. They are full of envy, murder, strife, deceit and malice. They are gossips, slanderers, God-haters, insolent, arrogant and boastful; they invent ways of doing evil; they disobey their parents; they are senseless, faithless, heartless, ruthless. Although they know God's righteous decree that those who do such things deserve death, they not only continue to do these very things but also approve of those who practice them (Rom. 1:18-32).

Or, as the apostle reminded the Philippians: 'As I have often told you before and now say again even with tears, many live as enemies of the cross of Christ. Their destiny is destruction, their god is their stomach, and their glory is in their shame. Their mind is on earthly things' (Phil. 3:18-19). And as he reminded the Colossians of their condition before conversion: 'Once you were alienated from God and were enemies in your minds because of your evil behaviour' (Col. 1:21).

As for the symptoms in the above paragraphs, they could have been drawn from tomorrow's newspapers – or the secret diaries (whether written or not) of countless men and women. But note my use of 'symptoms'. Men and women do these things – they commit sins – because they are sinners. Let me say that again: we sin because we are sinners; we are not sinners because we sin. This is the fundamental reason for the catalogue of sins: we are congenital and inveterate sinners. The Greeks realised it and acknowledged the ruin and degradation of the human race – witness the myths and legends of their gods and humanity. Of course, it takes the Bible to give us the reason for all this, the cause of the actions. And it does.

But before I get to that, let me glance at the obverse of the coin.

Sin brings shame

We are sinners. We sin against God. But in sinning against God, we often hurt and offend others, grievously, unspeakably, and permanently. In extreme cases, abusers inflict massive damage – massive in effect and duration – on others. Many victims carry a huge burden of shame. Take child abuse, sexual abuse, by a father. Satan has wrought havoc in many lives, not only by the father's original sin, but by the life-long sense of shame that the abused child carries. Take just one aspect of what I am trying to say: when that child has become an adult, and hears the gospel, and hears of the love of the Father, what a distorted picture that poor sinner has of God. A Father? A father to me is nothing but an ugly, abusive, cruel tyrant, one who strikes terror into me! And Satan laughs all the way to hell! I wonder how many are walking around, even as I write, even as you read, undergoing the abuse I speak of, or else bearing an intolerable sense of shame – not for their own sin (though they can wrongly blame themselves for it) – but for the sin of another, the sinful torment that another inflicted on them, twenty, fifty years ago?

Sexual abuse of a child is but one example of what I am talking about. Think of the victims of physical abuse, deprivation, enslavement, people-traffickers. Think of the victims of rape. Think of the mountain of shame there is in the world – shame, not, as I say, for one's own sin, but for the effect of the sin of another.

And sexual abuse is only one example of what I am talking about. Physical abuse, emotional abuse, psychological abuse, spiritual abuse... Think of the deep and long-lasting shadows cast by pride, gossip, religious bigotry, jealousy, malice, revenge, prejudice... Think of the physical, mental, emotional, psychological and spiritual scars hidden by a bandage of respectability and decorum, the pain cloaked in a veil of silence, secretly borne by the victim.

We are of course, all sinners. Now let the Bible tell us why.

Why do all men sin?

Why do I sin? Why do you sin? Why do we all sin? At this point, I need to move outside the immediate context of our passage. Since it does not suit his immediate purpose here – after all, he is dealing primarily with those who want to take believers under the law – Paul does not explicitly trace sin to its fundamental root; namely, the fall in Adam.[3] Rather, he centres his attention – his readers' attention – on Satan. Even so, by referring to Satan, Paul makes an implied reference to Genesis 3, and the serpent's part in the fall of Adam – especially bearing in mind what the apostle had already told his readers in his first letter. Remember the serpent's part: he promised Adam and Eve light, and although their eyes were certainly opened after eating the forbidden fruit, in reality they were now blinded spiritually (Gen. 3:1-24).[4]

Taking all that for granted, then, what am I trying to say? All men sin because all men are sinners, and this is because all men fell in Adam. Adam, when he sinned, dragged all the human race (apart from the incarnate Son of God) down into sin. All men, therefore, are born sinners; all men, therefore, sin. The following extract from William Tyndale's very important book,[5] written in 1525 and

---

[3] He does it elsewhere, of course – notably Romans 5:12-21 – but not here. It is not without significance, however, that he had already explained matters to the Corinthians – in his first letter to them (1 Cor. 15:21-22,47-49).

[4] Actually, one could read the rest of the Bible! Indeed, one could read the rest of history – including one's own!

[5] 'A cardinal document, standing as the very first welcome to the printed vernacular Scriptures in English' (James Simpson: *Burning to Read*, Harvard, 2007, p93).

revised and republished in 1530, puts it as clearly as anyone could wish:

By nature, through the fall of Adam, we are the children of wrath and heirs of the vengeance of God by birth – indeed, and this from our conception. And we have our fellowship with the damned devils, under the power of darkness and rule of Satan, while we are yet in our mother's womb. And although we do not show forth the fruits of sin as soon as we are born, yet we are full of the natural poison from which all sinful deeds spring. And we cannot help but sin outwardly (be we ever so young) as soon as we are able to act, if opportunity is given. For our nature is to do sin, as it is the nature of a serpent to sting. And like a serpent while still young, or even not yet born, is full of poison and later (when the time is come and occasion given) cannot help but bring forth the fruits thereof; and like an adder, a toad or a snake is hated by men not for the evil that it has done, but for the poison that is in it and hurt which it cannot help but do, so are we hated by God for that natural poison which is conceived and born with us before we do any outward evil. And like the evil of a venomous worm does not make it a serpent, but because it is a venomous worm it produces evil and poisons; and as the fruit does not make the tree evil, but because it is an evil tree it produces evil fruit when the season is right: just so our evil deeds do not make us evil. Though ignorance and blindness make us worse and worse, and evil working in us hardens us in evil, yet it is not by these but by nature that we are evil. Therefore by nature we both think and do evil, and by nature are under vengeance under the law, convicted to eternal condemnation by the law. And by nature we are contrary to the will of God in all our will, and in all things we consent to the will of the fiend.[6]

Men are sinners, then, by nature (Eph. 2:1-3). Again, as Jesus said (Mark 7:21-22), sin is rooted, ingrained in the human heart. And as Paul told us:

Men... suppress the truth... Although they knew God, they neither glorified him as God nor gave thanks to him, but their thinking became futile and their foolish hearts were darkened. Although they claimed to be wise, they became fools and exchanged the glory of the immortal God for images made to look like mortal man and birds and animals and reptiles... They exchanged the truth of God for a lie, and worshipped and served created things rather than the Creator... They

---

[6] William Tyndale: *A Pathway Into The Holy Scripture* (downloaded from newmatthewbible.org/pathway).

did not think it worthwhile to retain the knowledge of God (Rom. 1:18-28).

And sin shows itself in the way we think, the way we talk, and the way we act. In other words, the sin in our heart, our sinful heart, shows itself in our *sins*. As Paul could command believers not to live as they used to – the 'used to' being an apt description of the way of the man without God:

So I tell you this, and insist on it in the Lord, that you must no longer live as the Gentiles do, in the futility of their thinking. They are darkened in their understanding and separated from the life of God because of the ignorance that is in them due to the hardening of their hearts. Having lost all sensitivity, they have given themselves over to sensuality so as to indulge in every kind of impurity, with a continual lust for more (Eph. 4:17-19).

'Wait a minute! Where are you getting all this? – from the passage, I mean'. Let me answer that. Man is a sinner, lost and blinded, blinded by Satan, perishing, on the road to everlasting damnation: 'Our gospel is veiled'; 'it is veiled to those who are perishing. The god of this age has blinded the minds of unbelievers, so that they cannot see the light of the gospel of the glory of Christ, who is the image of God' (2 Cor. 4:3-4). Or as the AV put it, stressing the inwardness of the sinner's blindness: '*In whom* the god of this world hath blinded the minds of them which believe not, lest the light of the glorious gospel of Christ, who is the image of God, should shine unto them'.

Actually, I missed out a phrase. I did so deliberately. The fact is, I need to clear up a small – but not unimportant – technical matter. Let me draw your attention to the words I left out: '*And even if* our gospel is veiled'. The 'and even if', especially the 'if', could leave the impression that there is some doubt; perhaps the gospel is not veiled to some? To read the apostle's words in this way would be to make a serious mistake. Unfortunately, 'and even if' is the translation adopted in both the NIV and NASB; the NKJV has 'but even if'; the AV opted for 'but if'. This, as I say, is a pity. For what Paul actually wrote was *ei de kai*; tiny words, I agree, but words rich in meaning and nuance on their own; but especially so when joined, as here, in one phrase. This phrase can mean 'but even if', yes, but it can also mean 'but though', or 'though', as it does in '*though* we once regarded Christ...' (2 Cor. 5:16), 'even though' (NKJV, NASB), 'yea, though' (AV). And, of course, 'if' can have the connotation of 'since'. The point I am making is that 'and even if our gospel is veiled' does not hold within it the slightest hint of doubt. The fact is, our gospel *is* veiled to sinners, and they *are* perishing, lost. I think the clause would be better rendered 'even though our gospel is veiled' or 'since our gospel is veiled'. In short: sinners *are* blind, and they are perishing. They cannot see the light. The light is there, shining in all its glory, but they cannot see it. Not only so, 'there is no light in them' (Isa. 8:20, NKJV).

Now for one of those seeming contradictions we come across so frequently in Scripture. Have you noticed that, on the one hand, the trouble with us sinners is that Satan has blinded us (2 Cor. 4:4), yet, on the other hand, we as sinners refuse to recognise the obvious, and we deliberately suppress[7] the truth (Rom. 1:21,28)? Then again, I am a sinner because I am ruined in Adam (Rom. 5:12-21; 1 Cor. 15:21-22,47-49). What is more, God blinds sinners:

Even after Jesus had done all these miraculous signs in their presence, they still would not believe in him. This was to fulfil the word of Isaiah the prophet: 'Lord, who has believed our message and to whom has the arm of the Lord been revealed?' For this reason they could not believe, because, as Isaiah says elsewhere: 'He has blinded their eyes and deadened their hearts, so they can neither see with their eyes, nor understand with their hearts, nor turn – and I would heal them'. Isaiah said this because he saw Jesus' glory and spoke about him (John 12:37-41).

Take careful note of the precise words in the above. The Jews would not believe (verse 37), and this led to them being unable to believe, God having blinded them.

So which is it? I am a sinner; that is a fact! Is it Satan's responsibility or mine or Adam's or God's? All four. With sinners, it is precisely as it was with Pharaoh: God hardened Pharaoh's heart, and Pharaoh hardened his own heart; Pharaoh hardened his own heart, and God hardened Pharaoh's heart. This is what Scripture tells us, over and over again (Ex. 4:21; 7:3,13-14,22; 8:15,19,32; 9:7,12,34-35; 10:1,20,27; 11:10; 14:8).

---

[7] 'Suppress' from *katechō*, 'to restrain, hinder' (Thayer).

So why are men, as men, universally blinded? Man is in Adam; man, as a sinner, is blind; Satan blinds him; and he blinds himself; and God blinds him. Listen to Luke's account of the close of Paul's preaching the gospel to the Jewish leaders in Rome: 'From morning till evening he explained and declared to them the kingdom of God and tried to convince them about Jesus from the law of Moses and from the prophets. Some were convinced by what he said, but others would not believe. They disagreed among themselves and began to leave after Paul had made this final statement':

The Holy Spirit spoke the truth to your forefathers when he said through Isaiah the prophet: 'Go to this people and say: "You will be ever hearing but never understanding; you will be ever seeing but never perceiving". For this people's heart has become calloused; they hardly hear with their ears, and they have closed their eyes. Otherwise they might see with their eyes, hear with their ears, understand with their hearts and turn, and I would heal them' (Acts 28:23-27).

This was nothing new. Take Acts 4. Since the Jewish authorities 'could see the man who had been healed standing there with them, there was nothing they could say' (Acts 4:14); they had to admit that a miracle had been done. So... what was their reaction? Find out more? Not a bit of it! Silence the gospel-peddlers! Suppress the truth! Put a stop to its spread! Consider the Jews in Damascus when Paul preached there immediately following his conversion: 'Saul grew more and more powerful and baffled the Jews living in Damascus by proving that Jesus is the Christ'. So what was their reaction: 'The Jews conspired to kill him' (Acts 9:22-23)! How about trying to answer him? And when they failed to kill him, or his doctrine, how about yielding to the truth? Consider the leaders of the Jews when faced with Christ. They admitted that he was 'performing many miraculous signs'. So how did they react? He had to die; that is, he had to be assassinated! (John 11:45-53). Blindness, obdurate blindness!

Take another everyday example of this deliberate blindness, this deliberate refusal to recognise what is staring us all in the face:

The heavens declare the glory of God; the skies proclaim the work of his hands. Day after day they pour forth speech; night after night they display knowledge. There is no speech or language where their voice is not heard. Their voice goes out into all the earth, their words to the

64

ends of the world. In the heavens he has pitched a tent for the sun, which is like a bridegroom coming forth from his pavilion, like a champion rejoicing to run his course (Ps. 19:1-5).

Now what do men do with that inescapable proclamation, that endless speech from all nature? Nature is crying out to them, 'day after day, night after night', and unambiguously speaking in every man's language, throughout the world, it is telling them: 'There is a God. Look at his wisdom, his power! How good and great he must be! How he deserves our praise, thanksgiving and worship!' But how do men respond? Spiritually speaking, they stuff their fingers in their ears, and deliberately and defiantly close their eyes. They simply suppress the knowledge. They stifle nature's voice. They cannot see the hand of God in creation. Rather, they do not want to see the hand of God in creation. No! Let me say it as it is: they refuse to see it! They will not see it! They are determined not to see it! Instead, they prefer to ascribe all to blind luck, fate, chance – evolution. Instead of an all-wise God who has shown infinite goodness in creation (now ruined in the fall), men prefer to ascribe all that they see about them to that most cruel of tyrants: blind fate and 'the survival of the fittest'. And that mantra, worked out – as it ought to be, by its advocates – has produced what? The Nazis, and their unspeakable cult of National Socialism, for a start. And we know what that led to.[8]

---

8 On reading this, Andrew Rome helpfully directed me to Richard Weikart: *From Darwin to Hitler...*, Palgrave Macmillan, New York, 2004. Weikart met heavy criticism for his book. He responded: 'What I demonstrated in detail in my book is that many leading Darwinists themselves argued overtly that Darwinism did indeed undermine the sanctity-of-life ethic, and they overtly appealed to Darwinism when they promoted infanticide, euthanasia, racial extermination, *etc.* I specifically noted that not all Darwinists took this position, but those who did were leading Darwinian biologists, medical professors, psychiatrists, *etc.* They were not some fringe group of ignorant fanatics; they were mainstream Darwinists. Also, I did not simply show that leading Darwinists supported eugenics, infanticide, euthanasia, and racial extermination; I showed that they appealed overtly to Darwinism to justify their position. So, it is not Weikart who is reading Darwinism into the record. Darwinists themselves made these arguments. Therefore, critics of the position that Darwinism devalues human life should not attack me, but rather should attack those

Let us never forget it. Let me confront this evolution talk. 'Survival of the fittest', is it? Those who heard Richard Dimbleby's BBC report on entering Belsen in 1945 never could forget it. He couldn't! He recorded that it was the most horrible day of his life. Or what about Martin Gilbert's sudden and devastating realisation of what he was doing when he let the gritty dust trickle through his fingers on his visit to eastern Europe after the war? I shall not forget my own visit to Auschwitz. I hear the crunch of the gravel beneath my feet even as I write. I see the piles and piles of human hair in my mind's eye. 'The survival of the fittest'! I wonder if the commandant remembered that, and questioned his own fitness and future, as he faced his own gallows at Auschwitz, staring (surely in horror)[9] at the barracks where he had so cruelly imprisoned, gassed and incinerated thousands of Jews, Poles, Russians, gypsies and others? And what about the day he faces God at the great tribunal?

Here we have it. Blindness! For all their high-sounding sentiments, at bottom, men would prefer to have a god who produces Belsen and Auschwitz than the all-wise, all-gracious, all-loving, all-merciful God and Father of our Lord Jesus Christ! Could there be any greater manifestation of the wickedness of the human heart, and the utter stupidity to which sin has reduced us?

What is more, those who continue to hold to 'the survival of the fittest' should never be revolted at genocide or natural disaster – it is only 'the survival of the fittest'! Above all, never again should blinded sinners, deliberately self-blinded sinners, ever try to complain about God 'allowing' such things, and 'doing nothing about it'. Let 'the survival of the fittest' be their comfort! They want 'blind fate' as their god; they mustn't complain when blind fate does things they somehow don't like.

Darwinists I exposed in my work' (downloaded from the website csustan.edu/History/Faculty/Weikart/response-to-critics). Rome: 'I found the measured way in which he [Weikart] links the two devastatingly effective' (in a private email, 6th Nov. 2013).

[9] I say that, but, as I write, the death has been announced of Hitler's bodyguard, Rochus Misch, vainly denying to the last his master's part in the holocaust.

Evolution? Man is improving, on an upward course? How can men believe it? Degeneracy marks us all. Man is blind. Satan blinds him, and he blinds himself.

The path of the righteous is like the first gleam of dawn, shining ever brighter till the full light of day. But the way of the wicked is like deep darkness; they do not know what makes them stumble (Prov. 4:18-19).

Men are blinded by Satan; he blinds their minds, and this means ignorance

'The god of this age has blinded the minds of unbelievers, so that they cannot see the light of the gospel of the glory of Christ, who is the image of God' (2 Cor. 4:4). Because Satan has blinded the minds of those who do not believe, they cannot think straight, they cannot see what is staring them in the face, and they cannot believe God when he speaks to them, as he does – every day and every night, in everything around him. And this Satanic blindness begets and enforces the fundamental sin which, in turn, produces the catalogue of sins I have spoken of. Satan rules the roost. He is 'the prince of this world' (John 14:30). Paul spoke of 'the trap of the devil' – the one 'who has taken [sinners] captive to do his will' (2 Tim. 2:26). 'The whole world is under the control of the evil one' (1 John 5:19).[10] Yet men deny it! Even so, Christ and the apostles proclaim it.

Satan is the great deceiver:

The devil, or Satan, who *leads the whole world astray* (Rev. 12:9), Satan, who *deceives the whole world* (NKJV). The [second] beast... *deceived the inhabitants of the earth* (Rev. 13:14). The beast... and with him the false prophet who had performed the miraculous signs on his behalf. With these signs he had *deluded* those who had received the mark of the beast and worshipped his image (Rev. 19:20). The devil, or Satan, [was] bound... for a thousand years. [The angel] threw him into the Abyss and locked and sealed it over him, to keep him from *deceiving the nations* any more until the thousand years were ended... When the thousand years are over, Satan will be released from his prison and will go out to *deceive the nations* in the four corners of the earth... And the devil, who *deceived* them, was thrown into the lake of burning sulphur, where the beast and the false prophet had been

---

[10] See also John 17:15; Gal. 1:4.

thrown. They will be tormented day and night for ever and ever (Rev. 20:2-3,7-8,10).

Satan uses men to deceive others by their teaching (Matt. 24:4-5,11,24; Rom. 16:18; Eph. 4:14; 5:6; 2 Thess. 2:3; 2 Tim. 3:13; 1 Pet. 2:1-3; 1 John 3:7; 4:1-6; 2 John 7; Rev. 18:23). Not only that! He acts directly upon unbelievers so that when they hear the word of God, the gospel, he robs them of it. We have Jesus' explanation of his parable: 'The seed is the word of God. Those along the path are the ones who hear, and then the devil comes and takes away the word from their hearts, so that they may not believe and be saved' (Luke 8:11-12). And this was what I meant when I said there is a very good reason for the return of old error. Satan is ever bent on robbing men, not excluding believers, of the truth, and bringing them into error of every kind, into bondage of every kind – to the Mosaic law, the basic principles of the world, idols of every kind, 'special days and months and seasons and years', 'hollow and deceptive philosophy, which depends on human tradition and the basic principles of this world' – anything and everything except Christ (Gal. 3:23; 4:3,8-11; Col. 2:8,16,20-23; 1 John 2:22-23; 4:1-3); in particular, in the passage we are considering, trying to bring men under the law. Not least, and in the context of the Judaisers at Corinth, and elsewhere, we have the apostle's injunction to Titus:

There are many rebellious people, mere talkers and deceivers, *especially those of the circumcision group.* They must be silenced, because they are ruining whole households by teaching things they ought not to teach – and that for the sake of dishonest gain... Therefore, rebuke [the believers] sharply, so that they will be sound in the faith and will pay no attention to Jewish myths or to the commands of those who reject the truth... To those who are corrupted and do not believe, nothing is pure. In fact, both their minds and consciences are corrupted. They claim to know God, but by their actions they deny him. They are detestable, disobedient and unfit for doing anything good (Tit. 1:10-16).

In our passage, Paul takes Christ's doctrine and drives it home: 'The god of this age has blinded the minds of unbelievers' (2 Cor. 4:4). This spiritual blindness is a fact of life, the truth about all of us, Jews or not. All men, by nature, are blinded by Satan, and ignorant – ignorant of themselves, ignorant of God, ignorant of

Christ, ignorant of eternity, and ignorant of their danger. Admittedly, the sum of human knowledge has increased vastly this past century – but not in these vital areas. Man is still sitting in darkness on all the great issues, as much as ever he was – Satan sees to that.[11] Man is still in the place, spiritually speaking, where Christ began his ministry – 'in Capernaum... in the area of Zebulun and Naphtali'. And why did Christ begin his ministry there? In order:

To fulfil what was said through the prophet Isaiah: 'Land of Zebulun and land of Naphtali, the way to the sea, along the Jordan, Galilee of the Gentiles – the people *living in darkness* have seen a great light; on those *living in the land of the shadow of death* a light has dawned'. From that time on Jesus began to preach: 'Repent, for the kingdom of heaven is near' (Matt. 4:14-17; see also Isa. 9:1-7).

I will return to the question of the light dawning upon sinners in the gospel. For now I simply draw attention to the darkness in which sinners are plunged, and the darkness that is within them. Men are ignorant. Yes, even the most intellectual of them. The gospel, and all to do with it, seems nothing but nonsense to them. 'The fool says in his heart: "There is no God". They are corrupt, their deeds are vile; there is no one who does good' (Ps. 14:1; 53:1). In his heart, I stress. It's not just a question of knowledge, the mind; the will of man, his heart, is blinded. Paul confessed that though, before Christ converted him, he had been a Jewish rabbi, yet he had been ignorant, unbelieving, a blasphemer, and worse (1 Tim. 1:13). How much more this can be said of man in general. Peter could remind believers of 'the evil desires [they] had when [they] lived in ignorance', and 'the ignorant talk of foolish men' (1 Pet. 1:14; 2:15). Do not miss the link with 'the fool' just mentioned. Paul could talk of 'the Gentiles... in the futility of their thinking' who 'are darkened in their understanding and separated from the life of God because of the ignorance that is in them due to the hardening of their hearts' (Eph. 4:18). 'Their thinking [is] futile and their foolish hearts [are] darkened' (Rom. 1:21). That which Christ said of the time of his crucifixion can, I'm sure, be extended to this

---

[11] But, as I have shown, it also involves the sinner's willing suppression of the truth (Rom. 1:18,21,25,28).

present age: 'This is [the] hour... when darkness reigns' (Luke 22:53).

Satan is always about his work. Hugh Latimer:

And now I would ask a strange question: who is the most diligent bishop and prelate in all England that passes all the rest in doing his office? I can tell for I know... who it is; I know him well... There is one that passes all the other, and is the most diligent prelate and preacher in all England. And will ye know who it is? I will tell you: it is the devil. He is the most diligent preacher of all others; he is never out of his diocese; he is never from his cure; ye shall never find him unoccupied; he is ever in his parish; he keeps residence at all times; you shall never find him out of the way; call for him when you will he is ever at home; the most diligent preacher in all the realm; he is ever at his plough; no lording nor loitering can hinder him; he is ever applying his business; you shall never find him idle, I warrant you. And his office is to hinder religion, to maintain superstition, to set up idolatry, to teach all kind of popery. He is ready as he can be wished for to set forth his plough, to devise as many ways as can be to deface and obscure God's glory...O that our prelates would be as diligent to sow the corn of good doctrine as Satan is to sow cockle and darnel.[12]

'The devil prowls around like a roaring lion looking for someone to devour' (1 Pet. 5:8). Satan attacked Christ (Matt. 4:1-11). He certainly knew where Judas lived, and he turned him into a devil (Luke 22:3; John 6:70: 13:27). He went after Peter (Luke 22:31) and used Peter to tempt Christ (Matt. 16:23). He had his way with Ananias and Sapphira (Acts 5:3). (See also 1 Cor. 7:5; 2 Cor. 2:11; 11:14; 1 Thess. 2:18; 1 Tim. 5:15; Rev. 2:9,13,24; 3:9).

And men are not only blinded by Satan, and ignorant; they are slaves

When the synagogue ruler objected because Christ healed a crippled woman on the sabbath, Jesus retorted: 'Should not this woman, a daughter of Abraham, whom Satan has *kept bound* for eighteen long years, be set free on the sabbath day from what bound her?' (Luke 13:16). The same might be said of all sinners: they are 'kept bound', blinded by Satan.

---

[12] Hugh Latimer: 'Sermon on the Plough', preached 29th Jan. 1548 (wikiquote.org).

2. The Problem Confronting Humanity

Again, Jesus, addressing the Jews, spoke to them about their father. They retorted at once: 'Abraham is our father... The only Father we have is God himself'. Jesus responded:

If God were your Father, you would love me, for I came from God and now am here. I have not come on my own; but he sent me. Why is my language not clear to you? Because you are unable to hear what I say. You belong to your father, the devil, and you want to carry out your father's desire... You do not belong to God (John 8:38-47).

Reading the entire passage, you will soon see that Jesus spelled out exactly what he meant. The Jews were blind, deaf, unable to believe, ignorant. Yet they were the ancient people of God; they had God's law; they had the patriarchs; they had their great and wise leaders – Abraham, Moses, David, Solomon, and all the rest; they had the prophets; they had the Scriptures. Nevertheless, none of that kept them from blindness and sin. Every last Jew was a sinner. Jesus told them plainly that it was because Satan had blinded their hearts and minds that the Jews could not believe in him (Jesus); in fact, they hated him and wanted to kill him. They were in bondage; they were slaves of sin and Satan. So said Christ, addressing the Jews. I have just mentioned Paul's own case: his experience is a classic illustration of Christ's statement.

The Jews were in bondage; they were the slaves of sin and Satan. That is what Christ told them. They claimed they could see, even boasting of it, but their unfounded confidence made them yet more culpable. Compare the way Paul addressed Elymas at Paphos, calling him 'a child of the devil', the Lord immediately striking him blind (Acts 13:10-11). And if Christ's words were true of the Jews in his own day, how much more so for us all in our day. Millions are living and dying oblivious of the fact that they are sinners in darkness, or pretending that they are oblivious to it. Many openly deny it! Most simply suppress it. Satan has blinded their minds (2 Cor. 4:3-4). Indeed, many feel that they are right with God, can see perfectly well, thank you very much – bragging that they are master of their fate! How about this, by William Ernest Henley, for whistling in the dark?

2. The Problem Confronting Humanity

Out of the night that covers me,
Black as the pit from pole to pole,
I thank whatever gods may be
For my unconquerable soul.

In the fell clutch of circumstance
I have not winced nor cried aloud.
Under the bludgeonings of chance
My head is bloody, but unbowed.

Beyond this place of wrath and tears
Looms but the horror of the shade,
And yet the menace of the years
Finds, and shall find, me unafraid.

It matters not how strait the gate,
How charged with punishments the scroll.
I am the master of my fate:
I am the captain of my soul.

Take Algernon Charles Swinburne who spoke thus: 'Glory to Man in the highest! For Man is the master of things'.[13] Oh yes?

For another similar effort, take 'Ozymandias' by Percy Bysshe Shelley, who, at least, had the grace to admit the utter stupidity of his subject's vain claims:

I met a traveller from an antique land
Who said: 'Two vast and trunkless legs of stone
Stand in the desert. Near them on the sand,
Half sunk, a shattered visage lies, whose frown
And wrinkled lip and sneer of cold command
Tell that its sculptor well those passions read
Which yet survive, stamped on these lifeless things,
The hand that mocked them and the heart that fed.
And on the pedestal these words appear:
"My name is Ozymandias, King of Kings:
Look on my works, ye mighty, and despair!"
Nothing beside remains. Round the decay
Of that colossal wreck, boundless and bare,
The lone and level sands stretch far away'.

Take C.E.M.Joad who was honest enough to admit that though he had 'rejected the doctrine of original sin', he, along with many

---

[13] Babbage p21.

others, 'were always disappointed'. Disappointed in what? Disappointed in the failure of men to live in a reasonable way with other men. Still he held to 'the infinite perfectibility of man'. The final straw however, was the Second World War which brought him to face reality: 'Evil is endemic in man;... the Christian doctrine of original sin expresses a deep and essential insight into human nature'.[14] Men are slaves! Even the most advanced of men! Slaves to sin and to Satan!

Getting back to the Jews: they did not like Christ's rebuke, retorting: 'We are Abraham's descendants, and have never been slaves of anyone... Abraham is our father... The only Father we have is God himself'. Nevertheless, Jesus told them bluntly: 'You do not belong to God' (John 8:31-47). Let us learn the lesson: just because sinners feel no remorse, have no sense of danger, and are not concerned about their plight, because they are self-confident and presumptuous, because they can sneer at the Bible, it doesn't mean all is well, and that they aren't in a state of blindness and ruin and slavery. Quite the reverse! Their misguided boasting is nothing less than a consummate demonstration of their unregenerate state and, therefore, of the fact that they are sinners blinded by Satan, held captive by him.

Let me show that Scripture uniformly and repeatedly sets out the human plight in terms of blindness and slavery, and all under the power and cunning of Satan. As I have just shown, one grievous demonstration of this, of course, is the fact that most men simply dismiss the very idea with a wave of the hand and a laugh. If you are one such, reader, may I ask you: to what do you ascribe all the misery in the world – misery brought about by the sin of each and every man on the planet? Social conditions and the like won't do, as you well know. In fact, to blame transgression on poverty is a massive injustice to the many poor people who are anything but notorious sinners. No! I am asking you for your suggestion, a sensible, worthy suggestion, as to the root cause of the world's plight. What do you say it is? This is what the Bible says about it:

---

[14] See Babbage pp17-18.

2. The Problem Confronting Humanity

We know that... the whole world is under the control of the evil one (1 John 5:19), the prince of this world (John 12:31), the evil one (John 17:15).

The creation was subjected to frustration, not by its own choice, but by the will of the one who subjected it, in hope that the creation itself will be liberated from its bondage to decay and brought into the glorious freedom of the children of God. We know that the whole creation has been groaning as in the pains of childbirth right up to the present time (Rom. 8:20-22).

The Gentiles... in the futility of their thinking... are darkened in their understanding and separated from the life of God because of the ignorance that is in them due to the hardening of their hearts. Having lost all sensitivity, they have given themselves over to sensuality so as to indulge in every kind of impurity, with a continual lust for more... The fruitless deeds of darkness... It is shameful even to mention what the disobedient do in secret (Eph. 4:18-19; 5:11-12).

[False teachers] promise... freedom, while they themselves are slaves of depravity – for a man is a slave to whatever has mastered him (2 Pet. 2:19), slaves to sin (Rom: 6:17). I tell you the truth, everyone who sins is a slave to sin (John 8:34).

The man without the Spirit does not accept the things that come from the Spirit of God, for they are foolishness to him, and he cannot understand them, because they are spiritually discerned (1 Cor. 2:14).

The Spirit clearly says that in later times some will abandon the faith and follow deceiving spirits and things taught by demons. Such teachings come through hypocritical liars, whose consciences have been seared as with a hot iron (1 Tim. 4:1-2).

People [are] lovers of themselves, lovers of money, boastful, proud, abusive, disobedient to their parents, ungrateful, unholy, without love, unforgiving, slanderous, without self-control, brutal, not lovers of the good, treacherous, rash, conceited, lovers of pleasure rather than lovers of God – having a form of godliness but denying its power... These men oppose the truth – men of depraved minds, who, as far as the faith is concerned, are rejected (2 Tim. 3:2-4,8).

The heart is deceitful above all things and beyond cure. Who can understand it? (Jer. 17:9). Can the Ethiopian change his skin or the leopard its spots? Neither can you do good who are accustomed to doing evil (Jer.13:23).

You used to be slaves to sin... You used to offer the parts of your body in slavery to impurity and to ever-increasing wickedness... When you were slaves to sin, you were free from the control of righteousness. What benefit did you reap at that time from the things you are now ashamed of ? Those things result in death!... For the wages of sin is death (Rom. 6:17,19-21,23).

These dreamers pollute their own bodies, reject authority and slander celestial beings... These men speak abusively against whatever they do not understand; and what things they do understand by instinct, like unreasoning animals – these are the very things that destroy them. Woe to them! They have taken the way of Cain; they have rushed for profit into Balaam's error; they have been destroyed in Korah's rebellion... These men are blemishes... They are clouds without rain, blown along by the wind; autumn trees, without fruit and uprooted – twice dead. They are wild waves of the sea, foaming up their shame; wandering stars, for whom blackest darkness has been reserved forever. Enoch, the seventh from Adam, prophesied about these men: 'See, the Lord is coming with thousands upon thousands of his holy ones to judge everyone, and to convict all the ungodly of all the ungodly acts they have done in the ungodly way, and of all the harsh words ungodly sinners have spoken against him'. These men are grumblers and faultfinders; they follow their own evil desires; they boast about themselves and flatter others for their own advantage. But, dear friends, remember what the apostles of our Lord Jesus Christ foretold. They said to you: 'In the last times there will be scoffers who will follow their own ungodly desires'. These are the men who divide you, who follow mere natural instincts and do not have the Spirit (Jude 8 - 19).

But there were also false prophets among the people, just as there will be false teachers among you. They will secretly introduce destructive heresies, even denying the sovereign Lord who bought them – bringing swift destruction on themselves. Many will follow their shameful ways and will bring the way of truth into disrepute. In their greed these teachers will exploit you with stories they have made up. Their condemnation has long been hanging over them, and their destruction has not been sleeping (2 Pet. 2:1-3).

So much for Scripture. Now for you – what do you say? Many around us will instinctively disagree with Scripture, even to the point of anger. But what, I wonder, is their explanation of all the 'wrongness' in the human heart. We hear a great deal from gospel-opponents about the basic 'goodness' of man; what about the obvious 'badness'?

And thinking men do realise that something is fundamentally wrong with man, don't they? Take Jean Jacques Rousseau, who is usually thought to argue for the basic goodness of man. His idea of man's innate goodness has had a profound influence on the concept of the nature of man, not least in education. But consider this assessment of Rousseau, given by the *Stanford Encyclopaedia of Philosophy*:

Rousseau's own view of philosophy and philosophers was firmly negative, seeing philosophers as the *post-hoc* rationalisers of self-interest, as apologists for various forms of tyranny, and as playing a role in the alienation of the modern individual from humanity's natural impulse to compassion. The concern that dominates Rousseau's work is to find a way of preserving human freedom in a world where human beings are increasingly dependent on one another for the satisfaction of their needs. This concern has two dimensions: material and psychological, of which the latter has greater importance. In the modern world, human beings come to derive their very sense of self from the opinion of others, a fact which Rousseau sees as corrosive of freedom and destructive of individual authenticity. In his mature work, he principally explores two routes to achieving and protecting freedom: the first is a political one aimed at constructing political institutions that allow for the co-existence of free and equal citizens in a community where they themselves are sovereign; the second is a project for child-development and education that fosters autonomy and avoids the development of the most destructive forms of self-interest. However, though Rousseau believes the co-existence of human beings in relations of equality and freedom is possible, he is consistently and overwhelmingly pessimistic that humanity will escape from a dystopia [a society characterized by human misery, squalor, oppression, disease and overcrowding; the opposite of utopia] of alienation, oppression, and un-freedom.

Again:

Rousseau repeatedly claims that a single idea is at the centre of his world view, namely, that human beings are good by nature but are rendered corrupt by society. Unfortunately, despite the alleged centrality of this claim, it is difficult to give it a clear and plausible interpretation. One obvious problem is present from the start: since society, the alleged agent of corruption, is composed entirely of naturally good human beings, how can evil ever get a foothold? It is also difficult to see what 'natural goodness' might be. In various places Rousseau clearly states that morality is not a natural feature of human life, so in whatever sense it is that human beings are good by nature, it is not the moral sense that the casual reader would ordinarily assume.[15]

---

[15] plato.stanford.edu/entries/Rousseau

So much for Rousseau. Pretty damning (though realistic) for a man who thought 'that human beings are good by nature'!

What of Alexander Pope?

> *Know then thyself; presume not God to scan;*
> *The proper study of mankind is man.*
> *Plac'd on this isthmus of a middle state,*
> *A being darkly wise, and rudely great:*
> *With too much knowledge for the sceptic side,*
> *With too much weakness for the stoic's pride,*
> *He hangs between; in doubt to act, or rest,*
> *In doubt to deem himself a god, or beast;*
> *In doubt his mind or body to prefer,*
> *Born but to die, and reas'ning but to err;*
> *Alike in ignorance, his reason such,*
> *Whether he thinks too little, or too much:*
> *Chaos of thought and passion, all confus'd;*
> *Still by himself abus'd, or disabus'd;*
> *Created half to rise, and half to fall;*
> *Great lord of all things, yet a prey to all;*
> *Sole judge of truth, in endless error hurl'd:*
> *The glory, jest, and riddle of the world!*

Was Pope right or not? Time and space would fail me to quote the endless stream of writers who have expressed the misery and degradation within man. Take T.S.Eliot:

One thinks to escape... but one is still alone in an overcrowded desert,[16] jostled by ghosts... It's not being alone that is the horror... what matters is the filthiness... I can clean my skin...[17] but always there is the filthiness that lies a little deeper.[18]

---

[16] I know by personal experience the loneliness after bereavement – and this, most poignantly, when in a crowd. There is far more loneliness out there than many will admit – especially at seasons of supposed jollity!

[17] Echoes of Pilate and his bowl of water (Matt. 27:24), who should have read and acted upon: '"Although you wash yourself with soda and use an abundance of soap, the stain of your guilt is still before me", declares the Sovereign LORD' (Jer. 2:22; see also Job 14:17; Jer. 4:14; Hos. 13:12).

[18] Babbage pp14-15. See Babbage *passim* for a masterly overview of the way modern literature can set out man's 'ill', but is signally lacking when it comes to the cure. It takes God in the new covenant to provide that!

Let me turn to Martin Luther, who hit the biblical nail right on the head. In 1524, Desiderius Erasmus published his *The Freedom of the Will*. A year later, Luther responded with his *On the Bondage of the Will*, in which he pictured man as a horse – ridden either by Satan or by God! The substance of the *Bondage* has been summarised thus:

Luther... maintained that sin incapacitates human beings from working out their own salvation, and that they are completely incapable of bringing themselves to God. As such, there is no free will for humanity because any will they might have is overwhelmed by the influence of sin. Central... are Luther's beliefs concerning the power and complete sovereignty of God. Luther concluded that unredeemed human beings are dominated by Satan; Satan, as the prince of the mortal world, never lets go of what he considers his own unless he is overpowered by a stronger power, *i.e.* God. When God redeems a person, he redeems the entire person, including the will, which then is liberated to serve God.[19] No-one can achieve salvation or redemption through their own choices – people do not choose between good or evil, because they are naturally dominated by evil, and salvation is simply the product of God dominating a person and forcibly [working in them] turning them to good ends. Were it not so, Luther contended, God would not be omnipotent and would lack total sovereignty over creation, and... that arguing otherwise was insulting to the glory of God.[20]

In Luther's own words:

Now this I apprehend to be just the true state of the case: the natural man, having his understanding darkened, being alienated from the life of God, through the ignorance that is in him, because of the blindness of his heart, and being, moreover, possessed by the devil, whose energising consists in maintaining and increasing his blindness, forms his decisions and determinations upon partial and false evidence...
For to this belongs, what Christ and his Evangelists so often assert from Isaiah: 'Hearing, you shall hear and shall not naturally understand; and seeing, you shall see and shall not perceive'. What does this mean, but that the free will, or human heart, is so trodden under foot of Satan, that, except it be miraculously raised up by the Spirit of God, it cannot of itself either see or hear those things which strike upon the very eyes and ears, so manifestly as to be palpable to the hand? Such is the misery and blindness of the human race. For it is

---

[19] See 1 John 2:13-14; 4:4; 5:4-5.
[20] Wikipedia.

thus, that even the Evangelists themselves, after expressing their wonder how it should happen that the Jews were not taken with the works and words of Christ, which were absolutely irresistible and undeniable, reply to their own expressions of wonder, by citing this passage of Scripture: by suggesting, indeed, that man, left to himself, seeing sees not, and hearing hears not. What can be more marvellous? 'The light', says he, 'shines in darkness, and the darkness apprehends [comprehends] it not' [John 1:5]... Besides, it is nothing wonderful, that men of excellent understanding have for so many ages been blind to divine things... For what is the whole human race, without the Spirit, but the kingdom of the devil, as I have said; a confused chaos of darkness? Whence Paul calls the devils 'the rulers of this darkness'; and says (1 Cor. 2. 8): 'None of the princes of this world knew the wisdom of God!' What do you suppose that he thought of the rest [of mankind], when he asserts that the princes of the world were slaves of darkness? For, by princes, he means the first and highest persons in the world: whom you call men of excellent understanding... Why is Christ 'foolishness' to the Gentiles? Are there not among the Gentiles men of excellent understanding? Why is he to the Jews 'a stumbling-block'? Have there not been among the Jews men of excellent understanding? [Of course! But] 'God knows the thoughts of the wise', says Paul; 'for they are vain'. He... singles out 'the first and chiefest among men', that from these we may estimate the rest of them...

Satan [is]... the prince of this world, reigning (according to Christ and Paul) in the wills and minds of men, which are his captives and serve him... It has been proved by testimonies of Scripture, which are neither ambiguous nor obscure, that Satan is by far the most powerful and most crafty prince of the princes of this world. As I have said, under whose reign, the human will, which is now no longer free, and its own master, but the slave of sin and Satan, cannot will anything but what this prince of it shall be pleased to let it will. Nor will he allow it to will anything good: albeit, if Satan did not rule it, sin itself, whose servant man is, would be a sufficient clog upon it to prevent it willing good... Satan... is... called by Christ the prince of this world, and by Paul the god of this age; holding all men captive at his will, who have not been torn from him by the Spirit of Christ.[21]

Such was Luther's assessment of the human plight. I ask again: If you disagree with Luther, to what do you ascribe the universality of sin in mankind? Do you agree with Ovid? 'We know and approve

---

[21] Martin Luther: *On the Bondage of the Will*, openlibrary.org, li-lii, pp121-123,364,366,456.

the better, and do the worse'.[22] And what about the apostle: 'Although they know God's righteous decree that those who do such things deserve death, they not only continue to do these very things but also approve of those who practice them' (Rom. 1:32)?[23]

Though, as I have said, the vast majority will not face the stark and unpalatable truth, some are brought to recognise and admit it. Take John Newton, who, speaking of his unregenerate days, declared: 'When Satan's blind slave, I sported with death'.[24]

Isaac Watts was another to own it:

> *How sad our state by nature is!*
> *Our sin, how deep it stains!*
> *And Satan binds our captive souls*
> *Fast in his slavish chains.*

As was Charles Wesley:

> *Long my imprisoned spirit lay,*
> *Fast bound in sin and nature's night.*[25]

I will return to both hymns. And that's no throwaway remark! Rather, it illustrates what I am trying to say in this book about 'the glorious new-covenant ministry'. Satanic blindness of every man is a reality. But,[26] a *greater* reality is that *Christ*, in the new covenant, the gospel, *has the answer to man's need.*

Turning back to 2 Corinthians, when speaking of the unconverted, the apostle declares that to them 'our gospel is veiled'. What did he mean? 'Our gospel', he says 'is veiled to those who are perishing'. They cannot see; they cannot believe. In other words, as Paul reminded the Ephesians of what they once were, before their conversion:

As for you, you were dead in your transgressions and sins, in which you used to live when you followed the ways of this world and of the ruler of the kingdom of the air, the spirit who is now at work in those

---

[22] Babbage p36.

[23] Now read Rom. 7:15-24. Anticipating what is to come, now read Rom. 7:25 – 8:39, and do so out loud!

[24] 'Begone, unbelief,/ My Saviour is near'.

[25] 'And can it be that I should gain/ An interest in the Saviour's blood?'

[26] Allowing the linguistic *faux pas* – that one can have degrees of reality.

who are disobedient. All of us also lived among them at one time, gratifying the cravings of our flesh and following its desires and thoughts. Like the rest, we were by nature objects of wrath (Eph. 2:1-3).

And, as he told Titus:

We too were foolish, disobedient, deceived and enslaved by all kinds of passions and pleasures. We lived in malice and envy, being hated and hating one another (Tit. 3:3).

As John put it:

Cain... belonged to the evil one and murdered his brother. And why did he murder him? Because his own actions were evil and his brother's were righteous (1 John 3:12).

That's what believers used to be; that's what all unbelievers are, now. Decent, respectable, religious many of them might be, but in truth, every unbeliever is led captive by Satan, at his will, and to do his will (2 Tim. 2:26); every unbeliever is a sinner who cannot believe because Satan has blinded his mind. Quite a catalogue! Some problem!

But still we have not plumbed the depth of it.

Men are not only blinded by Satan, ignorant and slaves; they are helpless in their sin

This blindness not only includes ignorance and bondage. It strikes much deeper. It includes *power*; that is, the lack of spiritual power – the sinner *cannot* believe. Sinners are helpless, powerless to believe. Paul: 'No one can say: "Jesus is Lord", except by the Holy Spirit' (1 Cor. 12:3). Oh, they can mouth the words, like a parrot, but no man can truly say that Christ is Lord, and mean it in his heart. No man by nature can do as Thomas, and declare to Christ: 'My Lord and my God!' (John 20:28). Jesus put it starkly: 'No one can come to me unless the Father who sent me draws him' (John 6:44). Of course, by 'coming' to Christ he didn't mean they couldn't walk or whatever to meet him. Christ meant that sinners couldn't come to him spiritually – they couldn't believe in him (see also John 7:37-38). Nothing has changed. Man is still the same. He has a heart of stone' (Ezek. 36:26). As Jesus explained: 'The Spirit gives life; the flesh counts for nothing. The words I have spoken to you are spirit and they are life. Yet there are some of you who do not believe'. John added his own comment: 'For Jesus had known from the beginning which of them did not believe and who would betray him'. Jesus went on to say: 'This is why I told you that no one can come to me unless the Father has enabled him' (John 6:63-65). It is perfectly clear: 'coming to Christ' here means 'believing on Christ'. As Jesus declared: 'I am the bread of life. He who comes to me will never go hungry, and he who believes in me will never be thirsty' (John 6:35) – 'he who comes... he who believes'. But the main point I am making here is that sinners by nature cannot come to Christ, they cannot believe in Christ, they have no spiritual power to trust Christ: 'No one can come to me unless the Father who sent me draws him' (John 6:44). And as in Christ's day, so today. Sinners have no power to believe. Oh, sinners may like to think that believing is as easy as falling off a log, but they are sadly mistaken in their bravado.

Calvin on the verse:

[Christ] does not merely accuse them of wickedness, but likewise reminds them, that it is a peculiar gift of God to embrace the doctrine which is exhibited by him... Unbelievers... flattering themselves in their obstinacy, have the hardihood to condemn the gospel because it does not please them. On the contrary, therefore, Christ declares that the doctrine of the gospel, though it is preached to all without exception, cannot be embraced by all, but that a new understanding and a new perception are needed; and, therefore, that faith does not depend on the will of men, but that it is God who gives it.[27]

It goes deeper still.

Men are not only blinded by Satan, ignorant, slaves and helpless; they are wilful in their sin

The truth is, the inability, this sinnership, is a matter not only of lack of *knowledge* or *power*; it is a question of *will* also; the sinner *will not* believe. Satan holds them, grips them, in unbelief. As Jesus told the Jews: 'O Jerusalem, Jerusalem, you who kill the prophets and stone those sent to you, how often I have longed to gather your

---

[27] Calvin fell short here. 'No one can come to *me*', said Christ. It is not mere doctrine that sinners cannot believe; it is not mere doctrine that sinners must believe. It is Christ!

children together, as a hen gathers her chicks under her wings, *but you were not willing*' (Matt. 23:37). 'You *refuse* to come to me to have life' (John 5:40). 'Now, I told you that you have seen me but *will not* believe' (John 6:36) (GNB). 'Even after Jesus had done all these miraculous signs in their presence, they still *would not* believe in him' (John 12:37). At bottom, sin is heart-rebellion against God, wilful rebellion. As sinners, we defy him; we will not submit to him; we are determined to go our own way. 'Whoever believes in the Son has eternal life, but whoever rejects the Son will not see life, for God's wrath remains on him' (John 3:36).

Notice: unbelief is *rejection* of Christ, *refusal* to believe, *refusal* to receive him. And refusal of God's offer of salvation is, as Christ made plain, the highest sin, the damning sin.

John Gill on John 6:44:

They had neither power nor will of themselves; being dead in trespasses and sins, and impotent to everything that is spiritual: and while men are in a state of unregeneracy, blindness, and darkness, they see no need of coming to Christ, nor anything in him worth coming for; they are prejudiced against him, and their hearts are set on other things; and besides, coming to Christ and believing in Christ being the same thing, it is certain faith is not of a man's self, it is the gift of God, and the operation of his Spirit; and therefore efficacious grace must be exerted to enable a soul to come to Christ.[28]

Note Gill's assessment: 'They are prejudiced against [Christ], and their hearts are set on other things'. When Paul addressed the Jewish leaders at the start of his house-arrest in Rome, we read that 'some were convinced by what he said, but others would not believe' (Acts 28:24). Reader, can you spot the imbalance? Some were convinced; others were not convinced. Ah! But *that* is what Luke does *not* say! Some were convinced; the rest refused. That is what Luke says. Literally: 'Some indeed were persuaded... but some disbelieved'; that is, some believed; others would not believe. Their unbelief was a matter of the will, of the heart. Some were converted; others set themselves against it – they would not have it. You see the point: they *would not* believe.

---

[28] Notice how Gill was much better than Calvin here (see the previous note): no talk of *doctrine*, but all about *Christ*.

2. The Problem Confronting Humanity

Calvin on the verse:

Luke declares that this was at length the success of the disputation, that they did not all profit in the same doctrine. We know that the apostle was endued with such grace of the Spirit, that he ought to have moved stones; and yet he could not, after long disputing and testifying, win all men unto Christ. Wherefore, let us not marvel, if the unbelief of many do at this day resist the plain doctrine of the gospel, and if many remain obstinate, to whom the truth of Christ is no less made manifest than the sun at noonday. Moreover, those return from Paul blind and stupid, who came unto him willingly, as if they had been desirous to learn. If there were such stubbornness in voluntary hearers, what marvel is it if those refuse Christ with a malicious mind, who swell with pride and malice, [bitterness] and do openly fly and hate the light?

Do not miss Calvin's 'resist... obstinate... blind and stupid... stubbornness... a malicious mind... malice, [bitterness]... hate'. He was right!

Matthew Henry:

[Paul] not only expounded and testified the kingdom of God, but he persuaded them [that is, he tried to persuade them], urged it upon their consciences and pressed them with all earnestness to embrace the kingdom of God, and submit to it, and not to persist in an opposition to it. He followed his doctrine (the explication and confirmation of it) with a warm and lively application to his hearers, which is the most proper and profitable method of preaching. He persuaded them [as above] concerning Jesus. The design and tendency of his whole discourse were to bring them to Christ, to convince them of his being the Messiah, and to engage them to believe in him as he is offered in the gospel. He urged upon them... the things concerning Jesus... pointing at the Messiah... They being Jews, he dealt with them out of the Scriptures of the Old Testament... [Paul] was in good earnest, and his heart was upon it...

So much for the preacher that day. But what of the hearers?

What was the effect of this discourse? One would have thought that so good a cause as that of Christianity, and managed by such a skilful hand as Paul's, could not but carry the day, and that all the hearers would have yielded to it presently; but it did not prove so: the child Jesus is set for the fall of some and the rising again of others, a foundation stone to some and a stone of stumbling to others... Some of them thought Paul was in the right, others would not admit it. This is that division which Christ came to send, that fire which he came to

84

kindle (Luke 12:49,51). Paul preached with a great deal of plainness and clearness, and yet his hearers could not agree about the sense and evidence of what he preached. Some believed the things that were spoken, and some believed not. There was the disagreement. Such as this has always been the success of the gospel; to some it has been a savour of life unto life, to others a savour of death unto death. Some are wrought upon by the word, and others hardened; some receive the light, and others shut their eyes against it. So it was among Christ's hearers, and the spectators of his miracles; some believed and some blasphemed.

Paul did not leave it there:

'Your eyes you have closed', [he told them] (verse 27). This intimates an obstinate infidelity, and a willing slavery to prejudice... It was true of these unbelieving Jews that they were prejudiced against the gospel; they did not see, because they were resolved they would not, and [there are] none so blind as those that will not see. They would not prosecute their convictions, and for this reason would not admit them. They have purposely closed their eyes, lest they should see with their eyes the great things which belong to their everlasting peace, should see the glory of God, the amiableness of Christ, the deformity of sin, the beauty of holiness, the vanity of this world, and the reality of another. They will not be changed and governed by these truths, and therefore will not receive the evidence of them, lest they should hear with their ears that which they are loath to hear, the wrath of God revealed from heaven against them, and the will of God revealed from heaven to them. They stop their ears, like the deaf adder, that will not hearken to the voice of the charmer, charm he ever so wisely. Thus their fathers did; they would not hear (Zech. 7:11,12)... They kept their mind in the dark, or at least in a constant confusion and tumult, lest, if they should admit a considerate sober thought, they should understand with their heart how much it is both their duty and their interest... and they should be converted from the evil ways which they take pleasure in, to those exercises to which they have now an aversion.

Matthew Henry drew the application:

Observe: God's method is to bring people first to see and then so to understand with their hearts, and then to convert them, and bow their wills, and so heal them, which is the regular way of dealing with a rational soul; and therefore Satan prevents the conversion of souls to God by blinding the mind and darkening the understanding (2 Cor. 4:4). And the case is very sad when the sinner joins with him herein, and puts out his own eyes... they plunge into ignorance, that they may sin the more freely. They are in love with their disease, and are afraid lest God should heal them...[29] What with their resisting the grace of God and rebelling against the light, and God's withdrawing and withholding his grace and light from them – what with their not receiving the love of the truth, and God's giving them up for that to strong delusions, to believe a lie – what with their wilful [prejudice?] and what with their judicial hardness, the heart of this people is waxed gross, and their ears are dull of hearing. They are stupid and senseless, and not wrought upon by all that can be said to them. No medicine that can be given them operates upon them, nor will reach them, and therefore their disease must be adjudged incurable, and their case desperate. How should those be happy that will not be healed of a disease that makes them miserable?[30] And how should those be healed that will not be converted to the use of the methods of cure? And how should those be converted that will not be convinced either of their disease or of their remedy? And how should those be convinced that shut their eyes and stop their ears? Let all that hear the gospel, and do not heed it, tremble at this doom; for, when once they are thus given up to hardness of heart, they are already in the suburbs of hell; for who shall heal them, if God does not?

The upshot?

When Paul had said these words, he had said enough for them, and they departed, perhaps not so much enraged as some others of their nation had been upon the like occasion, but stupid and unconcerned, no more affected, either with those terrible words in the close of his discourse or all the comfortable words he had spoken before, than the seats they sat on. They departed, many of them with a resolution never to hear Paul preach again, nor trouble themselves with further enquiries about this matter.

I do not see how it could be put any clearer.

I am reminded of the time when the Jewish bigwigs were questioning Jesus, pestering him for his authority for the things he was doing. Jesus replied by telling them that he would answer their question if they would answer his. And what was his question? Just this: John the Baptist – his baptism – was it from heaven or men?

---

[29] Henry has put his finger on something here; deep down there are no atheists – they *know* but they *suppress* (Rom. 1:18,21,25,28). They do not want God to reign over them. See the following note.

[30] See the previous note. Suppression leads to misery.

The Jews chewed it over, privately. 'We can't say: "From heaven"', they said. 'If we do he'll want to know why we didn't believe John'. 'On the other hand, we can't say: "From men". If we do, the people will go berserk and do all sorts – they think John was a prophet'. So, returning to Jesus, this is what they said: 'We don't know'. Now that was a downright lie! They did know! *But they didn't want to say.* Jesus pounced: 'Neither will I tell you by what authority I am doing these things' (Matt. 21:23-27). Did you spot it? 'We don't know', they said. 'Oh no', retorted Christ, 'it's not a question of knowledge – you do know. It's all a question of *will.* You *will not* tell me, so I will not tell you'.

This is the point. Will not! Would not! Refusal of Christ is a question of *will.* It involves ignorance, yes; it involves spiritual inability, yes; but above all it involves resentment of Christ and the gospel (Rom. 8:7), an unwillingness to receive him, an unwillingness to be under his Lordship, and is a refusal of Christ. When Paul and Barnabas preached at Iconium, 'a great number of Jews and Gentiles believed'. But not all. Some 'Jews... refused to believe' (Acts 14:1-2). Again when he was at Ephesus, 'Paul entered the synagogue and spoke boldly there for three months, arguing persuasively about the kingdom of God. But some of them became obstinate; they refused to believe and publicly maligned the Way' (Acts 19:8-9). To say 'no' to Christ, therefore, is not something to be excused or pitied. In a sense, we should not feel sorry for those who hear the gospel and do not believe. We do, of course. But the truth is, they refuse to have Christ: 'We don't want this man to be our king' (Luke 19:14). Or, as it could be translated: 'We will not have this man to reign over us'. There it is: the will. When people say something like: 'I wish I could believe', what are they really saying? If anybody says that to me, he is paying me a massive insult – he wishes he could believe me? Really? He wishes he could trust me? Hmm! Well, then, think how it must sound to God. 'I wish I could believe', indeed![31] As I have just noted, it's all a question of suppression, stifling the truth. The intellectual atheists

---

[31] We must let them know that in the spiritual world sight follows faith, not the other way round (2 Cor. 5:7). Believing is seeing; not, as the world would have it, seeing is believing. See 2 Cor. 4:18.

claim that we believers suppress reality, will not face it, cannot face it; the boot is on the other foot.

In the book of Proverbs, Christ is personified as Wisdom (as a woman, I admit) addressing the crowd. What reaction does he get?

Wisdom calls aloud in the street, she raises her voice in the public squares; at the head of the noisy streets she cries out, in the gateways of the city she makes her speech: 'How long will you simple ones love your simple ways? How long will mockers delight in mockery and fools hate knowledge? If you had responded to my rebuke, I would have poured out my heart to you and made my thoughts known to you. But since you rejected me when I called and no one gave heed when I stretched out my hand, since you ignored all my advice and would not accept my rebuke, I in turn will laugh at your disaster; I will mock when calamity overtakes you – when calamity overtakes you like a storm, when disaster sweeps over you like a whirlwind, when distress and trouble overwhelm you. Then they will call to me but I will not answer; they will look for me but will not find me. Since they hated knowledge and did not choose to fear the LORD, since they would not accept my advice and spurned my rebuke, they will eat the fruit of their ways and be filled with the fruit of their schemes. For the waywardness of the simple will kill them, and the complacency of fools will destroy them; but whoever listens to me will live in safety and be at ease, without fear of harm' (Prov. 1:20-33).

God addressed Israel and Judah through the prophets. What was their response?

They refused to pay attention; stubbornly they turned their backs and stopped up their ears. They made their hearts as hard as flint and would not listen to the law or to the words that the LORD Almighty had sent by his Spirit through the earlier prophets. So the LORD Almighty was very angry. 'When I called, they did not listen; so when they called, I would not listen', says the LORD Almighty. 'I scattered them with a whirlwind among all the nations, where they were strangers. The land was left so desolate behind them that no one could come or go. This is how they made the pleasant land desolate' (Zech. 7:11-14).

And Christ was explicit in the parable:

A certain man was preparing a great banquet and invited many guests. At the time of the banquet he sent his servant to tell those who had been invited: 'Come, for everything is now ready'. But they all alike began to make excuses. The first said: 'I have just bought a field, and I must go and see it. Please excuse me'. Another said: 'I have just bought five yoke of oxen, and I'm on my way to try them out. Please excuse me'. Still another said: 'I have just got married, so I can't come'. The servant came back and reported this to his master. Then the owner of the house became angry and ordered his servant: 'Go out quickly into the streets and alleys of the town and bring in the poor, the crippled, the blind and the lame'. 'Sir', the servant said, 'what you ordered has been done, but there is still room'. Then the master told his servant: 'Go out to the roads and country lanes and make them come in, so that my house will be full. I tell you, not one of those men who were invited will get a taste of my banquet' (Luke 14:16-24).

In short, the problem with society, with men, women and children, with us all, is that we are sinners; that is, we are blinded by Satan, spiritually dead, slaves, unable to change, unwilling to change, with no desire for Christ. John recorded of Christ:

He was in the world, and though the world was made through him, the world did not recognise him. He came to that which was his own, but his own did not receive him (John 1:10-11).

As Isaiah explained:

He had no beauty or majesty to attract us to him, nothing in his appearance that we should desire him. He was despised and rejected by men, a man of sorrows, and familiar with suffering. Like one from whom men hide their faces he was despised, and we esteemed him not (Isa. 53:2-3).

Christ, speaking though the psalmist:

I am a worm and not a man, scorned by men and despised by the people. All who see me mock me; they hurl insults, shaking their heads (Ps. 22:6-7).

And speaking directly:

Jesus took the twelve aside and told them: 'We are going up to Jerusalem, and everything that is written by the prophets about the Son of Man will be fulfilled. He will be turned over to the Gentiles. They will mock him, insult him, spit on him, flog him and kill him' (Luke 18:31-32).

Paul broadened this view of the sinner's rebellion:

Those who live according to the flesh have their minds set on what the flesh desires... The mind of sinful man is death... the sinful mind is hostile to God. It does not submit to God's law, nor can it do so. Those controlled by the flesh cannot please God (Rom. 8:5-8).

We have a classic example of the wilful blindness of sinners when faced by Christ. I am thinking of the conference the Jewish leaders called in response to Christ's miracles – particularly in making the blind man to see (John 9:13-34,40-41), and the raising of Lazarus (John 11:45-53). If ever a meeting showed the deliberate blindness of sinners towards Jesus, the determination to suppress the truth, that one did! The Jews admitted that Jesus was doing miracles. How did they respond? What was their first thought? If this goes on, we shall lose our power, status, authority and following. More, the Romans will be provoked, they will step in and destroy us, our nation and temple. The solution? Get rid of him! At all costs, we must save the nation, save our religion, and save our skins and secure our position! So much so, they even drew up plans to kill Lazarus (John 12:9-11).

But they had already admitted that Jesus was doing miracles! So why not believe him? Why not trust God to work out his purpose? Why not throw in their lot with the miracle-worker and see where God would take them?

No! Stifle the evidence, get rid of the Christ! There is one further point: God shows his sovereignty even in this, but I will have more to say on that subject when it arises later on. For now, I simply want to bring out the defiance, the wilful suppression of the truth so clearly manifested in the way these Jews responded to the facts that they admitted. This is what we are dealing with when approaching sinners with the gospel.

We must not be fooled! Beware of pseudo-scientific jargon, not to say, babble. Any unbeliever can trot out: 'Science says', 'evolution proves', 'sexual perversion – lesbianism and homosexuality – along with a host of other forms of deviant behaviour, are all genetic'; and so on. Don't be fooled! Unbeliever, don't try to kid yourself! At bottom, sinners wilfully suppress the truth. If they can mask it with cod-science so much, they think, the better. The fool says in his heart: 'There is no God' (Ps. 14:1). These 'fools', as Gill commented, are:

Not such who are idiots, persons void of common sense and understanding; but such who are *fools in their morals*, without understanding in *spiritual* things; wicked profligate wretches, apostates from God, alienated from the life of God; and whose hearts are full of blindness and ignorance, and whose conversations are vile and impure, and they enemies of righteousness, though full of all wicked subtlety and mischief; these say in their hearts (which are desperately wicked, and out of which evil thoughts proceed, pregnant with atheism and impiety) [that 'there is no God']; these *endeavour to work themselves* into such a belief, and inwardly to conclude, *at least to wish* '[there is] no God' – though they do not express it with their mouths, yet *they would fain persuade their hearts* to deny the being of God; *that so having no superior to whom they are accountable, they may go on in sin with impunity*; however, to consider him as altogether such an one as themselves, and to remove such perfections from him, as may render him unworthy to be regarded by them; such as omniscience, omnipresence and to conceive of him as entirely negligent of and unconcerned about affairs of this lower world, having nothing to do with the government of it: and thus to deny his perfections and providence, is all one as to deny his existence, or that there is a God.[32]

Spot on! As the psalmist goes on, speaking of these fools: 'They are corrupt, their deeds are vile; there is no one who does good. The LORD looks down from heaven on the sons of men to see if there are any who understand, any who seek God. All have turned aside, they have together become corrupt; there is no one who does good, not even one. Will evil-doers never learn...?' (Ps. 14:1-4). Let's call a spade a spade!

Matthew Henry:

The sinner here described: he is one that says in his heart: 'There is no God'; he is a [virtual] atheist... [He] cannot doubt of the being of God, but will question *his dominion*. He says this in his heart; it is not his judgment, but his imagination. He cannot satisfy himself that there is none, but *he wishes there were none*, and pleases himself with the fancy that it is possible there may be none. He cannot be sure there is one, and therefore he is *willing* to think there is none... *for the silencing of the clamours of his conscience and the emboldening of himself in his evil ways*... The character of this sinner: he is a fool; he is simple and unwise, and this is an evidence of it; he is wicked and profane, and this is the cause of it. Note, atheistical thoughts are very foolish, wicked thoughts, and they are at the bottom of a great deal of the wickedness that is in this world. The word of God is a discerner of these thoughts,

---

[32] Emphasis mine.

and puts a just brand on him that harbours them... No man will say: 'There is no God' till he is so hardened in sin that *it has become his interest that there should be none to call him to an account.*[33]

And Calvin:

We commonly see that those who, in the estimation both of themselves and of others, highly excel in sagacity and wisdom, employ their cunning in laying snares, and exercise the ingenuity of their minds in despising and mocking God. It is therefore important for us, in the first place, to know that however much the world applauds these crafty and scoffing characters, who allow themselves to indulge to any extent in wickedness, yet the Holy Spirit condemns them as being fools; for there is no stupidity more brutish than forgetfulness of God... From this it follows, that when the ungodly allow themselves to follow their own inclinations, so obstinately and audaciously as they are here represented as doing, without any sense of shame, it is an evidence that they have cast off all fear of God... God from time to time causes even the most wicked of men to feel secret pangs of conscience, that they may be compelled to acknowledge his majesty and sovereign power; but whatever right knowledge God instils into them they partly stifle it by their malice against him, and partly corrupt it... They... fashion an idol in the room of God. As if the time would never come when they will have to appear before him in judgement, they endeavour, in all the transactions and concerns of their life, to remove him to the greatest distance, and to efface from their minds all apprehension of his majesty.

And still we have not got to the bottom of it all.

Sinners are lost, ruined, perishing under the wrath of God

As Paul declared: 'Our gospel is veiled'; 'it is veiled to those who are perishing' (2 Cor. 4:3); sinners are 'perishing'. Here we have unmistakable echoes of John 3:16: 'For God so loved the world that he gave his one and only Son, that whoever believes in him shall not *perish* but have eternal life'. But, of course, if they will not believe, they will perish! Let me re-quote the apostle writing to the Ephesians:

As for you, you were dead in your transgressions and sins, in which you used to live when you followed the ways of this world and of the ruler of the kingdom of the air, the spirit who is now at work in those

---

[33] Emphasis mine.

who are disobedient. All of us also lived among them at one time, gratifying the cravings of our flesh and following its desires and thoughts. Like the rest, we were by nature objects of wrath (Eph. 2:1-3).

It's all here. Sinners are spiritually dead; they are under Satan's domination; they are under the wrath of God; perishing. Jesus stated it as plainly as any man could ask; sinners are condemned in their unbelief. This is the fundamental problem – unbelief. And it leads to eternal condemnation. After speaking so warmly of the love of God for sinners (John 3:16), Jesus went on:

Whoever does not believe stands condemned already because he has not believed in the name of God's one and only Son. This is the verdict: Light has come into the world, but men loved darkness instead of light because their deeds were evil... [And] whoever rejects the Son will not see life, for God's wrath remains on him (John 3:18-19,36).

And Paul could not have been more explicit:

God is just: He will pay back trouble to those who trouble you [believers] and give relief to you who are troubled, and to us as well. This will happen when the Lord Jesus is revealed from heaven in blazing fire with his powerful angels. He will punish those who do not know God and do not obey the gospel of our Lord Jesus. They will be punished with everlasting destruction and shut out from the presence of the Lord and from the majesty of his power on the day he comes to be glorified in his holy people and to be marvelled at among all those who have believed... The secret power of lawlessness is already at work; but the one who now holds it back will continue to do so till he is taken out of the way. And then the lawless one will be revealed, whom the Lord Jesus will overthrow with the breath of his mouth and destroy by the splendour of his coming. The coming of the lawless one will be in accordance with the work of Satan displayed in all kinds of counterfeit miracles, signs and wonders, and in every sort of evil that deceives those who are perishing. They perish because they refused to love the truth and so be saved. For this reason God sends them a powerful delusion so that they will believe the lie and so that all will be condemned who have not believed the truth but have delighted in wickedness (2 Thess. 1:6-10; 2:7-12).

The root problem is unbelief, and the root of unbelief is Satanic blindness. Not only that. It brings in its wake the wrath of God for every sinner outside of Christ. Quite a problem, isn't it, humanity's plight? Sorting it all out is going to be a tall order, isn't it? It's more than enough to make us give up, isn't it? No, said the apostle, 'we do not lose heart' (2 Cor. 4:1); we do not give up; we keep pressing on. We have hope! And, do not forget, reader, the New Testament meaning of hope: confident expectation. 'Therefore, my dear brothers, stand firm. Let nothing move you. Always give yourselves fully to the work of the Lord, because you know that your labour in the Lord is not in vain' (1 Cor. 15:58). 'Let us not become weary in doing good, for at the proper time we will reap a harvest if we do not give up' (Gal. 6:9). We go on in this confident expectation, despite the fact that, unless they repent and trust Christ, sinners will perish, yet, even when they are told the truth, and in the most passionate and starkest of terms, they still by nature wilfully refuse to turn to Christ.

Before I leave this section, does anybody think: 'Well, I thought we were going to be told some glorious good news! Is *this* good news? Is this tale of misery and ugliness and ruination *good* news?' What is my answer? Just this: as we have seen, ignorance is at the root of the sinner's trouble. There are other factors involved, of course, but ignorance characterises every sinner. Now then, imagine that you go to the physician with a complaint, and he starts to tell you a joke, or talks about his holiday or whatever. You would be disappointed, angry, would you not? You want to be taken seriously; you want this professional, this expert, to give his undivided attention to you and to your problem. You want him to diagnose what's wrong, and start to put it right.

Again, imagine that the doctor sits there, obviously bewildered. Say he admits he is not sure, but suggests you 'have a go' at one 'cure' after another – and all fail. Imagine you get a second opinion, with the same result. Suppose you try again, and again... Finally, you meet a physician who assures you that he recognises the nature of your illness and its cause – and, moreover, knows its cure. Isn't that good news? Don't you feel better already? So it is with the gospel. It is good news because it first opens to us our distress, diagnoses our problem, and then it immediately leads us on to the cure. On the authority of Scripture, I know it to be the only place where we may find the right diagnosis of man's predicament, and, therefore, the only place where we may find a cure for it.

Nothing is more tragic than a man who is in deadly danger but is grossly ignorant of it; worse, that he stupidly brags of the very thing that is leading him to damnation. Such is the state of the natural man. 'Many live as enemies of the cross of Christ... their glory is in their shame. Their mind is on earthly things' (Phil. 3:18-19). 'There is a way that seems right to a man, but in the end it leads to death' (Prov. 14:12; 16:25). The sinner is lost in a fog of unbelief and ignorance. The best thing we can do for him – the first step on the road to his ultimate recovery – is to give him all the information we can. He needs a revelation – yes, a revelation! – from God. Yes, he needs to be utterly changed in his mind, heart and will, but the first step in that direction is to let him know the truth about his lost and ruined condition. *This* is good news indeed. Even in that, it goes without saying, only God can illumine the sinner's mind. We cannot do it, but we can and must tell him the truth – the truth about himself and about his eternity! The truth, this truth, is the last thing Satan wants him to hear and believe!

Let me remind you of John 9. Jesus made the blind man see physically. But what of the man's spiritual sight? After the Pharisees had questioned and re-questioned the man, and finally thrown him out, Jesus found him. He had cured him of his physical blindness; now for the spiritual. And this is how it came about:

Jesus heard that they had thrown him out, and when he found him, he said: 'Do you believe in the Son of Man?' 'Who is he, sir?' the man asked. 'Tell me so that I may believe in him'. Jesus said: 'You have now seen him; in fact, he is the one speaking with you'. Then the man said: 'Lord, I believe', and he worshipped him' (John 9:35-38).

Notice – the man needed information. 'Tell me...'. This is how it is with the gospel. Information alone will not save, but sinners must hear the truth in order to be saved. The truth! 'The statutes of the LORD are trustworthy, making wise the simple... The entrance of your words gives light; it gives understanding to the simple' (Ps. 19:7; 119:130). Paul could remind Timothy: 'From infancy you have known the holy Scriptures, which are able to make you wise for salvation through faith in Christ Jesus' (2 Tim. 3:15). Incidentally, what an encouraging example for godly parents to follow – Timothy's grandmother (Lois) and his mother (Eunice) teaching him the Scriptures from his infancy (2 Tim. 1:5; 3:14-15) – and look at the result! But note the scriptural emphasis: Lois and Eunice did not merely teach the lad the facts of Scripture; they aimed for his salvation. They wanted him 'wise unto salvation'. In other words, they weren't merely aiming for the mind and memory; they wanted the truth to penetrate his mind, and then his heart, will and life.

What the devil would prefer – if a man cannot be kept in complete ignorance – is that he be given a so-called cure that is nothing but poison or a soporific! And Satan has plenty of agents who are only too willing to fulfil their master's wishes. The gospel, of course, is the only solution to mankind's ills – it is the only place where a sinner will be told the truth about himself, about God and about eternity.

Finally, in this section, think what the world, society, would be like if everybody were a true disciple of the Lord Jesus, a true believer living in full submission by his Spirit to Christ in his law in Scripture. Shall I describe it? Can you imagine a society where there would be no locks or keys, no police force, no courts or prisons; where there would be no war, no armies, navies or military air forces; no security at airports; no tension or fear about nasty things somebody might do to you – can you imagine it, I ask?

The sad fact is, in our world we desperately need locks and keys, police, courts, chains and prisons, armies, weapons. As we all know, fear, anxiety, ignorance and misery reign in the world today. And sin is the cause of it all.

3. 'We Do not Lose Heart'

The heading for this section could be more fully expressed thus: Despite impossible odds, what is the only attitude for the new-covenant minister?

'We do not lose heart' (2 Cor. 4:1). So declared the apostle, fully confident. The new covenant brings this hope, confident expectation, assurance. As I have explained, in 2 Corinthians 3 and elsewhere in this letter (2 Cor. 11), Paul was vehement in his boasting and confidence. But here he is attempting to put nerve into the Corinthians. And, at times, he turns it into a command to all believers: 'Never be lacking in zeal, but keep your spiritual fervour, serving the Lord. Be joyful in hope' (Rom. 12:11-12). 'Therefore, my dear brothers, stand firm. Let nothing move you. Always give yourselves fully to the work of the Lord, because you know that your labour in the Lord is not in vain' (1 Cor. 15:58). And, although the apostle's injunction encompasses more than preaching to sinners, it certainly includes it: 'Let us not become weary in doing good, for at the proper time we will reap a harvest if we do not give up' (Gal. 6:9). In other words, we must keep exercising our 'ministry'. The world – lost men, women and children – desperately need what we have to offer them in Christ. They need Christ! We know they will refuse him (Isa. 6:9-10; Matt. 13:14-15; Acts 28:25-27), we know they are blinded by Satan, that they have no spiritual desire or power to turn to Christ because God has blinded them (John 12:37-41), but still we do not lose heart, still we continue to preach Christ to such people.

We do so for three very good reasons. *First*, we, ourselves, all of us, were in such a ruinous state, both in ourselves and before God (Eph. 2:1-3; Tit. 3:3), and yet God broke into our hearts and changed us by his Spirit in the gospel, did he not? This surely emboldens us in approaching others. More, it surely strengthens our witness to them. It also must make us sympathetic, even empathetic, to our fellow-men. Above all, it must encourage us to think that what God has done for us, done to us, and done in us, he can and will do for others.

And *secondly*, God gives all necessary grace to take up the task and complete it. I will come to this.

Before that, let me look at a *third* reason of why we do not lose heart, we dare not lose heart. Let me be politically incorrect, and be so in print: only Christ can save; only Christ can heal this sickness in humanity; only Christ can redeem. Law, rites, ceremonies, works, Judaism, Islam, Buddhism... all are useless. Christ alone can save sinners. The Lord Jesus himself declared it: 'I am the way and the truth and the life. No one comes to the Father except through me' (John 14:6). Peter enforced it: 'Salvation is found in no one else, for there is no other name under heaven given to men by which we must be saved' (Acts 4:12).

Isaac Watts expressed it thus:

> *Let everlasting glories crown*
> *Thy head, my Saviour and my Lord;*
> *Thy hands have brought salvation down,*
> *And writ the blessings in thy word.*

> *What if we trace the globe around,*
> *And search from Britain to Japan,*
> *There shall be no religion found*
> *So just to God, so safe for man.*

> *In vain the trembling conscience seeks*
> *Some solid ground to rest upon;*
> *With long despair the spirit breaks,*
> *Till we apply **to Christ alone**.*

> *How well thy blessèd truths agree!*
> *How wise and holy thy commands!*
> *Thy promises, how firm they be!*
> *How firm our hope and comfort stands.*

> *Should all the forms that men devise*
> *Assault my faith with treach'rous art,*
> *I'd call them vanity and lies,*
> *And bind the gospel to my heart.*

The gospel, the new covenant, Christ, is the only cure for mankind's ills. We must, therefore, continue with 'this ministry'; we must press on with it. Nothing else will do! There is no other saving ministry in all the world. Tremendous odds are against us, yes. An impossible task is before us – to get the blind to see, to get sinners ruled by Satan taken out of the kingdom of darkness and brought into the kingdom of Christ and light (Col. 1:13), to make unwilling and rebellious sinners submit to Christ. And we are faced all the while with apathy, if not open hostility (take Luke 21:17; John 7:7; 15:18 – 16:1-4,33; 17:14; 1 Thess. 2:2,14-16; 3:2-5; 2 Thess. 1:4-7; 3:1-3, as the merest sample).[1] And not only do we meet hostility from outside the church. After Paul had set out the contrast between the old and new covenants under the allegory of Sarah and Hagar, he came to this: 'At that time the son born in the ordinary way persecuted the son born by the power of the Spirit. *It is the same now*' (Gal. 4:29). The Judaisers had infiltrated the apostolic churches (Acts 15:1; Gal. 2:4; Jude 4).They have not gone away! All this we have to face as we exercise our ministry.[2]

It gets worse: in spreading the gospel, believers are called to suffer. Take 2 Timothy as just one book to speak of it:

God did not give us a spirit of timidity, but a spirit of power, of love and of self-discipline.[3] So do not be ashamed to testify about our Lord, or ashamed of me his prisoner. But join with me in suffering for the gospel, by the power of God... of this gospel I was appointed a herald and an apostle and a teacher. That is why I am suffering as I am. Yet I am not ashamed, because I know whom I have believed, and am convinced that he is able to guard what I have entrusted to him for that day... You know that everyone in the province of Asia has deserted me, including Phygelus and Hermogenes... Endure hardship with us like a good soldier of Christ Jesus... Jesus Christ... This is my gospel, for which I am suffering even to the point of being chained like a criminal. But God's word is not chained. Therefore I endure everything for the sake of the elect, that they too may obtain the salvation that is in Christ Jesus, with eternal glory... You, however, know all about my teaching, my way of life, my purpose, faith, patience, love, endurance,

---

[1] Note that hatred of us flows from hatred to, and ignorance of, Christ and his Father (John 16:1-4).

[2] For hatred of Christ by the religious leaders of the Jews, see Luke 19:47-48; 20:19 for instance. And although the crowd, at this time, seemed to be friendly towards Christ, never forget how quickly their 'Hosannas' turned to 'Crucify'.

[3] Note this 'self-discipline'. The believer is not law-less. While he is not under the law of Moses in the new covenant, God, by his Spirit, gives him the grace and spirit of self-discipline.

persecutions, sufferings – what kinds of things happened to me in Antioch, Iconium and Lystra, the persecutions I endured. Yet the Lord rescued me from all of them. In fact, everyone who wants to live a godly life in Christ Jesus will be persecuted, while evil men and impostors will go from bad to worse, deceiving and being deceived... In the presence of God and of Christ Jesus, who will judge the living and the dead, and in view of his appearing and his kingdom, I give you this charge: Preach the Word; be prepared in season and out of season; correct, rebuke and encourage – with great patience and careful instruction. For the time will come when men will not put up with sound doctrine. Instead, to suit their own desires, they will gather around them a great number of teachers to say what their itching ears want to hear. They will turn their ears away from the truth and turn aside to myths. But you, keep your head in all situations, endure hardship, do the work of an evangelist, discharge all the duties of your ministry. For I am already being poured out like a drink offering... Do your best to come to me quickly, for Demas, because he loved this world, has deserted me and has gone to Thessalonica. Crescens has gone to Galatia, and Titus to Dalmatia. Only Luke is with me... Alexander the metalworker did me a great deal of harm. The Lord will repay him for what he has done. You too should be on your guard against him, because he strongly opposed our message. At my first defence, no one came to my support, but everyone deserted me (2 Tim. 1:7-9,11-12,15; 2:3,8-10; 3:10-13; 4:1-6,9-16).

Let me stress some of those words, in order to show the connection between preaching the gospel and suffering for it: 'Of this gospel I was appointed a herald and an apostle and a teacher. *That is why I am suffering* as I am... my gospel, *for which I am suffering* even to the point of being chained like a criminal'. But as Paul makes perfectly clear, while he may be the supreme example, such a connection between suffering and the new-covenant ministry is inevitable for all believers: 'Join with me in suffering for the gospel, by the power of God... Of this gospel I was appointed a herald and an apostle and a teacher... Everyone who wants to live a godly life in Christ Jesus will be persecuted, while evil men and impostors will go from bad to worse, deceiving and being deceived' (2 Tim. 1:8,11; 3:12-13).

Suffering, conflict in the face of enormous odds coupled with hostility, then, is inevitable. But, even so, we do not lose heart! Why not? How can the great work be done? In face of this intractable problem, this deep-seated sin, this ingrained rebellion against God, this inevitable conflict and suffering, how can we do anything else but 'lose heart'? 'We do not lose heart', thundered the apostle, 'because we have this ministry'!

Let's hear his full argument: 'Therefore, since through God's mercy we have this ministry, we do not lose heart'. In other words, because we are ministers of the new covenant, even though 'we have this treasure in jars of clay' – in order 'to show that this all-surpassing power is from God and not from us' – even though 'we are hard pressed on every side... perplexed... persecuted ... struck down... always being given over to death for Jesus' sake', nevertheless as 'it is written: "I believed; therefore I have spoken"'. 'With that same spirit of faith we also believe and therefore speak'. And 'therefore we do not lose heart' (2 Cor. 4:1,7-16). We do not lose heart, because we have been given this new-covenant ministry. We do not lose heart, because we go armed with the provisions of the new covenant. We do not lose heart, full stop! This new covenant and its ministry must be something pretty special, don't you think?

Listen to the apostle again:

Finally, be strong in the Lord and in his mighty power. Put on the full armour of God so that you can take your stand against the devil's schemes. For our struggle is not against flesh and blood, but against the rulers, against the authorities, against the powers of this dark world and against the spiritual forces of evil in the heavenly realms (Eph. 6:10-12).

In exercising our 'ministry', this is precisely the battle we are engaged in. We are taking on rank wickedness, 'the spiritual forces of evil', Satanic delusion and darkness. So much for the opposition. Impossible odds, are they not? But let us not forget what Paul told the Corinthians:

The weapons we fight with are not the weapons of the world. On the contrary, they have divine power to demolish strongholds. We demolish arguments and every pretension that sets itself up against the knowledge of God, and we take captive every thought to make it obedient to Christ (2 Cor. 10:4-5).

Robert Hawker:

The faith of God's people is supposed by the gospel, to be a life of trust, assurance, and confirmation. The prophet, ages before the coming of Christ, declared, that the work of righteousness (Christ's righteousness) shall be peace; and the effect of righteousness, quietness, and assurance forever (Isa. 32:1). And to this purport, the promise runs along with it, and keeps pace together: 'You will keep him in perfect peace whose mind is stayed on you, because he trusts in you' (Isa. 26:3). If, therefore, there remained any uncertainty, in respect to the justified state of a child of God, whom God by sovereign grace hath called, with an holy calling; those blessed Scriptures lose their power. That man cannot be said to have quietness, and assurance forever, as an, effect of his interest in, and dependence upon, the righteousness of the Lord Jesus Christ; while the shadow of a doubt remains in his mind, whether he has received pardon, mercy, and peace, in the blood of the cross, and is justified by faith, throughout Lord Jesus Christ. Now the ground-work, on which the child of God, truly taught of God, rests his full assurance of faith, and which keeps him, as Paul says he was kept, from fainting, is the heart-felt conviction, that Christ, when he stood forth the surety of his church and people, truly, as the prophet said of him, finished the transgression, made an end of sin, made reconciliation for iniquity, and brought in an everlasting righteousness (Dan. 9:24). In all that high transaction, Christ acted as his peoples' sponsor and surety; and therefore, not an atom of guilt, either original, or actual, was left un-atoned, on his peoples' conscience. Now then, if I, or you, or any and every child of God, whom God hath effectually called by grace, believe the record, which God hath given of his dear Son, namely, that God hath given eternal life to his whole body the church, in his dear Son; and that, by virtue of the infinite value and preciousness of his righteousness and blood-shedding, they are justified from all things; how is it possible that there can be any suspense, doubt, or misgiving, on this grand assurance, of the redeemed child of God's hope? Reader, do look, again and again, at the blessed frame of mind Paul was in, and which wholly arose from this one cause: and recollect, that this high privilege, was not Paul's privilege only; but the whole church of God are equally begotten to it, and equally entitled to it, with the apostle; because it arises not from any merit, or services in Paul, but the sole gift of God in Christ... As we have received mercy, we faint not.[4]

Hawker was right. It wasn't only Paul who was given grace to serve Christ. He was: 'By the grace of God I am what I am, and his grace

---

[4] Hawker: *Commentary* (2 Cor. 4).

to me was not without effect. No, I worked harder than all of [the apostles] – yet not I, but the grace of God that was with me' (1 Cor. 15:10). 'We proclaim [Christ], admonishing and teaching everyone with all wisdom, so that we may present everyone perfect in Christ. To this end I labour, struggling with all his energy, which so powerfully works in me' (Col. 1:28-29). Yes, Paul was certainly enable to fulfil his ministry. *But so are all God's people.* And this is the second reason I spoke of earlier, the second reason why we do not lose heart. All God's people have the same sufficiency as the apostle:

God is able to make all grace abound toward you, that you, always having all sufficiency in all things, may have an abundance for every good work (2 Cor. 9:8, NKJV).
It is by grace you have been saved, through faith – -and this not from yourselves, it is the gift of God – not by works, so that no one can boast. For we are God's workmanship, created in Christ Jesus to do good works, which God prepared in advance for us to do (Eph. 2:8-10).
[God] is able to do immeasurably more than all we ask or imagine, according to his power that is at work within us (Eph. 3:20).

Let me return to the above extract from Colossians and take it a little further (the chapter division is appalling). Do not miss the remarkable juxtaposition:

We proclaim [Christ], admonishing and teaching everyone with all wisdom, so that we may present everyone perfect in Christ. To this end I labour, struggling with all his energy, which so powerfully works in me. I want you to know how much I am struggling for you and for those at Laodicea, and for all who have not met me personally (Col. 1:28 – 2:1).

What am I talking about? These words apply not only to Paul; they are true of us. And as new-covenant ministers, we have the 'energy'[5] of Christ, the 'power' of Christ, the Holy Spirit, the Spirit of Christ (Rom. 8:9; 1 Pet. 1:11); even so, we have to 'labour'[6] and

---

[5] The word is *dunamis*: 'strength, ability, power' (Thayer), the word from which we get 'dynamite'.

[6] The word is *kopiaō*: 'to labour with wearisome effort, to toil' (Thayer).

'struggle'.[7] That's the remarkable juxtaposition. It's not either/or; it's both (see Phil. 2:12-13). See also Ephesians 1:19-20 and Colossians 4:12-13. We don't lose heart, therefore. The struggle may be hard and wearisome, the enemies many and strong, but we have the power of Christ in and through it all.

Therefore, my dear brothers, stand firm. Let nothing move you. Always give yourselves fully to the work of the Lord, because you know that your labour in the Lord is not in vain (1 Cor. 15:58).
Let us not become weary in doing good, for at the proper time we will reap a harvest if we do not give up (Gal. 6:9).

With this ringing in our ears, it's high time we looked at what Paul means by this 'new-covenant ministry'. And, don't forget, as believers, we are all members of the new covenant, and, as priests, we are all ministers of the new covenant. 'This ministry', therefore, is *our* ministry. Reader, it is *your* ministry! You are engaged in this battle, you are taking on these enormous odds. Nevertheless, you are on this 'victory side'. 'The battle is the LORD's' (1 Sam. 17:47). You have the answer to mankind's ills, to your neighbour's ills, to your children's ills. You have the power of God's Spirit. Therefore do not lose heart!

---

[7] Paul uses two words: *agōvizomai*: 'to contend, struggle, with difficulties and dangers antagonistic to the gospel, to endeavour with strenuous zeal, strive'; *agōv*: 'intense solicitude, anxiety' (Thayer). We get 'agony' from the root word.

4. *The Only Hope for Sinners*

The heading for this section could be more fully expressed thus: What is it in particular about the new-covenant ministry that proves it to be the only way a sinner can be saved?

As we have seen, all men are, by nature, utterly lost and under the wrath of God. Is there a way out of all this misery and ruin by sin? Is there any hope for fallen man? There is; there is indeed! God's sovereign intervention in the new-covenant ministry is all that can save the sinner; that is, the work of the triune God in the gospel. God the Father, through Christ, by the Holy Spirit, works – intervenes – in the life of the sinner, and reverses – and more than reverses – all the ruin of the fall; more than reverses, I stress. Isaac Watts:

> *Jesus shall reign where'er the sun*
> *Does his successive journeys run;*
> *His kingdom stretch from shore to shore,*
> *Till moons shall wax and wane no more.*
>
> *Blessings abound where'er he reigns;*
> *The prisoner leaps to lose his chains;*
> *The weary find eternal rest,*
> *And all the sons of want are blessed.*
>
> *Where he displays his healing power,*
> *Death and the curse are known no more;*
> ***In him the tribes of Adam boast***
> ***More blessings than their father lost.***

The answer to the sinner's plight? God in the new covenant! Christ! God must take the initiative. And he does! Let me repeat the words:

God, who said: 'Let light shine out of darkness', made his light shine in our hearts to give us the light of the knowledge of the glory of God in the face of Christ (2 Cor. 4:6).

Note the reference to God's first – the first, I repeat – great act in creation: 'The earth was formless and empty, darkness was over the surface of the deep, and the Spirit of God was hovering over the waters. And God said: "Let there be light", and there was light'

(Gen. 1:2-3). That's it. Man, by nature, is like the earth was before God created light; man is in spiritual chaos, void, empty. Just as God, in creation, dispelled the darkness by creating light and commanding it to shine, so he, in the gospel, shines into the sinner's heart, dissipating the gloom that rules there. Is the sinner blind? God gives light! Is the sinner held fast in Satan's enslaving grip? God sets the prisoner free! God gives liberty! 'Loose him, and let him go!' (John 11:44, AV), runs his decree. Is the sinner ignorant? God enlightens the mind. Is the sinner helpless? God gives life and power. Is the sinner resolute in his hatred of Christ? God gives a new heart. Is the sinner ruined? God restores the locust years. We may justly apply these words to the case: 'I will... rebuild... Its ruins I will rebuild, and I will restore' (Acts 15:16). Is the sinner lost and perishing? God gives 'ever-surpassing glory' and 'inexpressible and glorious joy'! When God works on and in a sinner, that sinner comes into all the good of this:

Everything exposed by the light becomes visible, for it is light that makes everything visible. This is why it is said: 'Wake up, O sleeper, rise from the dead, and Christ will shine on you' (Eph. 5:13-14).

For that sinner, 'the sun of righteousness' truly has arisen, 'with healing in its wings' (Mal. 4:2). Or, changing the figure, as Paul told the Corinthians:

You yourselves are our letter, written on our hearts, known and read by everybody. You show that you are a letter from Christ, the result of our ministry, written not with ink but with the Spirit of the living God, not on tablets of stone but on tablets of human hearts (2 Cor. 3:2-3).

Yet again, changing the figure, as Paul told Timothy:

I thank Christ Jesus our Lord, who has given me strength, that he considered me faithful, appointing me to his service. Even though I was once a blasphemer and a persecutor and a violent man, I was shown mercy because I acted in ignorance and unbelief. The grace of our Lord was poured out on me abundantly, along with the faith and love that are in Christ Jesus. Here is a trustworthy saying that deserves full acceptance: Christ Jesus came into the world to save sinners – of whom I am the worst. But for that very reason I was shown mercy so that in me, the worst of sinners, Christ Jesus might display his unlimited patience as an example for those who would believe on him and receive eternal life. Now to the King eternal, immortal, invisible, the only God, be honour and glory for ever and ever. Amen (1 Tim. 1:12-17).

And this, it goes without saying, is true not only for Paul: it applies to every sinner who is regenerated and comes to Christ in faith:

This grace was given us in Christ Jesus before the beginning of time, but it has now been revealed through the appearing of our Saviour, Christ Jesus, who has destroyed death and has brought life and immortality to light through the gospel. And of this gospel I was appointed a herald and an apostle and a teacher (2 Tim. 1:9-11).

As the apostle reminded Titus:

We too were foolish, disobedient, deceived and enslaved by all kinds of passions and pleasures. We lived in malice and envy, being hated and hating one another. But when the kindness and love of God our Saviour appeared, he saved us, not because of righteous things we had done, but because of his mercy. He saved us through the washing of rebirth and renewal by the Holy Spirit, whom he poured out on us generously through Jesus Christ our Saviour, so that, having been justified by his grace, we might become heirs having the hope of eternal life (Tit. 3:3-7).

And Peter:

Simon Peter, a servant and apostle of Jesus Christ: To those who through the righteousness of our God and Saviour Jesus Christ have received a faith as precious as ours: Grace and peace be yours in abundance through the knowledge of God and of Jesus our Lord. His divine power has given us everything we need for life and godliness through our knowledge of him who called us by his own glory and goodness. Through these he has given us his very great and precious promises, so that through them you may participate in the divine nature and escape the corruption in the world caused by evil desires... We did not follow cleverly invented stories when we told you about the power and coming of our Lord Jesus Christ, but we were eyewitnesses of his majesty. For he received honour and glory from God the Father when the voice came to him from the majestic glory, saying: 'This is my Son, whom I love; with him I am well pleased'. We ourselves heard this voice that came from heaven when we were with him on the sacred mountain. And we have the word of the prophets made more certain, and you will do well to pay attention to it, as to a light shining in a dark place, until the day dawns and the morning star rises in your hearts (2 Pet. 1:1-4,16-19).

And John:

This is the message we have heard from him and declare to you: God is light; in him there is no darkness at all. If we claim to have fellowship with him yet walk in the darkness, we lie and do not live by the truth. But if we walk in the light, as he is in the light, we have fellowship with one another, and the blood of Jesus, his Son, purifies us from all sin... I am writing you a new command; its truth is seen in him and you, because the darkness is passing and the true light is already shining. Anyone who claims to be in the light but hates his brother is still in the darkness. Whoever loves his brother lives in the light, and there is nothing in him to make him stumble. But whoever hates his brother is in the darkness and walks around in the darkness; he does not know where he is going, because the darkness has blinded him. (1 John 1:5-7; 2:8-11).

I have already referred to the place where Christ began his ministry and why:

To fulfil what was said through the prophet Isaiah: 'Land of Zebulun and land of Naphtali, the way to the sea, along the Jordan, Galilee of the Gentiles – the people *living in darkness* have seen a great light; on those *living in the land of the shadow of death* a light has dawned'. From that time on Jesus began to preach: 'Repent, for the kingdom of heaven is near' (Matt. 4:14-17; see also Isa. 9:1-7).

Some thirty years before, Simeon had pronounced prophetic words over the Christ-child. Taking him in his arms, the old man had praised God, saying:

'Sovereign Lord, as you have promised, you now dismiss your servant in peace. For my eyes have seen your salvation, which you have prepared in the sight of all people, *a light for revelation* to the Gentiles and *for glory* to your people Israel'. The child's father and mother marvelled at what was said about him. Then Simeon blessed them and said to Mary, his mother: 'This child is destined to cause the falling and rising of many in Israel, and to be a sign that will be spoken against, so that the thoughts of many hearts will be *revealed*. And a sword will pierce your own soul too' (Luke 2:28-35).

Let me work these things out and establish them from Scripture; in particular, from this section of the passage we are considering.

I start with some negatives. What is the answer to all the sin in men, and all its consequent misery? Is it education? Better housing?

Universal social welfare? A good dose of religion or a series of morality lectures? Legislation? All these, and countless other 'solutions', have been suggested *and tried*. But none of them work. All fail! For years, the pioneer Moravians preached morality to the people of Greenland – and with no success. But as soon as they preached 'Christ and him crucified' they saw many convicted and converted. David Brainerd said much the same of his preaching among the Red Indians.[1] Nothing else will do! Better education will only produce better-educated sinners; better housing will only produce better-housed sinners. Indeed, better education *can* only produce better-educated sinners; better housing *can* only produce better-housed sinners. I'm not saying a word against education and good housing, of course: ignorance and insanitary conditions don't automatically produce saints. In fact, they are, for this purpose, irrelevant. As solutions to the problem of sin – education, housing, welfare, religion, morality – all are useless, and worse. What do I mean? An unconverted man who is religious, for instance, might well think that his religion makes him a spiritual man, and thus puts him right with God. A decent, respectable, upright citizen might well mistake his decency for true spiritual experience.

Let me illustrate. Field Marshal Montgomery, in his speech at the end of the war in 1945, recalled the fallen. He was confident they would hear God's welcome: 'Well done, good and faithful servant'. At the risk of being misunderstood, while I intend no slur (quite the opposite) on those who gave their life in that awful conflict, and did so for my freedom, the Field Marshal was talking through his double-badged beret! A man may do his duty, and more, as a soldier, and he deserves our gratitude, *but this is in no way saving*.

All such 'solutions' are, at best, the merest sticking plaster – and a plaster of that variety which annoyingly peels off within a few minutes. In fact, such 'antidotes' are better described as 'soporifics'. There is only one way out of the problem, only one cure for sinners. Christ! And he is brought to men by 'the new-covenant ministry'.

In particular, God must intervene in the lives of sinners, and do so in an act of sovereign power, an act that is equivalent to creation;

---

[1] See my *Christ* p518.

in truth, it *is* a work of creation (2 Cor. 5:17)! This is the only way that sinners can get their sin dealt with. This is the only solution to the 'problem', the plight of humanity; education, welfare, housing, law, regulations, rules, moral lectures are, all of them, utterly ineffective. It takes God to deal with sinners, and eradicate their sins. And when I say 'deal with' and 'eradicate', I mean 'deal with' and 'eradicate'. Sin and sinners do not need a pleasant-smelling ointment, or a fancy plaster to cover the sore. It's far worse than 'a sore'. Sin has ruined sinners, and sin will ruin them for ever, unless it is dealt with, and thoroughly dealt with at that. And this is precisely what God does in and through the new covenant! God, in his sovereign grace and power, regenerates the dead sinner, deals with his sin, eradicates his sin – its guilt, its condemning grip, its polluting vigour, and its presence. He breaks into the sinner's heart, gives him a new heart and a new spirit, and sets him free: 'If the Son sets you free, you will be free indeed' (John 8:36). This is the only way that sinners can be released from the guilt and condemnation of their sins. This is the only way that sinners can be released from the polluting power of their sin. This is the only way that sinners can be rid of the presence of sin. No works or rites invented and performed by man, no schemes dreamt up by man, will do the job. Indeed, even the law of God itself, the old covenant, could never deal with sin and its consequences; in the words of Paul to the Romans: 'What the law was powerless to do in that it was weakened by the flesh...' (Rom. 8:3). As the writer to the Hebrews declared:

The law is only a shadow of the good things that are coming – not the realities themselves. For this reason it can never, by the same sacrifices repeated endlessly year after year, make perfect those who draw near to worship. If it could, would they not have stopped being offered? For the worshippers would have been cleansed once for all, and would no longer have felt guilty for their sins. But those sacrifices are an annual reminder of sins, because it is impossible for the blood of bulls and goats to take away sins (Heb. 10:1-4).

And the law of God itself was not only inadequate when faced with the condemning power of sin; the law could never remove the polluting power of sin – it could never sanctify a saint, let alone save a sinner. Indeed, it could not make anyone perfect (that is, justify a sinner, and produce sanctification in a believer and lead him to glorification). It takes the new covenant to do all that:

The former regulation is set aside because it was weak and useless (for the law made nothing perfect), and a better hope is introduced, by which we draw near to God (Heb. 7:18-19).[2]

Christmas Evans:

The old covenant was an accuser and a judge, but offered no pardon to the guilty. It... provided no renovating and sanctifying grace. It was a national institution. It was a small vessel, trading only with the land of Canaan. It secured to the few the temporal blessing of the promised possessions, but never delivered a single soul from eternal death, never bore a single soul over to the heavenly inheritance. But the new covenant is a covenant of grace and mercy, proffering forgiveness and a clean heart... solely through faith in Jesus Christ... It is adapted to Gentiles as well as Jews, 'even as many as the Lord our God shall call'... The glorious high-priesthood of Christ has superseded the sacerdotal office among men... He that sits upon the throne has spoken: 'Behold, I make all things new!' The reformation includes not only the abrogation of the old, but also the introduction of the new... O, join the joyful multitude! The year of jubilee [release] is come. The veil is rent asunder. The way into the holiest is laid open. The blood of Jesus is on the mercy seat. The Lamb newly slain is in the midst of the throne. Go with boldness into his gracious presence... The covenant of Sinai cannot save you from wrath... 'You must be born again', 'born, not of the flesh, nor of the will of man, but of God'. You must have a new heart, and become a new creation in Christ Jesus. This is the promise of the Father.[3]

Now for a point of immense importance. As we have seen, conversion is likened to God's act in creation. Let us be clear: when, in creation, God said: 'Let there be light', there was light – at once! It had been darkness, nothing but darkness, and then it was light! God decreed light, and there was light – immediately! *Thus it is with conversion.*

---

[2] As I fully explained in my *Christ*, the law, being a part of God's word, still has a role in the life of the believer – as a paradigm, for instance. But the believer is not under the law! See 'The law as a paradigm' (in my *Christ* p289ff).

[3] Joseph Cross: *Sermons and Memoirs of Christmas Evans*, Kregel Publications, Grand Rapids, 1986 (first published 1856), pp19-22.

I do not base what I say now simply on this passage. As I have shown in other works, this biblical concept of conversion is being whittled down in more than one way these days, turning it from a 'climax', a 'crisis', into some drawn-out process. This is utterly wrong. If this process-concept gains ground, the consequences will be diabolical. We must be clear: to be converted, a sinner has to be born again (John 3:3-8), which is likened in our passage to God's fiat for the light to shine at creation. We must not imagine this to be akin to the gradual dawning of day with the measured rising of the sun, and the slow clearing of the morning mist. The sun was not created until the fourth day (Gen. 1:14-19). God's first-day fiat was the creation of *light itself* – not the sun and moon. At one 'moment' light did not exist – all was darkness; then there was... light! Thus it is with conversion.

That certain events may lead up to the conversion, and that the converted over time do increase in understanding, I do not for a moment deny, but there comes a 'time', a 'moment', when the sinner passes from death to life, when the sinner is translated from the kingdom[4] of darkness to the realm of light, and so on. He is a new creation (2 Cor. 5:17; Col. 1:13; 1 John 3:14). While I admit that natural birth is somewhat of a process, in the end a child is either born or it is not. Likewise, a sinner cannot be a child of God and a child of the devil (1 John 3:10). He cannot be in some sort of limbo, somehow in between death and life, in some sort of spiritual twilight or no-man's land. A sinner is either in darkness (unconverted), or he is in the light because the light is in him (converted).[5]

William T. Matson:

> *Lord, I was blind: I could not see*
> *In thy marred visage any grace;*
> *But now the beauty of thy face*
> *In radiant vision dawns on me.*

---

[4] I am grateful to the reader who pointed out that Scripture never calls Satan a king, but a prince. Strictly speaking, Satan's realm or dominion is a principality.

[5] Please see my other works, particularly my *Conversion*, for the full argument justifying these statements.

4. The Only Hope for Sinners

Lord, I was deaf: I could not hear
The thrilling music of thy voice;
But now I hear thee and rejoice,
And all thine uttered words are dear.

Lord, I was dumb: I could not speak
The grace and glory of thy name;
But now, as touched with living flame,
My lips thine eager praises wake.

Lord, I was dead: I could not stir
My lifeless soul to come to thee;
But now, since thou hast quickened me,
I rise from sin's dark sepulchre.

Lord, thou hast made the blind to see,
The deaf to hear, the dumb to speak,
The dead to live; and lo, I break
The chains of my captivity.

And, of course, John Newton:

Amazing grace, how sweet the sound,
That saved a wretch like me.
I once was lost, but now am found,
Was blind, but now I see.

We have seen how, in John 8, Jesus addressed the Jews, telling them of their blindness. It is not without significance that John 8 leads directly into John 9 – Jesus making the blind man see. If John 8 is about the spiritually blind, John 9 is about the physically blind – and by making the blind man see physically, Christ, as with all his miraculous signs (Mark 2:10-12; Heb. 2:1-4), illustrated the gospel. What he did for and to the physically blind man he can do for and to the spiritually blind – and by a miracle. As Jesus explained, the man had been born blind 'so that the work of God might be displayed in his life. As long as it is day, we must do the work of him who sent me. Night is coming, when no one can work. While I am in the world, I am the light of the world'. 'Having said this, he... So the man went and washed, and came home seeing' (John 9:3-7). As Christ told them all that day: 'For judgement I have come into this world, so that the blind will see and those who see will become blind' (John 9:39). Again, on a later occasion,

113

Jesus told the crowd: 'You are going to have the light just a little while longer. Walk while you have the light, before darkness overtakes you. The man who walks in the dark does not know where he is going. Put your trust in the light while you have it, so that you may become sons of light' (John 12:35-36).

How does God, shining in his sovereignty into the sinner's heart, bring about this conversion? Christ explained:

I tell you the truth, no one can enter the kingdom of God unless he is born of water and the Spirit. Flesh gives birth to flesh, but the Spirit gives birth to spirit. You should not be surprised at my saying: 'You must be born again'. The wind blows wherever it pleases. You hear its sound, but you cannot tell where it comes from or where it is going. So it is with everyone born of the Spirit (John 3:5-8).

All that the Father gives me will come to me, and whoever comes to me I will never drive away. For I have come down from heaven not to do my will but to do the will of him who sent me. And this is the will of him who sent me, that I shall lose none of all that he has given me, but raise them up at the last day. For my Father's will is that everyone who looks to the Son and believes in him shall have eternal life, and I will raise him up at the last day... No one can come to me unless the Father who sent me draws him, and I will raise him up at the last day. It is written in the prophets: 'They will all be taught by God'. Everyone who listens to the Father and learns from him comes to me... I tell you the truth, he who believes has everlasting life. I am the bread of life (John 6:37-48).

God shines in sinners' hearts; God inwardly (in the heart as well as the mind) teaches sinners. The result? The sinner comes to Christ, looks to Christ, trusts Christ, and is saved, is given eternal life. And this, of course, is all of a piece with the glorious provisions of the new covenant, promised, as Christ said, in the prophets – here Isaiah 54:13, but principally in Jeremiah 31:31-34; Ezekiel 36:22-29.

'The time is coming', declares the LORD, 'when I will make a new covenant with the house of Israel and with the house of Judah. It will not be like the covenant I made with their forefathers when I took them by the hand to lead them out of Egypt, because they broke my covenant, though I was a husband to them', declares the LORD. 'This is the covenant that I will make with the house of Israel after that time', declares the LORD. 'I will put my law in their minds and write it on their hearts. I will be their God, and they will be my people. No longer will a man teach his neighbour, or a man his brother, saying: "Know the LORD", because they will all know me, from the least of them to the greatest', declares the LORD. 'For I will forgive their wickedness and will remember their sins no more' (Jer. 31:31-34).

This is what the Sovereign LORD says: 'It is not for your sake, O house of Israel, that I am going to do these things, but for the sake of my holy name, which you have profaned among the nations where you have gone. I will show the holiness of my great name, which has been profaned among the nations, the name you have profaned among them. Then the nations will know that I am the LORD', declares the Sovereign LORD, 'when I show myself holy through you before their eyes. For I will take you out of the nations; I will gather you from all the countries and bring you back into your own land. I will sprinkle clean water on you, and you will be clean; I will cleanse you from all your impurities and from all your idols. I will give you a new heart and put a new spirit in you; I will remove from you your heart of stone and give you a heart of flesh. And I will put my Spirit in you and move you to follow my decrees and be careful to keep my laws. You will live in the land I gave your forefathers; you will be my people, and I will be your God. I will save you from all your uncleanness' (Ezek. 36:22-29).

As the writer to the Hebrews told us:

The ministry Jesus has received is as superior to [that of the priests of the old covenant] as the covenant of which he is mediator is superior to the old one, and it is founded on better promises. For if there had been nothing wrong with that first covenant, no place would have been sought for another. But God found fault with the people and said: 'The time is coming, declares the Lord, when I will make a new covenant with the house of Israel and with the house of Judah. It will not be like the covenant I made with their forefathers when I took them by the hand to lead them out of Egypt, because they did not remain faithful to my covenant, and I turned away from them, declares the Lord. This is the covenant I will make with the house of Israel after that time, declares the Lord. I will put my laws in their minds and write them on their hearts. I will be their God, and they will be my people. No longer will a man teach his neighbour, or a man his brother, saying: "Know the Lord", because they will all know me, from the least of them to the greatest. For I will forgive their wickedness and will remember their sins no more'. By calling this covenant 'new', he has made the first one obsolete; and what is obsolete and ageing will soon disappear...

By one sacrifice he has made perfect forever those who are being made holy. The Holy Spirit also testifies to us about this. First he says: 'This is the covenant I will make with them after that time, says the Lord. I will put my laws in their hearts, and I will write them on their minds'. Then he adds: 'Their sins and lawless acts I will remember no more'. And where these have been forgiven, there is no longer any sacrifice for sin (Heb. 8:6-13; 10:14-18).

Another thing. When God created light, and issued his fiat: 'Let there be light', he did not ask the darkness for permission to do it, nor for it to cooperate with him. He decreed light, and there was light. The darkness vanished. Thus it is with conversion. Not even Satan can thwart God in his decree to convert a sinner. When God decrees regeneration, the sinner is regenerate! God does not ask the sinner to cooperate. Rather, he takes a dead sinner and makes him live!

I would not be misunderstood. Although God is absolutely sovereign in all things – in particular, in conversion – this does not mean that he treats man as a robot, a stick or a stone; God does not 'violate' the humanity of man – he created it! What I am saying is this: while God in his sovereignty initiates, empowers and brings to full effect every aspect of salvation, the sinner has to repent and believe; not God! Indeed, the sinner has to choose Christ – compare Joshua's call to Israel (Josh. 24:15).[6] And he does! God wills, decrees the salvation of the sinner, but the sinner wills to have Christ as his Saviour. How is this possible? God constrains,

---

[6] Calvin on the verse: 'Joshua... [makes the Jews] free to choose what god they are willing to serve... Not without cause, therefore, does he give them freedom of choice, that they may not afterwards pretend to have been under compulsion, when they bound themselves by their own consent'. Matthew Henry: Joshua 'here puts them to their choice, not as if... they were at liberty to refuse his service, but because it would have a great influence upon their perseverance in religion if they embraced it with the reason of men and with the resolution of men... He brings them to embrace their religion rationally and intelligently, for it is a reasonable service. The will of man is apt to glory in its native liberty, and, in a jealousy for the honour of this, adheres with most pleasure to that which is its own choice and is not imposed upon it; therefore it is God's will that this service should be, not our chance, or a force upon us, but our choice. Accordingly... Joshua fairly puts the matter to their choice... He proposes the candidates that stand for the election. The Lord, Jehovah, on one side, and on the other side either the gods of their ancestors... or the gods of... the Amorites'.

regenerates, moves the will of man: 'Thy people shall be willing in the day of thy power' (Ps. 110:3, AV). He puts a new spirit within the elect, regenerating them and making them willing to be saved. I have already quoted Ezekiel, speaking for God in the new covenant: ' I will give you a new heart and put a new spirit in you; I will remove from you your heart of stone and give you a heart of flesh. And I will put my Spirit in you and move you to follow my decrees and be careful to keep my laws' (Ezek. 36:26).[7] Christ can say to every believer: 'You did not choose me, but I chose you' (John 15:16).[8]

Let me set all this out in a little more detail. Keeping in step with Paul in our passage, I want to show the contrast of the old covenant with the new – but making contemporary application as I go. Let me remind you, reader, that by 'legal preaching' I include not only overt calls to submit to the Mosaic law in its entirety, but the teaching (*à la* Calvin) that argues that we must preach the law (or, more usually, the ten commandments) in order to prepare sinners for Christ, and then we must preach the law (or, more usually, the ten commandments) as the means and motive of sanctification. What is more, I also include all teaching that asserts that grace is conveyed though rites, ceremonies or observances. In short, I deny all such claims for the law, rites, works or ceremonies. No amount of attendance at preaching services, no amount of water, no amount of participation in the Lord's supper, no amount of law preaching, will ever convert sinners or sanctify saints. With this firmly in mind, and reading into 'the law' every other system apart from the power of God in the new covenant, let me set out the leading principles of 'this ministry'.

As an appetiser, consider these scriptures, passages which declare that God sovereignly regenerates sinners in Christ, through the preaching of the gospel; in short, by the new-covenant ministry:

He chose to give us birth through the word of truth (Jas. 1:18).

---

[7] As I showed in my *Christ*, 'the law' in the new covenant is not the law of Moses but the law of Christ.

[8] I met a man who, so wanting to glorify God, said that God converted him against his will. He did not! He made him willing. Witness Saul's conversion on the Damascus road.

The message of the cross is foolishness to those who are perishing, but to us who are being saved it is the power of God (1 Cor. 1:18).

You also were included in Christ when you heard the word of truth, the gospel of your salvation. Having believed, you were marked in him with a seal, the promised Holy Spirit, who is a deposit guaranteeing our inheritance until the redemption of those who are God's possession – to the praise of his glory (Eph. 1:13-14).

Praise be to the God and Father of our Lord Jesus Christ! In his great mercy he has given us new birth into a living hope through the resurrection of Jesus Christ from the dead, and into an inheritance that can never perish, spoil or fade... Through him you believe in God, who raised him from the dead and glorified him, and so your faith and hope are in God. Now that you have purified yourselves by obeying the truth so that you have sincere love for your brothers, love one another deeply, from the heart. For you have been born again, not of perishable seed, but of imperishable, through the living and enduring word of God (1 Pet. 1:3-4,21-23).

By the truth of God and the power of God! *That* is how God fulfils his electing decree in delivering sinners though the new-covenant ministry. It is 'by the word of truth, by the power of God' (2 Cor. 6:7, NKJV)!

5. Sinners Brought to Glory

Reader, do not forget what Paul is doing in 2 Corinthians 4. He is working out his assertion that the old covenant – the law – while it had a glory, could never match the glory of the new covenant – the gospel. And in working out the principles of 'this ministry', the apostle now makes his first point: the law could never deal with the condemnation produced by sin; it could never bring remission. Never! In other words we are talking about justification.

Justification: The law could never redeem a sinner from condemnation; God, in the new covenant, does

This is the first great step[1] in the complete salvation of the sinner: justification. The law can never deal with the condemnation produced by sin. Never! It can never take away the sinner's guilt. Never! It can never justify:

No one will be declared righteous in his sight by observing the law; rather, through the law we become conscious of sin. But now a righteousness from God, apart from law, has been made known, to which the law and the prophets testify. This righteousness from God comes through faith in Jesus Christ to all who believe (Rom. 3:20-22).
The Gentiles, who did not pursue righteousness, have obtained it, a righteousness that is by faith; but Israel, who pursued a law of righteousness, has not attained it. Why not? Because they pursued it not by faith but as if it were by works... Brothers, my heart's desire and prayer to God for the Israelites is that they may be saved. For I can testify about them that they are zealous for God, but their zeal is not based on knowledge. Since they did not know the righteousness that comes from God and sought to establish their own, they did not submit to God's righteousness. Christ is the end of the law so that there may be righteousness for everyone who believes (Rom. 9:30 – 10:4).
[We] know that a man is not justified by observing the law, but by faith in Jesus Christ. So we, too, have put our faith in Christ Jesus that

---

[1] I am not going back on my assertion that conversion should not be thought of as a process, but rather as an event. Conversion is only one step in bringing the sinner from death to everlasting glory. But conversion, in itself, is a step, not a process.

we may be justified by faith in Christ and not by observing the law, because by observing the law no one will be justified (Gal. 2:16).

Only God, in the new covenant, can justify the sinner, and he uses 'this ministry' of that covenant to bring it about. As Paul has just declared, he is setting out 'the ministry that brings righteousness' (2 Cor. 3:9). 'Righteousness', here, as I have asserted, speaks of more than justification – but it does include justification. The fact is, the law could never justify a sinner, for the law was 'the ministry that brought death... the ministry that condemns men' (2 Cor. 3:7-8). It was not the fault of the law, let me hasten to add; the law was 'powerless' (Rom 8:3), 'weak' (NKJV), yes, but that was because of man, the flesh. If a man could keep the law perfectly, the law would justify (Lev. 18:5; Deut. 8:1; Luke 10:28; Rom. 7:10; 10:5; and so on), but since no sinner can keep the law, no sinner can be justified by observing the law. Listen to the apostle:

Therefore, there is now no condemnation for those who are in Christ Jesus, because through Christ Jesus the law of the Spirit of life set me free from the law of sin and death. For what the law was powerless to do in that it was weakened by the flesh, God did by sending his own Son in the likeness of sinful man to be a sin offering. And so he condemned sin in sinful man, in order that the righteous requirements of the law might be fully met in us, who do not live according to the flesh but according to the Spirit (Rom. 8:1-4).

I will return to this extract. For now, I simply want to draw out the following: *'For what the law was powerless to do in that it was weakened by the flesh'*. I apply these words in the first instance – as Paul did – to the question of condemnation: the law could not possibly justify a sinner – it was too weak. Deliverance from condemnation for the sinner comes only through Christ's sacrificial offering of himself upon the cross – he having lived perfectly under the law (Gal. 4:4-5) – and the application of that work to the sinner by the Holy Spirit, through faith; in other words, the new covenant! As Paul declared: 'Through Christ Jesus the law of the Spirit of life set [the believer] free from the law of sin and death' (Rom. 8:2). Through the rest of the chapter (Rom. 8:2-17,26-27), the apostle worked out this work of the Spirit.

Gill on Romans 8:2:

The gospel may be designated as 'the law of the Spirit of life in Christ Jesus'; which may be called a law, not... as requiring conditions to be performed, or as enjoining duties to be observed,[2] or as delivering out threatenings in case of disobedience; but as it is a doctrine, order, and chain of truths... It may be called the law, or doctrine 'of the Spirit', because the Spirit is the author of it, and makes it powerful and effectual to the good of souls; by it the Spirit of God is conveyed into the heart; and the substance of it is spiritual things: and the 'law of the Spirit of life', because it reveals the way of life and salvation by Christ. It is the means of quickening dead sinners, of working faith in them, by which they live on Christ, and of reviving drooping saints. And also it affords spiritual food, for the support of life. And this may be said to be 'in Christ', or by him, inasmuch as it comes from, and is concerning him; he is the sum, the substance, and subject matter of it.

And Matthew Henry:

The covenant of grace made with us in Christ is a treasury of merit and grace, and thence we receive pardon and a new disposition,[3] are freed from the law of sin and death, that is, both from the guilt and power of sin, from the curse of the law, and the dominion of the flesh. We are under another covenant, another master, another husband, under the law of the Spirit, the law that gives the Spirit, spiritual life to qualify us for eternal [life].

Notice, in these extracts, how both commentators go further than speaking about justification. They are quite right to do so, but at this stage I am trying to deal with the first step of the sinner's recovery only; namely, justification. The fact is, as we shall see throughout this section, the new covenant is so vast that it defies simple classification into neat watertight compartments. This, of course, is not a weakness of the new covenant; it is, in fact, one of its main glories.[4]

Let me confirm that when God works in a sinner, redeeming him from sin, the first step is to constitute him absolutely righteous in Christ. This, of course, includes full remission of all the sins

---

[2] In other works, I have dealt fully with the properly nuanced correctives to this statement from Gill.

[3] Henry had 'nature'.

[4] I made precisely the same point when setting out 'The Believer's Rule' in my *Christ*.

committed before conversion, *and after*. Although I have just quoted some of the passages, they bear repeating. Listen to Paul:

I want you to know that through Jesus the forgiveness of sins is proclaimed to you. Through him everyone who believes is justified from everything you could not be justified from by the law of Moses (Acts 13:38-39).

But now the righteousness of God apart from the law is revealed, being witnessed by the law and the prophets, even the righteousness of God, through faith in Jesus Christ, to all and on all who believe. For there is no difference; for all have sinned and fall short of the glory of God, being justified freely by his grace through the redemption that is in Christ Jesus, whom God set forth as a propitiation by his blood, through faith, to demonstrate his righteousness, because in his forbearance God had passed over the sins that were previously committed, to demonstrate at the present time his righteousness, that he might be just and the justifier of the one who has faith in Jesus. Where is boasting then? It is excluded. By what law? Of works? No, but by the law of faith. Therefore we conclude that a man is justified by faith apart from the deeds of the law... God will credit righteousness [to] us who believe in him who raised Jesus our Lord from the dead. He was delivered over to death for our sins and was raised to life for our justification... You see, at just the right time, when we were still powerless, Christ died for the ungodly. Very rarely will anyone die for a righteous man, though for a good man someone might possibly dare to die. But God demonstrates his own love for us in this: While we were still sinners, Christ died for us. Since we have now been justified by his blood, how much more shall we be saved from God's wrath through him!... Christ is the end of the law so that there may be righteousness for everyone who believes (Rom. 3:21-22,28, NKJV; 4:24-25; 5:6-9; 10:4).

We... know that a man is not justified by observing the law, but by faith in Jesus Christ... We... have put our faith in Christ Jesus that we may be justified by faith in Christ and not by observing the law, because by observing the law no one will be justified... Clearly no one is justified before God by the law, because: 'The righteous will live by faith'. The law is not based on faith; on the contrary: 'The man who does these things will live by them'. Christ redeemed us from the curse of the law by becoming a curse for us, for it is written: 'Cursed is everyone who is hung on a tree'. He redeemed us in order that the blessing given to Abraham might come to the Gentiles through Christ Jesus, so that by faith we might receive the promise of the Spirit (Gal. 2:15-16; 3:11-14).

So, confronted by man's sin, man's deep-seated sin, and the ruin of mankind by his sin, what message of hope does the new covenant offer? Let us shout it 'from the house-tops'! God, in the gospel, intervenes to release the sinner from condemnation. God, in the new covenant, breaks into the sinner's life to take away his (the sinner's) sin, washing away all his guilt, bringing him out of condemnation into a state of perfect and irreversible righteousness. This he does by imputing the sinner's sin to Christ, and imputing Christ's righteousness to the sinner:

For just as through the disobedience of the one man the many were made sinners, so also through the obedience of the one man the many will be made righteous (Rom. 5:19).

God made him [Christ] who had no sin to be sin for us, so that in him we might become the righteousness of God (2 Cor. 5:21).

Christ loved the church and gave himself up for her to make her holy, cleansing her by the washing with water through the word, and to present her to himself as a radiant church, without stain or wrinkle or any other blemish, but holy and blameless (Eph. 5:25-27).

When Christ came as high priest of the good things that are already here, he went through the greater and more perfect tabernacle that is not man-made, that is to say, not a part of this creation. He did not enter by means of the blood of goats and calves; but he entered the Most Holy Place once for all by his own blood, having obtained eternal redemption... Christ did not enter a man-made sanctuary that was only a copy of the true one; he entered heaven itself, now to appear for us in God's presence. Nor did he enter heaven to offer himself again and again, the way the high priest enters the Most Holy Place every year with blood that is not his own. Then Christ would have had to suffer many times since the creation of the world. But now he has appeared once for all at the end of the ages to do away with sin by the sacrifice of himself. Just as man is destined to die once, and after that to face judgement, so Christ was sacrificed once to take away the sins of many people; and he will appear a second time, not to bear sin, but to bring salvation to those who are waiting for him. (Heb. 9:11-12,24-28).

We have been made holy through the sacrifice of the body of Jesus Christ once for all (Heb. 10:10).

The blood of Jesus, [God's] Son, purifies us from all sin... If we confess our sins, he is faithful and just and will forgive us our sins and purify us from all unrighteousness (1 John 1:7-9).[5]

In short: God, in the new covenant, takes a guilty sinner and makes him as righteous as Christ in his standing before God. Now that really is dealing with the problem! Let me make the application once again. No law, not even the law of God, no rite or ceremony, nothing but God, acting in the new covenant, can ever justify a sinner. Only God's direct action can do it. But, of course, the vital point is that not only *can* God do it, this is precisely what he does; he takes dead sinners and makes them live; he takes blind sinners and makes them see; he takes defiant sinners, resolute against Christ, and makes them willing and submissive to Christ as Saviour and Lord; he takes guilty sinners and washes them from their sin; he takes ruined and enslaved sinners and makes them perfectly free from all condemnation:

I will sprinkle clean water on you, and you will be clean; I will cleanse you from all your impurities and from all your idols. I will give you a new heart and put a new spirit in you; I will remove from you your heart of stone and give you a heart of flesh. And I will put my Spirit in you and move you to follow my decrees and be careful to keep my laws (Ezek. 36:25-27).

And that's only the start! Intimately connected with justification, inevitably following on from justification, we have the believer's sanctification.

Sanctification: *The law could never sanctify; God, in the new covenant, does*
God, in the new covenant, pardons and justifies the sinner who trusts Christ. What next? I said I would return to Romans 8. I do so now:

Therefore, there is now no condemnation for those who are in Christ Jesus, because through Christ Jesus the law of the Spirit of life set me free from the law of sin and death. For what the law was powerless to

---

[5] In these passages, just as with the extracts from Gill and Henry, there are clear references to the following two sections also. As I say, the new covenant really defies neat compartmentalisation.

do in that it was weakened by the flesh, God did by sending his own Son in the likeness of sinful man to be a sin offering. And so he condemned sin in sinful man, in order that the righteous requirements of the law might be fully met in us, who do not live according to the flesh but according to the Spirit (Rom. 8:1-4).

Notice how Paul immediately takes his argument beyond justification: 'And so [God] condemned sin in sinful man, in order that the righteous requirements of the law might be fully met in us, who do not live according to the flesh but according to the Spirit' (Rom. 8:3-4). 'In order that the righteous requirements of the law might be fully met in us, who do not live according to the flesh but according to the Spirit' is clearly the language of sanctification. Romans 8, of course, follows hard upon Romans 6 and 7. Remember, reader, these are not isolated texts; they constitute one continuous argument. Paul, writing to believers – those whom God has justified through faith in Christ under the new covenant – declares:

Our old self was crucified with him so that the body of sin might be done away with, that we should no longer be slaves to sin – because anyone who has died has been freed from sin. Now if we died with Christ, we believe that we will also live with him. For we know that since Christ was raised from the dead, he cannot die again; death no longer has mastery over him. The death he died, he died to sin once for all; but the life he lives, he lives to God. In the same way, count yourselves dead to sin but alive to God in Christ Jesus. Therefore do not let sin reign in your mortal body so that you obey its evil desires. Do not offer the parts of your body to sin, as instruments of wickedness, but rather offer yourselves to God, as those who have been brought from death to life; and offer the parts of your body to him as instruments of righteousness. For sin shall not be your master, because you are not under law, but under grace...
So, my brothers, you also died to the law through the body of Christ, that you might belong to another, to him who was raised from the dead, in order that we might bear fruit to God. For when we were controlled by the flesh, the sinful passions aroused by the law were at work in our bodies, so that we bore fruit for death. But now, by dying to what once bound us, we have been released from the law so that we serve in the new way of the Spirit, and not in the old way of the written code (Rom. 6:6-14; 7:4-6).

Paul said the very same, though in different terms, to the believers in Galatia:

We... know that a man is not justified by observing the law, but by faith in Jesus Christ. So we... have put our faith in Christ Jesus that we may be justified by faith in Christ and not by observing the law, because by observing the law no one will be justified... Through the law I died to the law so that I might live for God. I have been crucified with Christ and I no longer live, but Christ lives in me. The life I live in the body, I live by faith in the Son of God, who loved me and gave himself for me... You foolish Galatians! Who has bewitched you? Before your very eyes Jesus Christ was clearly portrayed as crucified. I would like to learn just one thing from you: Did you receive the Spirit by observing the law, or by believing what you heard? Are you so foolish? After beginning with the Spirit, are you now trying to attain your goal[6] by human effort?... So I say, live by the Spirit, and you will not gratify the desires of the flesh. For the flesh desires what is contrary to the Spirit, and the Spirit what is contrary to the flesh. They are in conflict with each other, so that you do not do what you want. But if you are led by the Spirit, you are not under law (Gal. 2:15 – 3:3; 5:16-18).

And the writer to the Hebrews had something to say on the matter:

When Christ came as high priest of the good things that are already here, he went through the greater and more perfect tabernacle that is not man-made, that is to say, not a part of this creation. He did not enter by means of the blood of goats and calves; but he entered the Most Holy Place once for all by his own blood, having obtained eternal redemption. The blood of goats and bulls and the ashes of a heifer sprinkled on those who are ceremonially unclean sanctify them so that they are outwardly clean. How much more, then, will the blood of Christ, who through the eternal Spirit offered himself unblemished to God, cleanse our consciences from acts that lead to death, so that we may serve the living God! For this reason Christ is the mediator of a new covenant, that those who are called may receive the promised eternal inheritance – now that he has died as a ransom to set them free from the sins committed under the first covenant... [Christ] has appeared once for all at the end of the ages to do away with sin by the sacrifice of himself. Just as man is destined to die once, and after that to face judgement, so Christ was sacrificed once to take away the sins

---

[6] In the first instance, sanctification; but, of course, the apostle includes perfection and glorification – the third point in this section.

of many people; and he will appear a second time, not to bear sin, but to bring salvation to those who are waiting for him... We have been made holy through the sacrifice of the body of Jesus Christ once for all (Heb. 9:11-15,26-28; 10:10).[7]

It is clear: God, in the new covenant, takes a guilty sinner and makes him as righteous as Christ in his standing before God. But not only that! He then takes that justified sinner, and sanctifies him, making him progressively holy in his daily life, more and more Christ-like in fulfilment of his eternal purpose to take ruined sinners, convert them, and make them increasingly and ultimately 'to be conformed to the likeness of his Son' (Rom. 8:29). God makes saved sinners godly. He imputes Christ's righteousness to them in justification, and imparts it to them in sanctification. Sin has ruined every man. God, in the new covenant, not only justifies sinners, but he makes them holy. I have already quoted the apostle:

Through Christ Jesus the law of the Spirit of life set [believers] free from the law of sin and death. For what the law was powerless to do in that it was weakened by the flesh, God did by sending his own Son in the likeness of sinful man to be a sin offering. And so he condemned sin in sinful man, in order that the righteous requirements of the law might be fully met in us, who do not live according to the flesh but according to the Spirit (Rom. 8:2-4).

So I say, live by the Spirit, and you will not gratify the desires of the flesh... If you are led by the Spirit, you are not under law (Gal. 5:16-18).

I will sprinkle clean water on you, and you will be clean; I will cleanse you from all your impurities and from all your idols. I will give you a new heart and put a new spirit in you; I will remove from you your heart of stone and give you a heart of flesh. And I will put my Spirit in you and move you to follow my decrees and be careful to keep my laws (Ezek. 36:25-27).

'The time is coming', declares the LORD, 'when I will make a new covenant with the house of Israel and with the house of Judah. It will not be like the covenant I made with their forefathers when I took them by the hand to lead them out of Egypt, because they broke my covenant, though I was a husband to them', declares the LORD. 'This is the covenant I will make with the house of Israel after that time', declares the LORD. 'I will put my law in their minds and write it on

---

[7] As before, some of these passages have a reference to the final point in this sub-chapter.

their hearts. I will be their God, and they will be my people. No longer will a man teach his neighbour, or a man his brother, saying: "Know the LORD", because they will all know me, from the least of them to the greatest', declares the LORD. 'For I will forgive their wickedness and will remember their sins no more' (Jer. 31:31-34).

Now that really is dealing with the problem!

Once again, let me stress the contemporary application. It's useless thinking that the law or rites or ceremonies will ever sanctify a child of God. Take the law. The law can never do it. In fact, as we have seen, according to the apostle, the sinner has to die to the law in order to be sanctified:

So, my brothers, you also died to the law through the body of Christ, that you might belong to another, to him who was raised from the dead, in order that we might bear fruit to God. For when we were controlled by the flesh, the sinful passions aroused by the law were at work in our bodies, so that we bore fruit for death. But now, by dying to what once bound us, we have been released from the law so that we serve in the new way of the Spirit, and not in the old way of the written code (Rom. 7:4-6).

Through the law I died to the law so that I might live for God. I have been crucified with Christ and I no longer live, but Christ lives in me. The life I live in the body, I live by faith in the Son of God, who loved me and gave himself for me (Gal. 2:19-20).

And, in the new covenant, in regenerating the dead sinner, and justifying him through faith, this is precisely what happens: God breaks into the sinner, and the sinner, in Christ, dies to the law, and therefore can then be sanctified. Now that really is worth shouting about! God, in his grace, takes sinners, and justifies them, and then, through his Spirit, progressively sanctifies them.

But even that's not the end of it! The believer, being united to Christ by faith, is justified: he is perfect once and for all time in the work of Christ, free from all sin (Rom. 5:19; 8:1; Eph. 5:25-27; Heb. 10:14). Moreover, in Christ Jesus the law of the Spirit of life has set him free from the law of Moses. More! In being liberated from the law, having died to the law, the believer is married to Christ and thus produces fruit to the glory of Christ – the righteous requirements of the law being fully met in him (Rom. 7:4; 8:1 – 4; Heb. 10:14). What next? Glory! But this glory begins here and now – the believer does not have to wait for heaven!

Glorification: The law cannot bring a sinner to glory; God, in the new covenant, brings glory to the believer, and, at last, will take him to glory and fully glorify him

Glory! In converting a sinner, God brings glory to the believer. As Paul told the Corinthians in our passage, having been converted, having received the Spirit, they are now free in Christ. But this is not all:

Now the Lord is the Spirit, and where the Spirit of the Lord is, there is freedom. And we, who with unveiled faces all reflect the Lord's glory, are being transformed into his likeness with ever-increasing glory, which comes from the Lord, who is the Spirit (2 Cor. 3:17-18).

Do not miss the apostle's talk of 'freedom'. This 'freedom' is a massive part of the believer's glory: we might well look upon it as eternal glory begun while here below.[8] As Jesus declared: 'I have come that they may have life, and have it to the full' (John 10:10); in other words, for the believer, eternal life begins here and now. Eternal life is not just an *endless* life; it is an endless *life!* When we talk about *eternal* life, we should not be thinking of merely a matter of *length*; supremely, we should be thinking of its *quality*! People talk about 'quality time': 'I would like some "quality time"'. Very well. Once a sinner is in Christ, eternal life, glory has begun – here and now. Now that really is quality! Peter could not have been more explicit:

Praise be to the God and Father of our Lord Jesus Christ! In his great mercy he has given us new birth into a living hope through the resurrection of Jesus Christ from the dead, and into an inheritance that can never perish, spoil or fade – kept in heaven for you, who through faith are shielded by God's power until the coming of the salvation that is ready to be revealed in the last time. In this you greatly rejoice, though now for a little while you may have had to suffer grief in all kinds of trials. These have come so that your faith – of greater worth than gold, which perishes even though refined by fire – may be proved genuine and may result in praise, glory and honour when Jesus Christ

---

[8] 'The men of grace have found,/ Glory begun below' (Isaac Watts' hymn: 'Come we that love the Lord,/ And let our joys be known'). 'Grace is but glory begun, and glory is but grace perfected' (Christopher Love: *Grace: The Truth and Growth and Different Degrees Thereof...*, London, 1652, p80 (Google Books). This is often attributed to Jonathan Edwards.

is revealed. Though you have not seen him, you love him; and even though you do not see him now, you believe in him and are filled with an inexpressible and glorious joy, for you are receiving the goal of your faith, the salvation of your souls (1 Pet. 1:3-9).

Despite trials and sufferings, afflictions and temptations, the believer has glory now. He will be taken into glory, yes; he will be given eternal glory, yes; but his glory has begun even now. Heaven has come to earth, giving the converted sinner a foretaste of what is to come. Every believer has 'a living hope'; 'you believe in [Christ] and are filled with an inexpressible and glorious joy, for you are receiving the goal of your faith, the salvation of your souls': a living hope, a glorious freedom, and the gift of the Spirit!

And Paul could not be more emphatic upon the power of God in the new covenant to liberate a sinner, and all in stark contrast to the bondage of the old covenant, the law:

Tell me, you who want to be under the law, are you not aware of what the law says? For it is written that Abraham had two sons, one by the slave woman and the other by the free woman. His son by the slave woman was born in the ordinary way; but his son by the free woman was born as the result of a promise. These things may be taken figuratively, for the women represent two covenants. One covenant is from Mount Sinai and bears children who are to be slaves: This is Hagar. Now Hagar stands for Mount Sinai in Arabia and corresponds to the present city of Jerusalem, because she is in slavery with her children. But the Jerusalem that is above is free, and she is our mother. For it is written: 'Be glad, O barren woman, who bears no children; break forth and cry aloud, you who have no labour pains; because more are the children of the desolate woman than of her who has a husband'. Now you, brothers, like Isaac, are children of promise. At that time the son born in the ordinary way persecuted the son born by the power of the Spirit. It is the same now. But what does the Scripture say? 'Get rid of the slave woman and her son, for the slave woman's son will never share in the inheritance with the free woman's son'. Therefore, brothers, we are not children of the slave woman, but of the free woman. It is for freedom that Christ has set us free. Stand firm, then, and do not let yourselves be burdened again by a yoke of slavery (Gal. 4:21 – 5:1).

Christ had already set down the marker: 'If you hold to my teaching, you are really my disciples. Then you will know the truth, and the truth will set you free... I tell you the truth, everyone who sins is a slave to sin... If the Son sets you free, you will be free indeed' (John 8:31-36; see also Rom. 8:2; 2 Cor. 3:17; Gal. 5:1,13; Jas. 2:12; 1 Pet. 2:16). This freedom is to be 'led by the Spirit' (Gal. 5:18), to 'live by the Spirit' or 'walk in the Spirit' (Gal. 5:16) – virtually synonymous. Believers are under the influence of the Spirit, empowered by the Spirit, guided by the Spirit, and enabled to live their life by the grace of the Spirit. This 'glory' of the new covenant Paul explained and expounded:

Thanks be to God that, though you used to be slaves to sin, you wholeheartedly obeyed the form of teaching to which you were entrusted. You have been set free from sin and have become slaves to righteousness. I put this in human terms because you are weak in your natural selves. Just as you used to offer the parts of your body in slavery to impurity and to ever-increasing wickedness, so now offer them in slavery to righteousness leading to holiness. When you were slaves to sin, you were free from the control of righteousness. What benefit did you reap at that time from the things you are now ashamed of ? Those things result in death! But now that you have been set free from sin and have become slaves to God, the benefit you reap leads to holiness, and the result is eternal life. For the wages of sin is death, but the gift of God is eternal life in Christ Jesus our Lord (Rom. 6:17-23).

Moreover, God not only justifies the sinner who believes, and then sanctifies him, and brings glory to him now, but, at last, he will eternally glorify him, and glorify him completely. The writer to the Hebrews again:

Christ is the mediator of a new covenant, that those who are called may receive the promised eternal inheritance – now that he has died as a ransom to set them free from the sins committed under the first covenant... [Christ] has appeared once for all at the end of the ages to do away with sin by the sacrifice of himself. Just as man is destined to die once, and after that to face judgement, so Christ was sacrificed once to take away the sins of many people; and he will appear a second time, not to bear sin, but to bring salvation to those who are waiting for him (Heb. 9:15,26-28).

And John:

How great is the love the Father has lavished on us, that we should be called children of God! And that is what we are! The reason the world does not know us is that it did not know him. Dear friends, now we are children of God, and what we will be has not yet been made known.

But we know that when he appears, we shall be like him, for we shall see him as he is (1 John 3:1-2).

And Paul:

Those God foreknew he also predestined to be conformed to the likeness of his Son, that he might be the firstborn among many brothers. And those he predestined, he also called; those he called, he also justified; those he justified, he also glorified. What, then, shall we say in response to this? If God is for us, who can be against us? He who did not spare his own Son, but gave him up for us all – how will he not also, along with him, graciously give us all things? Who will bring any charge against those whom God has chosen? It is God who justifies. Who is he that condemns? Christ Jesus, who died – more than that, who was raised to life – is at the right hand of God and is also interceding for us. Who shall separate us from the love of Christ? Shall trouble or hardship or persecution or famine or nakedness or danger or sword?... No, in all these things we are more than conquerors through him who loved us. For I am convinced that neither death nor life, neither angels nor demons, neither the present nor the future, nor any powers, neither height nor depth, nor anything else in all creation, will be able to separate us from the love of God that is in Christ Jesus our Lord (Rom. 8:29-39).

Writing to the Thessalonians, Paul declared that Christ will come again in glory:

To be glorified in his holy people and to be marvelled at among all those who have believed. This includes you, because you believed our testimony to you. With this in mind, we constantly pray for you, that our God may count you worthy of his calling, and that by his power he may fulfil every good purpose of yours and every act prompted by your faith. We pray this so that the name of our Lord Jesus may be glorified in you, and you in him, according to the grace of our God and the Lord Jesus Christ... We ought always to thank God for you, brothers loved by the Lord, because from the beginning God chose you to be saved through the sanctifying work of the Spirit and through belief in the truth. He called you to this through our gospel, that you might share in the glory of our Lord Jesus Christ (2 Thess. 1:10-12; 2:13-14).

Well, that's what God can do in the new covenant. It's what he's doing now! It's what he will do! He takes blinded sinners, dead sinners, rebellious sinners, ungodly sinners, hopeless sinners, enslaved sinners, Satan-dominated sinners, and, by his Spirit,

132

applying Christ's work, he redeems them from all their sin, he releases them from the grip and polluting power of sin and Satan, he progressively sanctifies them, he brings them into everlasting liberty and glory – begun here and now – and he will at last take them into eternity to live for ever in the new heavens and new earth – where they will be vindicated and glorified to perfection. Is there any ministry to compare with this? Of course there isn't! The gospel, the new covenant, is a glorious ministry indeed! Conversion is not merely a change of habit or view or outlook. It is, of course, but is far, far more than that. Using the proverb of the Ethiopian and the leopard (Jer. 13:23), the impossible has happened: the leopard *has* changed its spots, and the Ethiopian his skin! Chaos, emptiness, bondage, ruin, shame, guilt and death have gone – and order, meaning, joy and life have come. Nothing but God in the new covenant can do this work. Law can't; ceremonies can't; sacraments (horrible word!) can't; works can't; only God, by his Spirit can. And he does! Spurgeon:

Coming to sacraments may condemn you! Coming to priests will ruin you! But coming to Christ will save you! If your simple faith takes hold of Christ's salvation, there is life in that grip. If your thoughts think of him, if your heart embraces him, if your soul trusts him, however weakly and imperfectly you do it, he will not cast you out![9] Oh, this is glorious truth to my mind – is it not so to yours? So long as we but come to him, our Saviour will not cast us away! I feel glad to be preaching this gospel in Exeter Hall – are you not glad to hear it? If you are not, you are a sorry lot.[10]

May I add my pennyworth? I am glad to be preaching this gospel in this book, now. I hope, reader, that you are glad to hear it!

---

[9] John 6:37. Do not limit this to the initial coming. This text has a far greater application than to the unconverted. Christ will never cast out or drive away any of his believing elect. I know legal teachers will shudder as I say it, but whatever Satan, the world, or the church may say, nothing – and, like Paul, I mean 'nothing' – can bring a believer into condemnation or sever him from Christ. Let me be accused of encouraging antinomianism, but I stand with the apostle (Rom. 8, especially verses 28-39).

[10] *Metropolitan Tabernacle Pulpit* Vol. 30 number 1762.

Incidentally, contrary to the thinking and practice of many, the preaching of judgement is far from converting. Oh, I know Jonathan Edwards will be cited against me – and there is much that could be said about that! – but let me ask you, reader, to go through the New Testament and see how many preachers brought sinners to Christ by preaching hell-fire. In saying this, I hope I will not be accused of denying everlasting perdition – though I fear I shall be tarred with that particular brush – but I ask you to do as I said, and see for yourself. Moreover, consider the following passages; note how even the *infliction* of actual judgement – not merely the preaching of it – failed to produce repentance:

A third of mankind was killed by the three plagues of fire, smoke and sulphur that came out of their mouths. The power of the horses was in their mouths and in their tails; for their tails were like snakes, having heads with which they inflict injury. The rest of mankind that were not killed by these plagues still did not repent of the work of their hands; they did not stop worshipping demons, and idols of gold, silver, bronze, stone and wood – idols that cannot see or hear or walk. Nor did they repent of their murders, their magic arts, their sexual immorality or their thefts...
The fourth angel poured out his bowl on the sun, and the sun was given power to scorch people with fire. They were seared by the intense heat and they cursed the name of God, who had control over these plagues, but they refused to repent and glorify him. The fifth angel poured out his bowl on the throne of the beast, and his kingdom was plunged into darkness. Men gnawed their tongues in agony and cursed the God of heaven because of their pains and their sores, but they refused to repent of what they had done (Rev. 9:18-21; 16:8-11).

I admit that 'there was a severe earthquake and a tenth of the city collapsed. Seven thousand people were killed in the earthquake, and the survivors were terrified and gave glory to the God of heaven' (Rev. 11:13-14), but I'm not at all convinced that this was saving. After all, we know that sinners 'show contempt for the riches of [God's] kindness, tolerance and patience, not realising that God's *kindness* leads [them] towards repentance' (Rom. 2:4). And what drew the prodigal back (Luke 15)? Was it not the sense of his father's kindness and goodness?

But what about 2 Corinthians 5:11, AV: 'Knowing therefore the terror of the Lord, we persuade men'? That would certainly seem to imply that because we know that the unconverted will suffer eternal torment, we seek to persuade as many as possible: conversion is the only way that they will be delivered from that wrath. I agree! And I think the thought of it should come very high upon our hearts as we approach sinners with the gospel. But that does not mean we should thump eternal torment, and do so in extended and graphic detail in our preaching. What is more, 'terror' might not be the best translation of *phobos*. The word can mean 'fear, dread, terror', 'that which strikes terror' or 'reverence, respect'.[11] The latter, I think, is the best translation here. We, having respect for God, knowing we are answerable to God, seek to persuade men. Paul might well be making us think of 'terror' (reverence) as it concerns *us*, not the sinners we're trying to persuade. Gill thought this a distinct possibility, though he preferred the other view:

The fear of the Lord; by which is meant either the grace of the fear of the Lord, implanted in the hearts of the apostles, and in which they acted in their ministry, faithfully dispensing to men the mysteries of grace; from which they could by no means be moved, because the fear of God was before their eyes, and upon their hearts. Or rather, [it may mean] the terror of the Lord in the last judgement, which will be very great, considering the awfulness of the summons: 'Arise you dead, and come to judgement'; the appearance of the Judge, which will be sudden, surprising, and glorious... the position of the wicked, the dreadful sentence pronounced on them, and the immediate execution of it... And therefore [we] persuade men... [that is] [we] endeavour to persuade them.

Calvin, in his *Commentary*, thought that Paul was talking of the fear that he had of God – not the dreadful judgements upon sinners. The NIV and NASB both opt for 'fear'. And this, of course, fits the context: 'We must all appear before the judgement seat of Christ, that each one may receive what is due him for the things done while in the body, whether good or bad' (2 Cor. 5:10); that is, we as believers will have to answer to God. Having said that, we know 'it is a dreadful thing to fall into the hands of the living God' (Heb. 10:31) and 'our "God is a consuming fire"' (Heb. 12:29). Even so it is 'Christ's love [that] compels us' (2 Cor. 5:14). Gill understood this to speak of Christ's love to us, as did Calvin.

---

[11] Thayer.

All in all, in short, knowing that sinners are under the wrath of God even as they stand now, knowing that one day they will have to face an angry God in judgement with everlasting damnation to follow, and having a sense of responsibility towards them (even love towards them), and knowing we have to answer to God for all our ways (including what we fail to do), we seek to persuade sinners to trust Christ.

Getting back to the main point: remember what we have seen: Satan has his children – all the unconverted – locked in his grip in delusion and darkness. God, in his sovereignty, delivers sinners from blindness by shining into their hearts. And all, in Scripture, is ascribed to God's sovereign initiative:

I will sprinkle clean water on you, and you will be clean; I will cleanse you from all your impurities and from all your idols. I will give you a new heart and put a new spirit in you; I will remove from you your heart of stone and give you a heart of flesh. And I will put my Spirit in you and move you to follow my decrees and be careful to keep my laws (Ezek. 36:25-27).

I praise you, Father, Lord of heaven and earth, because you have hidden these things from the wise and learned, and revealed them to little children. Yes, Father, for this was your good pleasure (Matt. 11:25-26; Luke 10:21-22).

Because of his great love for us, God, who is rich in mercy, made us alive with Christ even when we were dead in transgressions (Eph. 2:4-5).

You were once darkness, but now you are light in the Lord (Eph. 5:8).

Christ Jesus took hold of me (Phil. 3:12).

He has rescued us from the dominion of darkness and brought us into the kingdom of the Son he loves, in whom we have redemption, the forgiveness of sins (Col. 1:13-14).

Once you were alienated from God and were enemies in your minds because of your evil behaviour. But now he has reconciled you by Christ's physical body through death to present you holy in his sight, without blemish and free from accusation (Col. 1:21-22).

But you, brothers, are not in darkness... You are all sons of the light and sons of the day. We do not belong to the night or to the darkness (1 Thess. 5:4-5).

Since the children have flesh and blood, he too shared in their humanity so that by his death he might destroy him who holds the power of death – that is, the devil – and free those who all their lives were held in slavery by their fear of death (Heb. 2:14-15).

5. *Sinners Brought to Glory*

But you are a chosen people, a royal priesthood, a holy nation, a people belonging to God, that you may declare the praises of him who called you out of darkness into his wonderful light (1 Pet. 2:9).

Of course, Satan does not give up without a fight. Nevertheless, although he is powerful, Christ is all powerful: 'All authority in heaven and on earth has been given to me', he declares (Matt. 28:18; see also Dan. 7:13-14; Matt. 11:27; John 13:3; 17:2; Rom. 14:9; Eph. 1:20-22; Phil. 2:9-11; Col. 2:10; 1 Pet. 3:22). The devil may grip the sinner in blind enslavement, but 'God, who said: "Let light shine out of darkness", made his light shine in our hearts to give us the light of the knowledge of the glory of God in the face of Christ' (2 Cor. 4:6). And, just as on the first day of creation, the darkness had to flee with the coming of the light, so the dead sinner has to live, the deaf sinner has to hear, the blind sinner has to see. Satan may kick and fight, but he has to give up his prey.

Isaiah foretold it:

The desert and the parched land will be glad; the wilderness will rejoice and blossom. Like the crocus, it will burst into bloom; it will rejoice greatly and shout for joy. The glory of Lebanon will be given to it, the splendour of Carmel and Sharon; they will see the glory of the LORD, the splendour of our God. Strengthen the feeble hands, steady the knees that give way; say to those with fearful hearts: 'Be strong, do not fear; your God will come, he will come with vengeance; with divine retribution he will come to save you'. Then will the eyes of the blind be opened and the ears of the deaf unstopped. Then will the lame leap like a deer, and the mute tongue shout for joy. Water will gush forth in the wilderness and streams in the desert. The burning sand will become a pool, the thirsty ground bubbling springs. In the haunts where jackals once lay, grass and reeds and papyrus will grow. And a highway will be there; it will be called the Way of Holiness. The unclean will not journey on it; it will be for those who walk in that Way; wicked fools will not go about on it. No lion will be there, nor will any ferocious beast get up on it; they will not be found there. But only the redeemed will walk there, and the ransomed of the LORD will return. They will enter Zion with singing; everlasting joy will crown their heads. Gladness and joy will overtake them, and sorrow and sighing will flee away (Isa. 35).

And we know that this prophecy was fulfilled in Christ in the new covenant:

5. Sinners Brought to Glory

When John heard in prison what Christ was doing, he sent his disciples to ask him: 'Are you the one who was to come, or should we expect someone else?' Jesus replied: 'Go back and report to John what you hear and see: the blind receive sight, the lame walk, those who have leprosy are cured, the deaf hear, the dead are raised, and the good news is preached to the poor' (Matt. 11:2-5).

Let me complete the verse from Charles Wesley, which I partly quoted earlier:

> *Long my imprisoned spirit lay,*
> *Fast bound in sin and nature's night;*
> *Thine eye diffused a quickening ray –*
> *I woke, the dungeon flamed with light;*
> *My chains fell off, my heart was free,*
> *I rose, went forth, and followed thee.*

And Horatius Bonar:

> *I heard the voice of Jesus say,*
> *'I am this dark world's light;*
> *Look unto me, thy morn shall rise,*
> *And all thy day be bright'.*
> *I looked to Jesus, and I found*
> *In him my star, my sun;*
> *And in that light of life I'll walk*
> *Till trav'lling days are done.*

And, at the end of the age, when the battle between Christ and Satan reaches its climax, what then?

And then the lawless one will be revealed... The coming of the lawless one will be in accordance with the work of Satan displayed in all kinds of counterfeit miracles, signs and wonders, and in every sort of evil that deceives those who are perishing. They perish because they refused to love the truth and so be saved. For this reason God sends them a powerful delusion so that they will believe the lie and so that all will be condemned who have not believed the truth but have delighted in wickedness (2 Thess. 2:8-12).

Ah! But I've deliberately left out the vital bit: 'And then the lawless one will be revealed, *whom the Lord Jesus will overthrow with the breath of his mouth and destroy by the splendour of his coming*' (2 Thess. 2:8). The victory is already gained and certain. Christ said:

5. Sinners Brought to Glory

'I saw Satan fall like lightning from heaven' (Luke 10:18). Just before his death, Jesus declared:

The hour has come for the Son of Man to be glorified. I tell you the truth, unless a grain of wheat falls to the ground and dies, it remains only a single seed. But if it dies, it produces many seeds. The man who loves his life will lose it, while the man who hates his life in this world will keep it for eternal life. Whoever serves me must follow me; and where I am, my servant also will be. My Father will honour the one who serves me. Now my heart is troubled, and what shall I say? 'Father, save me from this hour'? No, it was for this very reason I came to this hour. Father, glorify your name!

'Then a voice came from heaven'. And what did God say in that thundering voice? 'I have glorified it, and will glorify it again'. 'The crowd that was there and heard it said it had thundered; others said an angel had spoken to him. Jesus said: "This voice was for your benefit, not mine. Now is the time for judgement on this world; now the prince of this world will be driven out. But I, when I am lifted up from the earth, will draw all men to myself"' (John 12:20-32).

Christ, when comforting his disciples just before his death, told them that he would send the Holy Spirit:

I tell you the truth: It is for your good that I am going away. Unless I go away, the Counsellor will not come to you; but if I go, I will send him to you. When he comes, he will convict the world of guilt in regard to sin and righteousness and judgement: in regard to sin, because men do not believe in me; in regard to righteousness, because I am going to the Father, where you can see me no longer; and in regard to judgement, because the prince of this world now stands condemned (John 16:7-11).

Here it is. Anticipating his triumph on the cross, Christ cried out: 'The prince of this world now stands condemned'! Christ, just before his death, promised the gift of the Spirit and spoke of what he would do: 'When he comes, he will convict the world of guilt in regard to sin and righteousness and judgement: in regard to sin, because men do not believe in me; in regard to righteousness, because I am going to the Father, where you can see me no longer; and in regard to judgement, because the prince of this world now stands condemned' (John 16:8-11). The judgement, of course, is

139

not the judgement 'to come' (a frequent gloss), but Christ's 'judgement' of – his triumph over – Satan on the cross and in his resurrection. Gill offered this as one possible explanation of those words:

[It could mean] the judgement, or condemnation and destruction of Satan, the prince of the world, for Christ, by his death, has destroyed him and his works, has spoiled his principalities and powers, and by his resurrection from the dead, and ascension to heaven, has carried him and them captive, triumphing over them; and, through the effusion of the Holy Spirit upon the apostles, and the power of it attending their ministry, Satan was judged, condemned, and cast out of the heathen world, their temples, and the souls of men, the prey was taken from the mighty, and the lawful captive delivered.

And Matthew Henry saw at least this:

It appears that Christ is stronger than Satan, and can disarm and dispossess him, and set up his throne upon the ruin of his... [The Spirit] shall show that Christ's errand into the world was to set things to rights in it, and to introduce times of reformation and regeneration; and he proves it by this, that the prince of this world, the great master of misrule, is judged and expelled. All will be well when his power is broken who made the mischief... He shall convince the world that all judgement is committed to [Christ], and that he is the Lord of all, which is evident by this, that he has judged the prince of this world, has broken the serpent's head, destroyed him that had the power of death, and spoiled principalities. If Satan be thus subdued by Christ, we may be sure no other power can stand before him.

As the writer to the Hebrews explained: 'Since the children have flesh and blood, [Christ] too shared in their humanity so that by his death he might destroy him who holds the power of death – that is, the devil – and free those who all their lives were held in slavery by their fear of death' (Heb. 2:14-15). 'The reason the Son of God appeared was to destroy the devil's work' (1 John 3:8). While Satan is powerful, Christ is all powerful, and victory over Satan is secure (Rom. 16:20; 2 Thess. 3:3).

In short, Christ triumphed over Satan on the cross, and now we, as ministers of the new covenant go out to a fallen world in the confidence and assurance of this triumph. No wonder the Holy

Spirit is the Comforter! This new-covenant ministry is amazing, is it not? Even so, there is yet more for us to look into.

6. God Shines in the Heart

God shines in the heart (2 Cor. 4:6); in the heart, I stress. God, in the new-covenant ministry, works on the heart. Note also the reference to the conscience: 'By setting forth the truth plainly we commend ourselves to every man's conscience in the sight of God' (2 Cor. 4:2). And. of course, in speaking of the heart and conscience, the apostle is showing us the inwardness of the new covenant. God, therefore, works in the will also. The whole man is affected. Here we meet no Sandemanian[1] view of the gospel. The new-covenant ministry is a whole-man ministry, primarily a work in and on the heart.

How different is this to legal preaching, legal preaching in all its various forms, dealing as it does in externals, mere conformity to rules and rites. We want, we must have, preaching to the heart. The heart is reached, of course, through the mind, but the heart has to be reached and moved. As James taught us: 'Humbly accept the word planted in you, which can save you. Do not merely listen to the

---

[1] A Sandemanian thinks saving faith is nothing more than mental assent. If a sinner accepts the facts of the gospel, he is saved. To talk about the heart or feelings is to introduce works, and ruin the grace of God in salvation. The name comes from Robert Sandeman (1718-1771). It is, perhaps, the most common error to blight the churches today, with debilitating – not to say, devastating – effect. Here is an example: 'Saving faith... A person either believes the offer of eternal life or he doesn't... If someone does believe the offer of eternal life – as the Bible presents this offer – he will also be sure that he has eternal life. This is what we mean when we say that assurance is of the essence of saving faith... Let me just restate the matter in order to make it clear. The nature of the gospel message is such that, when a person believes it, he necessarily has assurance of eternal salvation. No matter what else he might believe, if he is not assured, he has not believed the gospel'. And what is saving faith? Mental assent: 'To believe in Jesus is shorthand for to believe that Jesus is the Christ... There is no difference in kind between believing that Elvis [Presley] is alive and believing that Jesus is the Christ. Both are acts of faith. Of course, the former faith is unfounded. The latter is divinely sanctioned. The former is misplaced faith. The latter is saving faith' (Zane C.Hodges: 'Assurance: Of The Essence Of Saving Faith', faithalone.org).

word, and so deceive yourselves. Do what it says' (Jas. 1:21-22). The word has to enter the ear and eye; then it must reach the mind; then it must reach the will; it must reach the heart; above all, it must reach the experience. It is in the heart that the work is done, leading to the experience:

God be thanked that though you were slaves of sin, yet you obeyed from the heart that form of doctrine to which you were delivered (Rom. 6:17, NKJV).

If you confess with your mouth: 'Jesus is Lord', and believe in your heart that God raised him from the dead, you will be saved. For it is with your heart that you believe and are justified, and it is with your mouth that you confess and are saved (Rom. 10:9-10).

As Peter put it:

Through [Christ] you believe in God, who raised him from the dead and glorified him, and so your faith and hope are in God. Now that you have purified yourselves by obeying the truth... For you have been born again, not of perishable seed, but of imperishable, through the living and enduring word of God. For: 'All men are like grass, and all their glory is like the flowers of the field; the grass withers and the flowers fall, but the word of the Lord stands forever'. And this is the word that was preached to you (1 Pet. 1:21-25).

As I have just noted, but it bears repetition, Sandemanianism (almost entirely incipient or unrecognised) is probably the most common blight affecting the churches today. How desperately we need to recover 'the glorious new-covenant ministry', with its powerful emphasis upon the heart, upon heart-experience, God shining in his sovereign grace and power into sinners' hearts!

Joseph Hart:

> *Let us ask th'important question,*
> *Brethren, be not too secure,*
> *What it is to be a Christian?*
> *How we may our heart assure!*
> *Vain is all our best devotion,*
> *If on false foundations built;*
> *True religion's more than notion,*
> *Something must be known and felt.*

Let us remind ourselves of the ground we have covered. The sinner, as we first meet him, is locked in sin, dead in sin, blinded by Satan, ruined, hopeless and helpless, under the wrath of God. The law, in all its forms, can never set him free. God, and God alone, in the new covenant, can, by his sovereign intervention, redeem and release him: he can justify him, sanctify him, liberate him, and glorify him. He can wash him from his sin, he can make him holy; he can change him completely, irreversibly and for ever. Because God has worked within him, he can now, by God's Spirit, work out his salvation in daily life (Phil. 2:12-13). As Paul told the Ephesians:

As for you, you were dead in your transgressions and sins, in which you used to live when you followed the ways of this world and of the ruler of the kingdom of the air, the spirit who is now at work in those who are disobedient. All of us also lived among them at one time, gratifying the cravings of our sinful nature and following its desires and thoughts. Like the rest, we were by nature objects of wrath. But because of his great love for us, God, who is rich in mercy, made us alive with Christ even when we were dead in transgressions – it is by grace you have been saved. And God raised us up with Christ and seated us with him in the heavenly realms in Christ Jesus, in order that in the coming ages he might show the incomparable riches of his grace, expressed in his kindness to us in Christ Jesus. For it is by grace you have been saved, through faith – and this not from yourselves, it is the gift of God – not by works, so that no one can boast. For we are God's workmanship, created in Christ Jesus to do good works, which God prepared in advance for us to do (Eph. 2:1-10).

All this is nothing less than a miracle, a new creation, amazing beyond words. Under the new covenant, the sinner is not moved a few microns across a spectrum; he is radically changed. It's life from the dead! It's an utter transformation and translation from the kingdom of darkness to the kingdom of light and love (Col. 1:13). The converted sinner is now a new man, living – not existing – liberated from sin, death and law, living, not in Satan's bondage, but a free man in Christ, living for the glory and praise of God:

You are all sons of the light and sons of the day. We do not belong to the night or to the darkness. So then, let us not be like others, who are asleep, but let us be alert and self-controlled. For those who sleep, sleep at night, and those who get drunk, get drunk at night. But since we belong to the day, let us be self-controlled, putting on faith and love as a breastplate, and the hope of salvation as a helmet. For God did not appoint us to suffer wrath but to receive salvation through our Lord Jesus Christ. He died for us so that, whether we are awake or asleep, we may live together with him. Therefore encourage one another and build each other up, just as in fact you are doing (1 Thess. 5:5-11).

But how, precisely, is the sinner to come into the good of all this in the new covenant? How can we, as believers, help to bring other sinners into all this liberty in Christ?

Well, in one sense, we can do nothing. As I have said, it takes God's sovereign intervention to do the work, in fulfilment of his sovereign decree by the operation of the Holy Spirit, even a new creation – superseding the work of creation, itself. 'For God, who said: "Let light shine out of darkness", made his light shine in our hearts to give us the light of the knowledge of the glory of God in the face of Christ' (2 Cor. 4:6). When 'God said: "Let there be light", and there was light' (Gen. 1:3), that was a sovereign act, an act of sheer power. Thus it is with the gospel. Sinners are dead; they can do nothing. The saints, too, are powerless to take dead sinners and make them live. But God, in his fiat – 'Let him live!' – makes dead sinners live (Ezek. 16:6; 37:1-14). 'I will sprinkle clean water on you, and you will be clean; I will cleanse you from all your impurities and from all your idols. I will give you a new heart and put a new spirit in you; I will remove from you your heart of stone and give you a heart of flesh. And I will put my Spirit in you and move you to follow my decrees and be careful to keep my laws' (Ezek. 36:25-27). He raises living saints out of stones (Luke 3:8). Stones! He does it directly by a sovereign decree: 'Let these live!' He does it in the (in the fullest sense of the word) preaching of the gospel (1 Cor. 1:18; 4:15). God declares to every cleansed sinner, as he declared to Joshua the high priest: 'I have taken away your sin, and I will put rich garments on you' (Zech. 3:4). 'I have': that is, God does it, he *has* done it, it is a finished act, a once-for-all act, and it is an act of sovereignty. More, it is an act of grace, free grace.

As William Gadsby put it:

> *Salvation! O my soul rejoice!*
> *Salvation is of God;*
> *He speaks, and that almighty voice*
> *Proclaims his grace abroad.*

6. God Shines in the Heart

The Father loved us e'er we fell,
And will for ever love;
Nor shall the pow'rs of earth or hell
His love from Zion move.

'Twas love that moved him to ordain
A Surety just and good,
And on his heart inscribed the name
Of all for whom he stood.

Nor is the Surety short of love;
He loves beyond degree;
No less than love divine could move
The Lord to die for me.

And oh, what love the Spirit shows!
When Jesus he reveals
To men oppressed with sin and woes,
He all their sorrows heals.

The Three-in-One and One-in-Three
In love for ever rest;
His people shall in glory be,
And with his love be blessed.

Gill, commenting on 'God, who... made us alive with Christ even when we were dead in transgressions' (Eph. 2:4-5), said of 'regeneration', that:

When a soul that is dead in a moral or spiritual sense is quickened and made alive, a principle of life is infused, and acts of life are put forth. Such have their spiritual senses, and these are in exercise, [so that] they can feel the load and weight of sin, see their lost state and condition, the odiousness of sin, and the beauty of a Saviour, the insufficiency of their own righteousness, and the fullness and suitableness of Christ's. [They] breathe after divine and spiritual things... move towards Christ, exercise grace on him, act for him, and walk on in him: and this life they have not from themselves, for previous to it they are dead, and in this quickening work are entirely passive. Nor can... unregenerate sinners [quicken themselves], but this is God's act, the act of God the Father; though not exclusive of the Son, who quickens whom he will; nor of the Spirit, who is the Spirit of life from Christ. And it is an instance of the exceeding greatness, both of his power and love. And this may be said to be done with Christ, because he is the procuring and meritorious cause of it, by his death and resurrection from the dead, and is the author and efficient cause cf it. And he is the matter [substance] of it; it is not so much the quickened persons that live, as Christ that lives in them, and it is the same life he himself lives. And because he lives, they shall live also. It is [all] in him as in the fountain, and in them as in the stream.

Here we have it: regeneration is an act of God in his sovereign grace and power. As John 1:13 puts it: Believers are 'children born not of natural descent, nor of human decision or a husband's will, but born of God'. Or as James tells us, God 'chose to give us birth through the word of truth' (Jas. 1:18). This 'word of truth', I am sure, speaks in the first instance of God's fiat, his decree, his sovereign pronouncement. And this is God's great initial act within the sinner in the new covenant!

But, let us not forget, although God is sovereign and does not need any human hand to help him in his work, 'through God's mercy we have [received] this ministry' (2 Cor. 4:1). '*We* have...', please note: it is *our* ministry! We, therefore, as believers have a part to play in bringing many other sinners out of darkness into the marvellous light of the gospel. Amazing. is it not? Yes, God is sovereign, but he is graciously pleased to use his people in 'this ministry'. It is '*through God's mercy* [that] we have this ministry', and, moved by the sense of God's mercy to us, we, as new men and women in Christ, take our place in the line, and play our part in the glorious ministry of the new covenant.

This, of course, means that we can and must pray that God will exercise his sovereignty in the saving of sinners. Yes. But that is not what the apostle stresses – or even mentions – here. Prayer, there is no doubt about it, is a vital part of 'our ministry', but, sticking to our passage, while prayer is not questioned, neither is it mentioned. What does Paul set out here? We must get to grips with this if we want to engage fully in our ministry. So let us now explore what our part in 'this ministry' is; that is, let us see what our privileges and duties are in serving God in the gospel of his Son.

7. Our Privilege and Duty

I open this section by returning to James 1:18. This verse, in the first instance, teaches that regeneration is a sovereign, direct act of God, in power and grace, upon the dead sinner. But that's not quite the whole story; not quite! I do not think that it exhausts the meaning of the words. Let Matthew Henry give us his opinion:

Here let us take notice: (1) A true Christian is a creature begotten anew. He becomes as different a person from what he was before the renewing influences of divine grace as if he were formed over again, and born afresh. (2) The original of this good work is here declared: it is of God's own will; not by our skill or power; not from any good foreseen in us, or done by us, but purely from the goodwill and grace of God. (3) The means whereby this is effected are pointed out: 'the word of truth', that is, the gospel, as Paul expresses it more plainly: 'I have begotten you in Jesus Christ through the gospel' (1 Cor. 4:15). This gospel is indeed a word of truth, or else it could never produce such real, such lasting, such great and noble effects. We may rely upon it, and venture our immortal souls upon it. And we shall find it a means of our sanctification as it is a word of truth (John 17:17).

And Gill was sure that James was speaking of the preaching of the gospel:

The gospel, [Gill said,] which is the word of truth, and truth itself, and contains nothing but truth; and by this souls are begotten and born again (see Eph. 1:13; 1 Pet. 1:23). And hence ministers of it are accounted spiritual fathers. Faith, and every other grace in regeneration, and even the Spirit himself, the regenerator, come this way.

Calvin had no doubt:

'Of his own will'. [James] now brings forward a special proof of the goodness of God which he had mentioned, even that he has regenerated us unto eternal life. This invaluable benefit every one of the faithful feels in himself. Then the goodness of God, when known by experience, ought to remove from them all a contrary opinion respecting him. When he says that God of his own will, or spontaneously, has begotten us, he intimates that he was induced by no other reason, as the will and counsel of God are often set in opposition

148

to the merits of men. What great thing, indeed, would it have been to say that God was not constrained to do this? But he impresses something more, that God according to his own goodwill hath begotten us, and has been thus a cause to himself. It hence follows that it is natural to God to do good.

But this passage teaches us, that as our election before the foundation of the world was gratuitous, so we are illuminated by the grace of God alone as to the knowledge of the truth, so that our calling corresponds with our election. The Scripture shows that we have been gratuitously adopted by God before we were born. But James expresses here something more, that we obtain the right of adoption, because God does also call us gratuitously (Eph. 1:4-5). Further, we hence learn, that it is the peculiar office of God spiritually to regenerate us; for that the same thing is sometimes ascribed to the ministers of the gospel [that is, all believers! – DG], means no other thing than this, that God acts through them; and it happens indeed through them, but he nevertheless alone does the work.

The word 'begotten' means that we become new men, so that we put off our former disposition or spirit [Calvin had 'nature'] when we are effectually called by God. He adds how God begets us, even by the word of truth, so that we may know that we cannot enter the kingdom of God by any other door.

As Peter put it:

For you have been born again, not of perishable seed, but of imperishable, through the living and enduring word of God. For: 'All men are like grass, and all their glory is like the flowers of the field; the grass withers and the flowers fall, but the word of the Lord stands forever'. And this is the word that was preached to you (1 Pet. 1:23-25).

Paul: 'You also were included in Christ when you heard the word of truth, the gospel of your salvation. Having believed...' (Eph. 1:13). 'The word of truth' certainly means 'Scripture' (John 17:17; Eph. 1:13; 2 Tim. 2:15). As the apostle put it:

[It is] with your heart that you believe and are justified, and it is with your mouth that you confess and are saved. As the Scripture says: 'Anyone who trusts in him will never be put to shame'... The... Lord... richly blesses all who call on him, for: 'Everyone who calls on the name of the Lord will be saved'. How, then, can they call on the one they have not believed in? And how can they believe in the one of whom they have not heard? And how can they hear without someone preaching to them? And how can they preach unless they are sent?... Consequently, faith comes from hearing the message, and the message is heard through the word of Christ (Rom. 10:10-17).

Thus regeneration, while it is a sovereign act of God – which he can do directly – is an act which he usually performs through the preaching of the gospel.

In other words, here we have the makings of yet another first-class contradiction! We have the sinner – dead, ruined, blind, deluded by Satan, helpless and hopeless. Only God, in an act of sovereign grace and power, can re-create, regenerate this dead sinner. While he can do it directly, absolutely independently, at his good will and pleasure, even so, he is pleased to 'tie' himself to working through his servants, his people, in the 'preaching' (I use the word in its fullest and widest biblical meaning) of the gospel to these dead sinners. As dead sinners hear the gospel call, God, in his sovereignty, regenerates his elect; they fly to Christ by faith, and the work is done: they are everlastingly saved. It's not God's sovereignty alone; it's not preaching alone; it's not saving faith alone. All three are linked – unbreakably – together. All this I see plainly set out in the Scriptures. But how can our feeble preaching to dead sinners have the slightest effect on them? And how is it possible that God's free sovereignty should be tied to our efforts? How can a deaf sinner hear, a dead sinner live, a dumb sinner speak? How can our preaching have any bearing on this impossible task?

The same goes for prayer. Why pray, when God has decreed all things from before the beginning of time? Well, for a start, because God has commanded it. He had his plans prepared for Israel; even so he wanted Israel to pray: 'I will do it... I will yet for this be enquired of by the house of Israel, to do it for them' (Ezek. 36:36-37, AV). In addition, there is a host of other reasons why we should pray – it increases our faith, our sense of dependence, our joy in participating with God, the worship of God, our submission to God, *etc*. Nevertheless, the mystery remains.

Quite a number of pretty tough questions there! More than enough to be going on with! Let me tell you what I propose to do about it: I will leave others to sort out the logic as best they can, and simply get on and set out the biblical principles as I see them –

leaving all the seeming paradoxes or antinomies for God to explain in his good time. I see all parts of the paradox clearly revealed in Scripture. Consequently, while I cannot fully reconcile them, I simply maintain each aspect of the antinomy, trying to give each its proper scriptural weight. I am of Isaac Watts' mind. Let me complete my quotation of his hymn:

How sad our state by nature is!
Our sin how deep its stains!
And Satan binds our captive minds
Fast in his slavish chains.

But there's a voice of sovereign grace
Sounds from the sacred word;
'Ho, ye despairing sinners, come,
And trust upon the Lord!'

My soul obeys th'almighty call,
And runs to this relief;
I would believe thy promise, Lord,
Oh, help my unbelief!

To the dear fountain of thy blood,
Incarnate God, I fly;
Here let me wash my spotted soul
From sins of deepest dye.

Stretch out thine arm, victorious King,
My reigning sins subdue,
Drive the old dragon from his seat,
With all his hellish crew.

A guilty, weak, and helpless worm,
On thy kind arms I fall;
Be thou my strength and righteousness,
My Jesus, and my all.

Note how Watts rightly links the ruined state of man, the sovereignty of God, the call of the gospel and personal response in saving faith in Christ – and all without trying to reconcile all the parts.

The point is this: one of the great privileges which God affords his people in the new covenant is to take them into his service. On their conversion, they become 'God's fellow-workers' (1 Cor. 3:9;

2 Cor. 6:1; see also Mark 16:20). And Paul leaves us in no doubt as to what he is talking about:

All this is from God, who reconciled us to himself through Christ and gave us the ministry of reconciliation: that God was reconciling the world to himself in Christ, not counting men's sins against them. And he has committed to us the message of reconciliation. We are therefore Christ's ambassadors, as though God were making his appeal through us. We implore you on Christ's behalf: Be reconciled to God. God made him who had no sin to be sin for us, so that in him we might become the righteousness of God. As God's fellow-workers we urge you not to receive God's grace in vain. For he says: 'In the time of my favour I heard you, and in the day of salvation I helped you'. I tell you, now is the time of God's favour, now is the day of salvation (2 Cor. 5:18 – 6:2).

This, of course, reinforces what the apostle has already declared in our passage:

Therefore, since through God's mercy we have this ministry, we do not lose heart. Rather, we have renounced secret and shameful ways; we do not use deception, nor do we distort the word of God. On the contrary, by setting forth the truth plainly we commend ourselves to every man's conscience in the sight of God. And even if our gospel is veiled, it is veiled to those who are perishing. The god of this age has blinded the minds of unbelievers, so that they cannot see the light of the gospel of the glory of Christ, who is the image of God. For we do not preach ourselves, but Jesus Christ as Lord, and ourselves as your servants for Jesus' sake. For God, who said: 'Let light shine out of darkness', made his light shine in our hearts to give us the light of the knowledge of the glory of God in the face of Christ (2 Cor. 4:1-6).

Christ made all this perfectly clear to Paul right at the outset of his Christian pilgrimage, immediately at his conversion, even as he was telling him of his life's work:

I am sending you to [the Gentiles] to open their eyes and turn them from darkness to light, and from the power of Satan to God, so that they may receive forgiveness of sins and a place among those who are sanctified by faith in me (Acts 26:17-18).

Let me trace out the relevant points. While we are not in the same league as the apostle, nevertheless, as I have explained, as new-covenant ministers, all believers have received 'this ministry'; all believers are able to participate in bringing sinners to Christ. And what is 'this ministry'? Although, as the New Testament makes clear, the believer's 'ministry' is far wider than 'preaching', sticking close to our passage, I limit the discussion here to 'preaching'. 'This ministry' is, said Paul, to 'preach'; it is 'to set forth the truth; it is to 'preach Jesus Christ'; it is to 'preach Jesus Christ as Lord'; and it is to let sinners know that we are 'their servants for Jesus' sake'. I want to bring this home by using the singular. In the new covenant, every believer, each believer, has received 'this ministry'. Believer, you are to preach, to preach Jesus Christ, to preach Jesus Christ as Lord, and to let sinners know that you are here to serve them in the gospel, and all for Jesus' sake. This is your duty and your privilege.

Let me work out these points in a little more detail.

Every believer is to preach

This does not mean, of course, that every believer is to stand in a pulpit and maintain a regular stated ministry of the gospel. Now, in saying this I do not want to be misunderstood. Of course, a preacher can stand in a pulpit or on a platform to preach. I'm not saying a word against 'preaching' in that regard. Indeed, I could say a great deal for it; please see the Appendix. But we must not limit the word 'preach' to such. Sinners can hear of Christ in many ways other than by a formal preacher. Why, I am preaching to you now as you read this book. I don't apologise for it. That's why I write! As a member of the new covenant, I should always be engaged in 'this ministry'. Again, a believer preaches when he engages someone in spiritual conversation. When the early church was persecuted, the believers were driven out of Jerusalem, and we know that 'those who had been scattered, preached the word wherever they went' (Acts 8:4); that is, they talked to people, they told them about Christ, they 'gossiped' the gospel. If you are a Christian, then you, in this sense, are a preacher. It is your job and your privilege to tell others about Christ and his gospel. Conversation might lead to conversion!

Let me remind you of some scriptural examples of what I am talking about. After he had healed a demon-possessed man, as 'Jesus was getting into the boat' to cross the lake, 'the man who had been demon-possessed begged to go with him'. But Jesus refused. He was adamant: 'Go home to your family', he said, 'and tell them how much the Lord has done for you, and how he has had mercy on you'. And the man did it (Mark 5:18-20). Well, that's clear enough. I believe we can and should apply this to ourselves. I know that, on occasion, and for special local reasons, Jesus commanded those whom he had healed to say nothing about it (Mark 1:43-45; Luke 5:14; 8:56, for instance), but these hard cases, as always, make bad law for us today. In any case, while we have plain commands and scriptural examples concerning the promiscuous spread of the gospel, we have no specific command from Christ to tell us to be silent under this or that special circumstance. This we should need, but this, as far as I can judge, we do not have. The evidence of the New Testament is that silence by believers is culpable. Now you know, believer, that you must tell your family and friends what Christ means to you, and what he has done for you, and done in you. Have you told them? If not, why not? Since you are a believer, you have received 'this ministry', and part of 'this ministry' is telling of your experience of Christ.

Of course, we must rid ourselves of the usual (Christendom, institutional) view of preaching – a man standing in a pulpit, lecturing a silent audience, using a certain kind of jargon, and all heavily (overtly) structured. Rather, take the example of Jesus at the well with the Samaritan woman. As for talking with one's family, one's children, or whatever, surely it must be counter-productive to lambast relatives with 'sermons'. Remember Queen Victoria's complaint against William Ewart Gladstone: 'He speaks to me as if I were a public meeting!'

Take a leaf out of Andrew's book. John the Baptist directed him to Jesus as the Lamb of God. Andrew followed Jesus, and had his eyes and heart opened; he discovered that Jesus was the promised Messiah, the Christ. What did he do next? 'The first thing Andrew did' – note that – 'the first thing Andrew did was to find his brother Simon and tell him: "We have found the Messiah" (that is, the Christ). And he brought him to Jesus' (John 1:41-42). This is a vital part of 'this ministry'. So, reader, I ask: What about you? You have come to know Jesus as your Saviour and Lord? You have? Well then, have you gone back home and told your family about him? Have you tried to 'bring them to Jesus'? If not, why not? When you were converted, you became a new-covenant minister; testifying of Jesus is part of 'this ministry'.

Take another case: Philip. Jesus called Philip. Philip followed him. 'Philip found Nathaniel and told him: "We have found the one Moses wrote about in the law, and about whom the prophets also wrote – Jesus of Nazareth"'. When Nathaniel doubted, Philip had his answer ready: 'Come and see', he said (John 1:44-46). You see: the early believers were all at it! 'Come to Jesus!' 'Come and see!' What about you? You have found in the Lord Jesus all that the Scriptures promise, haven't you? Well then, have you told your friends about him? Have you answered all their questions, fears and doubts by telling them to 'come to Jesus and see' for themselves? If not, why not? Once again, it is all part of 'this ministry' which Christ has given you in the new covenant.

Let's go back to the woman at Jacob's well in Samaria. After she had met Jesus, what did she do? 'Leaving her water jar, the woman went back to the town and said to the people: "Come, see a man who told me everything I ever did. Could this be the Christ?"'. Notice how she was so occupied with her meeting with Christ, and her experience of him, and her immediate desire to tell others, that she forgot why she had come out to the well in the first place – the vital task of fetching water – and, leaving her water pot, she went back into the town to tell the rest (John 4:28-29). Remarkable! That took some courage! She had come out to the well at midday (John 4:6), probably to avoid people, because, as we learn from the account in John 4, she was a woman with a notorious reputation. But whatever the rights and wrongs of that, having met with Jesus, she couldn't help herself. Leaving her water pot, she went back to speak to the people, and invited – encouraged – them to come to meet him, too. We read: 'They came out of the town and made their way towards him'. Later, we are told, 'many of the Samaritans from that town believed in him because of the woman's testimony'. As a result of their confession, Jesus stayed with the Samaritans and spoke to many others: 'And because of his words, many more became believers. They said to the woman: "We no longer believe just because of what you said; now we have heard for ourselves, and we know that this man really is the Saviour of the world"' (John 4:30,39-42).

Do you not see, believer, that – just like this woman – your word of testimony might be used by God to bring many others to know and trust the Saviour, too? Don't you feel challenged and encouraged by her example? She didn't know the terminology of course, but she had become a new-covenant minister – and so, as a believer, have you. She carried out her ministry; do you carry out yours? I don't think for a moment that she felt it was her duty; her heart was so full, she simply couldn't help herself – she had to share it with others. A few minutes before she had been talking vehemently, resisting Christ, in terms of the old covenant (John 4:9,12,19-20), even though she knew that the old covenant predicted the coming of the Messiah (John 4:25). Now that her eyes and her heart had been opened, what was the topic of her conversation? Christ (John 4:29,39)! No more racial talk, no more talk of 'our father Jacob', no more talk of places of worship, What was her concern? What was uppermost in her mind and heart? Christ! Not water; but the water of life, Christ! And after they had met the Lord, and been changed, the same could be said of many in that place (John 4:40-42).

Surely Charles Wesley captured the thought:

> *My heart is full of Christ, and longs*
> *The glorious matter to declare!*
> *Of him I make my loftier song,*
> *I cannot from his praise forbear;*
> *My ready tongue makes haste to sing*
> *The glories of my heavenly King.*

And 'praise' is not to be limited to singing hymns in a meeting!

Take Philip with the Ethiopian eunuch. Philip saw the Ethiopian reading the Scriptures. At God's bidding, he ran to the man and spoke to him about what he was reading. The Ethiopian said he didn't understand, but wanted to know. 'Then Philip began with that very passage of Scripture, and told him the good news about Jesus'. 'Then Philip opened his mouth, and began at the same scripture, and preached unto him Jesus' (Acts 8:35, AV). And what happened? The Ethiopian believed and was baptised (Acts 8:26-38)! Can you not see, believer, how a word from you can bring a sinner to Christ, and lead him to obedience to the Lord? Notice how this thought has come up time and again. And what a thought it is! Somebody might be converted through my testimony! Will you not speak about your Saviour to others? Don't you realise, you are a minister of the new covenant? Philip wasn't standing in a pulpit that day; he was in a chariot, sitting alongside another man, an open Bible (that is, in those days, the Old Testament) before them, and talking of Christ. This is what we must understand by 'this ministry'.

Let me encourage you with this thought of seeing a sinner in glory – converted though your ministry. Samuel Rutherford laboured at Anwoth. Listen to Anne Cousin's rendering of Rutherford's letters:

> *Fair Anwoth by the Solway,*
> *To me thou still art dear.*
> *Ev'n from the verge of heaven*
> *I drop for thee a tear.*
> *O, if one soul from Anwoth*
> *Meet me at God's right hand,*
> *My heaven will be two heavens*
> *In Immanuel's land.*

And one final case; namely, Saul of Tarsus. Saul was converted on the road to Damascus. God certainly 'shined' that day – into Saul's heart – and with physical light (Acts 9:3; 22:6; 26:13)! Notice how this fact – God shining with an intense light – is recorded in all three accounts. Did this play a part in Paul's words in 2 Corinthians 4:5-6? I'm sure of it.

Let me expand on this a little. In what follows, do not miss the emphasis on 'light' and 'seeing', especially in the last two extracts – which are drawn from Paul's own testimony:

As he neared Damascus on his journey, suddenly a *light* from heaven flashed around him... The men travelling with Saul stood there speechless; they heard the sound but did not see anyone. Saul got up from the ground, but when he opened his eyes he could *see* nothing... For three days he was blind... In Damascus there was a disciple named Ananias... The Lord told him: '...In a vision [Saul] has *seen* a man named Ananias come and place his hands on him to restore his *sight*'... Then Ananias went to the house and entered it. Placing his hands on Saul, he said: 'Brother Saul, the Lord – Jesus, who appeared to you on the road as you were coming here – has sent me so that you may *see* again and be filled with the Holy Spirit'. Immediately, something like scales fell from Saul's *eyes*, and he could *see* again (Acts 9:3,7-18).

About noon as I came near Damascus, suddenly a bright *light* from heaven flashed around me... My companions saw the light, but they did not understand the voice of him who was speaking to me... My companions led me by the hand into Damascus, because the brilliance of the *light* had blinded me... Ananias... stood beside me and said: 'Brother Saul, receive your *sight*!' And at that very moment I was able to *see* him. Then he said: 'The God of our fathers has chosen you to know his will and to *see* the Righteous One and to hear words from his mouth. You will be his witness to all men of what you have *seen* and heard' (Acts 22:6-15).

I saw a *light* from heaven, brighter than the sun, blazing around me and my companions... Then I asked: 'Who are you, Lord?' 'I am Jesus, whom you are persecuting', the Lord replied. 'Now get up and stand on your feet. I have *appeared* to you to appoint you as a servant and as a witness of what you have *seen* of me and what I will show you. I will rescue you from your own people and from the Gentiles. I am sending you to them to *open their eyes* and turn them from darkness to *light*, and from the power of Satan to God, so that they may receive forgiveness of sins and a place among those who are sanctified by faith in me'. So then, King Agrippa, I was not disobedient to the vision from heaven... I am saying nothing beyond what the prophets and Moses said would happen – that the Christ would suffer and, as the first to rise from the dead, would proclaim *light* to his own people and to the Gentiles (Acts 26:13-26).

Doesn't it stand out a mile? Saul had been confronted by the living Lord Jesus. He submitted to him, trusted him and was baptised. And that which impressed him most of all was this question of 'light' and 'sight'. What happened next? He wanted as many others as possible to have their *blindness* removed so that they could *see*! So, 'at once he began to preach... that Jesus is the Son of God' (Acts 9:1-20). Paul wasn't fulfilling 'an engagement to preach'. Nobody rang him and 'gave him a date'! He just got on and did it. He may have been invited to speak (as in Acts 13:14-16); he may not; I certainly have my doubts that he would have been asked to speak of Christ in the synagogue at Damascus! He may have done just as he would later do in Athens (Acts 17:16-17). I don't know. It doesn't matter. He just got on and did it, instinctively, it seems to me. And he preached Christ (Acts 9:20).

You may not be a preacher in the formal sense, but if you are a Christian, you must tell others. You cannot keep it a secret. Furthermore, granted that you are a preacher in the formal sense, do you confine your preaching to the pulpit? Are you only able to preach when confined to a pulpit, buttressed by the trappings of Christendom, secure in the institution, far beyond the participation (what a thought!), let alone contradiction, of the congregation? Shame on you!

But, as before, let me remind you that we must not approach the individual the way most preachers approach a congregation, lecturing blotting paper. A little more conversational approach in the pulpit would not come amiss, coupled with a lot more response from the hearers! So, reader, don't let Christendom's pattern put you off trying to 'preach' the gospel. Read the Bible – not Christendom! There is a place for the usual kind of preaching, yes, but it's not the only form – not by a long chalk. In any case, I'm referring here to the conversational approach to individuals. I'm trying to encourage you to have a go at it! Speak to your family, friends and neighbours about Christ, and speak as you would in normal conversation. Imagine confiding in your physician in the same way as the 'normal' preacher addresses his congregation! And, Mr Preacher, when you get into the pulpit, try to use a bit more of your normal twang and approach, and less of the 'professional', programmed and expected.

What is more, dear friend, don't think you have to be a MTh before you can speak. Don't be afraid to tell the person you are conversing with that you don't know. I was asked to see a 'difficult' man in the States. After about an hour of pretty close questioning, he told me this: 'You're the first minister who's come here who's admitted he doesn't know the answer to every question I ask. I'll come and hear you!' Experience – that's what you've got of Christ. Speak of *that*! Speak of him! Here are a couple of hymns:

> *Stop; and let me tell you*
> *What the Lord has done for me.*

And:

> *I love to tell the story of unseen things above,*
> *Of Jesus and his glory, of Jesus and his love.*
> *I love to tell the story, because I know 'tis true;*
> *It satisfies my longings as nothing else can do.*

And surely every godly parent could make good use of the psalmist's words: 'Come, my children, listen to me; I will teach you the fear of the LORD' (Ps. 34:11).

So I say again, every believer must speak for Christ. We cannot be silent. Why not? Why should you speak for Christ? Because God commands you to confess with your mouth that which you believe in your heart: 'If you confess with your mouth, "Jesus is Lord", and believe in your heart that God raised him from the dead, you will be saved. For it is with your heart that you believe and are justified, and it is with your mouth that you confess and are saved' (Rom. 10:9-10). This confession, of course, has nothing to do with the nonsense of confessing your sins to a priest. It means telling others what Christ has done for you. It is a vital factor in the new-covenant ministry, one of the inestimable privileges Christ has bestowed upon you as a believer. As I have stressed throughout this book, all believers have 'this ministry'. All believers! Every believer! Each believer! How little this is understood and encouraged. And with what loss to the individual believer, to the church – and to sinners.

Charles Wesley:

> *O for a thousand tongues to sing*
> *My great Redeemer's praise,*
> *The glories of my God and King,*
> *The triumphs of his grace!*

> *My gracious Master and my God,*
> *Assist me to proclaim,*
> *To spread through all the earth abroad*
> *The honours of thy name.*

> *Jesus! the name that charms our fears,*
> *That bids our sorrows cease;*
> *'Tis music in the sinner's ears,*
> *'Tis life, and health, and peace.*

> *He breaks the power of cancelled sin,*
> *He sets the prisoner free;*
> *His blood can make the foulest clean,*
> *His blood availed for me.*

7. Our Privilege and Duty

He speaks, and, listening to his voice,
New life the dead receive,
The mournful, broken hearts rejoice,
The humble poor believe.

Hear him, ye deaf; his praise, ye dumb,
Your loosened tongues employ;
Ye blind, behold your Saviour come,
And leap, ye lame, for joy.

Of course, if we want to confine those words to the singing of hymns within our hallowed meeting house... but I for one cannot see how this view of the hymn can be maintained. It seems to me that Wesley included the promiscuous preaching of the gospel wherever men would hear, and preaching by every believer. Moreover, if we think that preaching is reserved for 'the minister' in the usual sense of the word, may I suggest that in future only such 'ministers' sing the hymn? Nonsense! Let us all sing it, and let us all sing it with the full New Testament meaning of the word 'minister' and 'preach'. Let's do our bit in bringing to pass that which Moses longed for: 'I wish that all the LORD's people were prophets and that the LORD would put his Spirit on them!' (Num. 11:29). Make no mistake: God has certainly put his Spirit on and in you, believer (Isa. 54:13; Jer. 31:33-34; Ezek. 36:25-27; John 6:45; 14:17; Rom. 8:9)! That which Christ told his disciples, he surely tells us:

When the Counsellor comes, whom I will send to you from the Father, the Spirit of truth who goes out from the Father, he will testify about me. And you also must testify, for you have been with me from the beginning (John 15:26-27; see also Luke 24:47-48).

'You ... must testify'! Earlier, I spoke of the sovereign intervention and fiat of God, and how he is pleased to carry out his decree, and perform his sovereign pleasure in and through his people as they preach Christ. Paul certainly experienced it. When he and Barnabas preached in the synagogue at Pisidian Antioch:

Almost the whole city gathered to hear the word of the Lord. When the Jews saw the crowds, they were filled with jealousy and talked abusively against what Paul was saying. Then Paul and Barnabas answered them boldly: 'We had to speak the word of God to you first. Since you reject it and do not consider yourselves worthy of eternal life, we now turn to the Gentiles. For this is what the Lord has commanded us: "I have made you a light for the Gentiles, that you may bring salvation to the ends of the earth"'. When the Gentiles heard this, they were glad and honoured the word of the Lord; and all who were appointed for eternal life believed (Acts 13:44-48).

There it is: Paul preached (doing his duty) and 'and all who were appointed for eternal life believed' (God working out his decree).

As the Scriptures show us:

Then the disciples went out and preached everywhere, and the Lord worked with them and confirmed his word by the signs that accompanied it (Mark 16:20).
What, after all, is Apollos? And what is Paul? Only servants, through whom you came to believe – as the Lord has assigned to each his task. I planted the seed, Apollos watered it, but God made it grow. So neither he who plants nor he who waters is anything, but only God, who makes things grow. The man who plants and the man who waters have one purpose, and each will be rewarded according to his own labour. For we are God's fellow-workers; you are God's field, God's building (1 Cor. 3:5-9).
By the grace of God I am what I am, and his grace to me was not without effect. No, I worked harder than all of them – yet not I, but the grace of God that was with me. Whether, then, it was I or they, this is what we preach, and this is what you believed (1 Cor. 15:10-11).

Or, as the apostle declares in our passage, God works through us as we exercise 'our ministry'. Paul could point to the Corinthians as a living example of it:

You show that you are a letter from Christ, the result of our ministry, written not with ink but with the Spirit of the living God, not on tablets of stone but on tablets of human hearts. Such confidence as this is ours through Christ before God. Not that we are competent in ourselves to claim anything for ourselves, but our competence comes from God. He has made us competent as ministers of a new covenant – not of the letter but of the Spirit; for the letter kills, but the Spirit gives life (2 Cor. 3:3-6).

In short, Philippians 2:13 may be applied to this: 'It is God who works in you to will and to act according to his good purpose'.

Calvin, commenting on Mark 16:20, 'the Lord worked with them':

By which he means that this was truly a divine work. And yet by this mode of expression he does not represent them as sharing their work or labour with the grace of God, as if they contributed anything to it of themselves; but simply means that they were assisted by God, because, according to the flesh, they would in vain have attempted what was actually performed by them. The ministers of the word [that is, all believers! – DG], I acknowledge, are called fellow-workers[1] with God (1 Cor. 3:9) because he makes use of their agency; but we ought to understand that they have no power beyond what he bestows, and that by planting and watering they do no good, unless the increase come from the secret efficacy of the Spirit.

Spot on! We work, but it is God who really does the work.

Let C.H.Spurgeon, preaching on the raising of Lazarus (John 11:43-44), bring these two points – God's decree and our labours – together:

I assert that it [the raising of Lazarus] is a *type* of what the Lord Jesus is constantly doing at this hour in the realm of mind and spirit. Did he raise the *naturally* dead? So does he still raise the *spiritually* dead! Did he bring back a body from corruption? So does he still deliver men from loathsome sins! The life-giving miracle of grace is as truly astounding as the quickening miracle of power...

Now, there are some men who are symbolized by this case – they are not only devoid of all spiritual life, but corruption has set in – their character has become abominable, their language is putrid, their spirit is loathsome. The pure mind desires to have them put out of sight! They cannot be endured in any decent society. They are so far gone from original righteousness as to be an offence to all and it does not seem *possible* that they should ever be restored to purity, honesty, or hope. When the Lord, in infinite compassion, comes to deal with them and makes them to live, then the most sceptical are obliged to confess: 'This is the finger of God!' What else can it be? Such a profane wretch become a believer? Such a blasphemer a man of prayer? Such a proud, conceited talker, receive the kingdom as a little child? Surely God himself must have worked this marvel! Now is fulfilled the word of the Lord by Ezekiel: 'And you shall know that I am the Lord, when I have opened your graves, O my people, and brought you up out of your graves'. We bless our God that he does thus quicken the dry bones whose hope was lost! However far gone a man may be, he cannot be

---

[1] Do not miss this idea of 'fellow-workers'. Paul is very fond of including all believers in the work (Rom. 16:3,9,21; 2 Cor. 8:23; Phil. 2:25; 4:3; Col. 4:11; 1 Thess. 3:2; Philem. 1,24, *etc.*)

beyond the reach of the Lord's right arm of mighty mercy! The Lord can change the vilest of the vile into the most holy of the holy! Blessed be his name, we have seen him do this and, therefore, we have cheering hope for the worst of men!

Nothing was used by our Lord but his own word of power. Jesus cried with a loud voice: 'Lazarus, come forth!' He simply repeated the dead man's name and added two commanding words. This was a simple business enough. Dear friends, a miracle seems all the greater when the means used are apparently feeble and little adapted to the working of so great a result. It is so in the salvation of men! It is marvellous that such poor preaching should convert such great sinners. Many are turned unto the Lord by the simplest, plain, most unadorned preaching of the gospel. They hear little, but that little is from the lips of Jesus! Many converts find Christ by a single short sentence.[2] The divine life is borne into their hearts upon the wings of a brief text. The preacher had no eloquence. He made no attempt at it, but the Holy Spirit spoke through him with a power which eloquence could not rival! Thus said the Lord: 'You dry bones, live', and they did! I delight to preach my Master's gospel in the plainest terms. I would speak still more simply if I could. I would borrow the language of Daniel concerning Belshazzar's robe of scarlet and his chain of gold, and I would say to rhetoric: 'Let your gifts be to yourself and give your rewards to another'. The power to quicken the dead lies not in the wisdom of *words* but in the Spirit of the living God! The voice is Christ's voice and the word is the word of him who is the resurrection and the life and, therefore, men live by it! Let us rejoice that it is not necessary that you and I should become orators in order that the Lord Jesus should speak by us – let the Spirit of God rest upon us and we shall be endowed with power from on high so that even the spiritually *dead* shall, through us, hear the voice of the Son of God – and they that hear shall *live*!

The result of the Lord's working must not be passed over, for it is a main element of wonder in this miracle. Lazarus did come forth and that immediately. The thunder of Christ's voice was attended by the lightning of his divine power and, forthwith, life flashed into Lazarus and he came forth. Bound as he was, the power which had enabled him to live enabled him to shuffle forth from the ledge of rock where he lay – and there he stood with nothing of death about him but his grave clothes! He left the close air of the sepulchre and returned to know,

---

[2] A reader wrote to me: 'O knew a boy in Singapore – a Buddhist – who had never heard the name of Jesus. He went to a Christian meeting and believed the very first time he heard his name!'

once more, the things which are done under the sun – and that at once. To me it is one of the great glories of the gospel that it does not require weeks and months to quicken men and make new creatures of them! Salvation can come to them at once!

Spurgeon proposed a hypothetical case (but one which was not infrequently real in his experience):

The man who stepped into this Tabernacle this morning, steeped in rebellion against his God and apparently impervious to divine truth, may, nevertheless, go down those steps with his sins forgiven and with a new spirit imparted to him – in the strength of which he shall begin to live unto God as he never lived before! Do you speak of a nation being born, at once, as if it were impossible? It is possible with God! The divine power can send a flash of life all round the world at any instant to quicken myriads of his chosen! We are dealing now with *God* – not with men! Man must have time to prepare his machinery and get it into working order, but it is not so with the Lord. We, on our part, must seek after a preacher and find for him a place where the people may be gathered. But when the Lord Jesus works, straightway the deed is done – with or without the preacher – and inside or outside the place of assembly!

If you and I had to feed 5,000, we would need to grind the corn at the mill, bake the bread in the oven – and then we would be a long time in bringing the loaves in baskets! But the Master takes the barley cakes and breaks – and as he breaks – the food is multiplied! Likewise he handles the fish and lo, it seems as if a shoal had been in his hands instead of 'a few small fishes'. Behold, the vast multitude receives refreshment from the little stock which has been so abundantly increased! Trust in God, my brothers! In all your work of love, trust in the unseen power which lay at the back of the manhood of Christ – and still lies at the back of the simple gospel which we preach! The everlasting word of God may seem to be weak and feeble. It may groan and weep and seem as if it could do no more. But it can raise the dead and raise them at once! You can be sure of this.[3]

I think the point is fairly made: God is sovereign, but in his sovereignty he is pleased, by the foolishness (that is, the weakness, the utter impotency, in itself) of our preaching, or through the foolishness (that is, in the eyes of the unconverted) of what we preach, to save sinners: 'Since in the wisdom of God the world

---

[3] spurgeongems.org/vols28-30/chs1776.pdf, emphasis his.

through its wisdom did not know him, God was pleased through the foolishness of what was preached to save those who believe' (1 Cor. 1:21). So, brother and sister, go on. Preach! Preach the gospel! This is God's revealed will for us as believers. As for God's secret will (Deut. 29:29), God can use our feeble words to regenerate sinners and bring them to repentant trust in Christ, and thus everlastingly save them. Let us never forget what Christ did with five small loaves and two fish, something recorded in all four Gospels (Matt. 14:13-21; Mark 6:32-44; Luke 9:10-17; John 6:1-13). You and I have to carry out the revealed will of God, and leave God to look after his decree.[4] More, we must go on obeying God in his revealed will, trusting that, according to his good pleasure, he might well be pleased to use our meagre efforts to save sinners and edify his saints. This is what it means to be in the new covenant, and to be a minister of the new covenant. This is, indeed, a glorious ministry! And it is ours! Surely we can all see the spiritual lessons conveyed by these words, and feel the encouragement of them:

Cast your bread upon the waters, for after many days you will find it again... Whoever watches the wind will not plant; whoever looks at the clouds will not reap. Sow your seed in the morning, and at evening let not your hands be idle, for you do not know which will succeed, whether this or that, or whether both will do equally well (Eccles. 11:1,4,6).

In face of this, we may well feel and cry with the man in the Gospels: 'I do believe; help me overcome my unbelief!' (Mark 9:24).

But what do believers have to preach?
It is as Paul stated: our work is 'setting forth the truth plainly' (2 Cor. 4:2). The word he uses is *phanerōsis*, 'manifestation'. In other words, our work is to tell men the truth, to make the truth known to

---

[4] Samuel Rutherford: 'Duties are ours; events are God's. When our faith meddles with events, and holds account upon God's providence, and asks: "How will you do this or that?" we lose ground; we have nothing to do there; it is our part to let the Almighty exercise his own office, and steer his own helm; there is nothing left for us, but to see how we may be approved of him, and how we roll the weight of our weak souls upon him who is God omnipotent' (cf. ccel.org).

them, 'to tell it as it is'. Men are ignorant. They need truth. We must preach the truth, the only truth, the gospel. We preach the good news, the only good news there is for fallen man. But we need to be very clear at this point. *In the ultimate, it is not 'what' we preach, but 'whom' we preach.* The new-covenant preaching ministry is nothing more and nothing less than preaching Christ. We do not preach theology or doctrine; we do not preach a creed; we do not preach a Confession of Faith; we do not preach the law – either overtly as the law of Moses, or incipiently by way of 'recipe-preaching'; we preach Christ. Look to Christ, come to Christ, believe on Christ (Isa. 45:22; 55:1-7; Matt. 11:28; John 7:37; Acts 8:35; 16:31, *etc.*), must be our theme. Christ is all (Col. 3:11).

Let me recast that sentence I just wrote: We *ought not to* preach theology or doctrine; we *ought not to* preach a creed; we *ought not to* preach a Confession of Faith; we *ought not to* preach the law; *we ought to* preach **Christ**. Sad to say, not a few do preach theology, creeds, Confessions or law. This is quite wrong. We must preach Christ from Scripture, not from man-made systems, however good, however ancient and hallowed by tradition. Sinners need to come to Christ (Matt. 11:28; John 6:35;37,44-45). Listen to Peter's response to Christ when he asked them if they also wanted to leave him: 'Lord, to *whom* shall we go? *You* have the words of eternal life. We believe and know that *you* are the Holy One of God' (John 6:68-69).

Consider Paul's final address to the elders of the church in Ephesus. It is all here: the apostle warned of the danger to which we are always exposed, and stressed the paramount need of preaching the gospel. 'From Miletus, Paul sent to Ephesus for the elders of the church. When they arrived, he said to them':

You know how I lived the whole time I was with you, from the first day I came into the province of Asia. I served the Lord with great humility and with tears, although I was severely tested by the plots of the Jews. You know that I have not hesitated to preach anything that would be helpful to you but have taught you publicly and from house to house. I have declared to both Jews and Greeks that they must turn to God in repentance and have faith in our Lord Jesus. And now, compelled by the Spirit, I am going to Jerusalem, not knowing what will happen to me there. I only know that in every city the Holy Spirit warns me that prison and hardships are facing me. However, I consider my life worth nothing to me, if only I may finish the race and complete the task the Lord Jesus has given me – the task of testifying to the gospel of God's grace. Now I know that none of you among whom I have gone about preaching the kingdom will ever see me again. Therefore, I declare to you today that I am innocent of the blood of all men. For I have not hesitated to proclaim to you the whole will of God. Keep watch over yourselves and all the flock of which the Holy Spirit has made you overseers. Be shepherds of the church of God, which he bought with his own blood. I know that after I leave, savage wolves will come in among you and will not spare the flock. Even from your own number men will arise and distort the truth in order to draw away disciples after them. So be on your guard! Remember that for three years I never stopped warning each of you night and day with tears. Now I commit you to God and to the word of his grace, which can build you up and give you an inheritance among all those who are sanctified (Acts 20:17-32).

This matter of preaching the gospel – let me unpack it a little further. In so doing, I will say something which will mark me as a heretic: in a sense we do not preach Scripture – we do of course – but we do not preach merely the text of Scripture. We preach Christ! I fear that so many stop at setting out the meaning of a passage of Scripture, thinking that when they have done that, then their work is done. This is a very bad mistake. Having got that far, they have only just begun. We should set out the meaning of the text, of course, *but expound the text in order to find* **Christ** *and preach* **him**: 'Just as Moses lifted up the snake in the desert, so the Son of Man must be lifted up, that everyone who believes in him may have eternal life' (John 3:14-15). The Son of Man – Christ, himself – has to be lifted up – not merely the truth *about* the Son of Man. As Jesus declared: 'When you have lifted up the Son of Man, then you will know that I am [the one I claim to be] and that I do nothing on my own but speak just what the Father has taught me... I, when I am lifted up from the earth, will draw all men to myself' (John 8:28; 12:32). I know this refers to the manner of his death, but I don't for a moment think it can be confined to that. I am convinced that Christ must be 'lifted up' in our preaching. Christ! Not a creed, not a Confession, not law, not sacraments. Christ! Notice how often we meet the phrase 'preach Christ', or its equivalent (Acts 3:20; 5:42; 8:5,35; 9:20; 17:3; Rom. 16:25; 1 Cor. 1:23; 2:2; 15:12; 2 Cor. 1:19; 4:5; Phil. 1:15-18; Col. 1:28; 1 Tim.

3:16, for instance). The Greeks got it right: 'We would like to see Jesus' (John 12:21). Jesus! Not the five points! Jesus! Remember the outcome of Christ's transfiguration: 'When they looked up, they saw no one except Jesus' (Matt. 17:8); or: 'When they looked around, they no longer saw anyone with them except Jesus' (Mark 9:8).[5] *That* ought to be the ethos of every new-covenant preacher; *that* ought to be the driver for our ministry; *that* ought to *be* our ministry! Paul could not have put it more succinctly and categorically: 'We preach Christ crucified... I resolved to know nothing... except Jesus Christ and him crucified' (1 Cor. 1:23; 2:2). He certainly preached Jesus from the law and prophets when under house-arrest in Rome (Acts 28:24,31). 'Christ is all, and is in all' is the sum and substance of Christianity. If we would see sinners saved, saints edified and sanctified, God glorified, we must preach Christ. This was Paul's manifesto: 'Nothing but Christ!'

In this, the apostle was following Christ himself who, on the Emmaus road, instructed the two disciples:

Beginning with Moses and all the prophets, he explained to them what was said in all the Scriptures concerning himself... They asked each other: 'Were not our hearts burning within us while he talked with us on the road and opened the Scriptures to us?' (Luke 24:27-32).

And, later that same day, meeting with the disciples in Jerusalem, he instructed them: 'Everything must be fulfilled that is written about me in the law of Moses, the prophets and the psalms'. 'Then he opened their minds so they could understand the Scriptures' (Luke 24:44-45). And what – whom – did they find in the Scriptures? Christ, of course!

Why should we preach Christ? Sinners are blind; they need light. And who is the light of the world? Jesus:

In the beginning was the Word, and the Word was with God, and the Word was God. He was with God in the beginning. Through him all things were made; without him nothing was made that has been made. In him was life, and that life was the light of men. The light shines in the darkness, but the darkness has not understood it. There came a man

---

[5] I am not trying to be clever, nor despise learning, but Jesus was crucified under Aramaic (or Hebrew), Latin and Greek (John 19:20). The fact is, Christ can be buried under theology.

who was sent from God; his name was John. He came as a witness to testify concerning that light, so that through him all men might believe. He himself was not the light; he came only as a witness to the light. The true light that gives light to every man was coming into the world (John 1:1-9).

As Christ himself declared:

I am the light of the world. Whoever follows me will never walk in darkness, but will have the light of life... While I am in the world, I am the light of the world (John 8:12; 9:5).

Do not miss the full import of Jesus' repeated words: he is not merely *a* light in this world; he is this world's *only* light. Islam has no light to offer; secularism has no light; atheism is gross darkness. *Christ alone, Christ only*, is the light of the world. He is the truth. He is the life (John 14:6). 'What is truth?' demanded Pilate, cynically I have no doubt. Let me tell him: Christ!

Remember, reader, that we are talking about the new-covenant ministry to deliver sinners from their sins. That this deliverance includes justification – that it begins with justification – nobody denies; or, if they do, they fly directly in the face of abundant New Testament testimony. But, as we have seen, we are talking about deliverance not only from the *condemnation* of sin, but from the *pollution* of sin, from the *power* of sin, and from the *presence* of sin. We are talking about justification, progressive sanctification and eternal glorification. And what does the believer have to do to bring sinners to redemption – to release them from sin in its condemning power, its polluting power, and its enslaving power? He has to preach Christ and him crucified! This is 'the glorious new-covenant ministry'.

Notice what the apostle does *not* say in 2 Corinthians 4 – nor anywhere else, for that matter! He does not urge the preaching of the law! Remember the context. Paul is confronting Judaisers who want to bring believers under the law: 'Unless you are circumcised, according to the custom taught by Moses, you cannot be saved'. 'The Gentiles must be circumcised and required to obey the law of Moses' (Acts 15:1,5). Paul will not stand it for a moment. He expressly states that we have received a very different ministry (2 Cor. 4:1). The law had a glory, yes, but in comparison with the new covenant it has no glory at all:

Now if the ministry that brought death, which was engraved in letters on stone, came with glory, so that the Israelites could not look steadily at the face of Moses because of its glory, fading though it was, will not the ministry of the Spirit be even more glorious? If the ministry that condemns men is glorious, how much more glorious is the ministry that brings righteousness! For what was glorious has no glory now in comparison with the surpassing glory. And if what was fading away came with glory, how much greater is the glory of that which lasts! Therefore, since we have such a hope, we are very bold. Therefore, since through God's mercy we have this ministry, we do not lose heart... We... preach... Jesus Christ as Lord... God, who said: 'Let light shine out of darkness', made his light shine in our hearts to give us the light of the knowledge of the glory of God in the face of Christ (2 Cor. 3:7-12; 4:1-6).

The law can never justify; the law can never sanctify; the law cannot bring liberty and glory. Only Christ, Christ crucified – the new covenant – can deliver the sinner. So whatever you preach, believer, preach Christ! I consciously – deliberately – repeat myself on this point; it is so important. Don't preach law, sacraments, works. Paul never did anything of the sort, at any time, to any people. Preach Christ! Don't preach Bible reading, attendance at meetings, prayer... all excellent in their place, of course – but we must preach Christ! If we want to see sinners saved, if we want to see saints edified and sanctified, we must preach Christ!

Charles Wesley:

> *Jesus, the name high over all,*
> *In hell, or earth, or sky;*
> *Angels and men before it fall,*
> *And devils fear and fly.*
>
> *Jesus! the name to sinners dear,*
> *The name to sinners given;*
> *It scatters all their guilty fear,*
> *It turns their hell to heaven.*
>
> *Jesus! the prisoner's fetters breaks,*
> *And bruises Satan's head;*
> *Power into strengthless souls it speaks,*
> *And life into the dead.*

7. Our Privilege and Duty

O that the world might taste and see,
The riches of his grace;
The arms of love that compass me,
Would all mankind embrace.

His only righteousness I show,
His saving truth proclaim;
'Tis all my business here below
To cry: 'Behold the Lamb!'

Happy, if with my latest[6] breath
I may but gasp his name:
Preach him to all, and cry in death,
'Behold, behold the Lamb!'

I cannot overstate this: preach Christ! To preach the gospel is not merely to preach the facts of the gospel, nor even preach in praise of the gospel – it is to preach Christ!

Let me say yet again that this business of preaching the good news is both a privilege and a duty. Paul certainly felt it himself:

I am bound both to Greeks and non-Greeks, both to the wise and the foolish. That is why I am so eager to preach the gospel also to you who are at Rome. I am not ashamed of the gospel, because it is the power of God for the salvation of everyone who believes: first for the Jew, then for the Gentile (Rom. 1:14-16).[7]

I am compelled to preach. Woe to me if I do not preach the gospel! If I preach voluntarily, I have a reward; if not voluntarily, I am simply discharging the trust committed to me. What then is my reward? Just this: that in preaching the gospel I may offer it free of charge, and so not make use of my rights in preaching it. Though I am free and belong to no man, I make myself a slave to everyone,[8] to win as many as possible. To the Jews I became like a Jew, to win the Jews. To those under the law I became like one under the law (though I myself am not under the law), so as to win those under the law. To those not having the law I became like one not having the law (though I am not free from God's law but am under Christ's law), so as to win those not having the law. To the weak I became weak, to win the weak. I have

---

[6] That is, 'final'.

[7] Note the 'obligated' – duty – and 'so eager' – privilege.

[8] Note the progression: the sinner is a slave to sin; he is converted and becomes a slave to Christ; he then becomes a slave to all men, as a minister of the new covenant.

become all things to all men so that by all possible means I might save some. I do all this for the sake of the gospel, that I may share in its blessings (1 Cor. 9:16-23).

Notice further, that it is the *gospel* we must preach; that is, good news. Preaching law, or works of any kind, or sacraments, in no way can be construed as preaching good news. The only good news is that God in Christ has done all that is necessary, he has finished the work (John 19:30). To preach law, works or sacraments, is to preach anything but *good* news! We dare not preach what men have to do; we declare what God in Christ has done and will do! Notice how men always want to do something (John 6:28; Acts 16:30). We dare not reinforce that prejudice. God has given us 'the ministry of reconciliation'; namely:

That God was reconciling the world to himself in Christ, not counting men's sins against them. And he has committed to us the message of reconciliation. We are therefore Christ's ambassadors, as though God were making his appeal through us. We implore you on Christ's behalf: Be reconciled to God. God made him who had no sin to be sin for us, so that in him we might become the righteousness of God (2 Cor. 5:18-21).

Now *that* is good news! God has reconciled! We appeal to sinners to trust the Saviour, to look to Christ. And we appeal to saints to go on trusting the Saviour and looking to Christ. This is *good* news indeed. No wonder 'Jesus cried out':

When a man believes in me, he does not believe in me only, but in the one who sent me. When he looks at me, he sees the one who sent me. I have come into the world as a light, so that no one who believes in me should stay in darkness (John 12:44-46).

Good news? The best of all news! And all this is just a foretaste, a down payment, the 'earnest' (2 Cor. 1:22; 5:5; Eph. 1:14) of what is to come in all its fullness. Speaking of the new Jerusalem, John declared:

I did not see a temple in the city, because the Lord God Almighty and the Lamb are its temple. The city does not need the sun or the moon to shine on it, for the glory of God gives it light, and the Lamb is its lamp. The nations will walk by its light, and the kings of the earth will bring their splendour into it. On no day will its gates ever be shut, for there

173

will be no night there. The glory and honour of the nations will be brought into it. Nothing impure will ever enter it, nor will anyone who does what is shameful or deceitful, but only those whose names are written in the Lamb's book of life... No longer will there be any curse. The throne of God and of the Lamb will be in the city, and his servants will serve him. They will see his face, and his name will be on their foreheads. There will be no more night. They will not need the light of a lamp or the light of the sun, for the Lord God will give them light. And they will reign for ever and ever (Rev. 21:22-27; 22:3-5).

I say it again, this is the best of all news! Ruined, blinded, dead, Satan-dominated sinners not only saved and sanctified, but everlastingly glorified in and with and through the Lord Jesus Christ!

As Joseph Irons expressed it:

> *No news can suit a ruined race*
> *But sov'reign, free, eternal grace;*
> *No other gospel can impart*
> *Joy, peace and comfort to the heart.*
>
> *But those are tidings good indeed,*
> *Which tell me Jesus deigned to bleed,*
> *To vanquish Satan, cancel sin,*
> *And bring eternal glory in.*
>
> *The only gospel we can own*
> *Sets Jesus Christ upon his throne;*
> *Proclaims salvation full and free,*
> *Obtained on Calvary's rugged tree.*
>
> *The gospel is the news from heaven,*
> *Of grace bestowed and sins forgiven –*
> *Redeeming blood – electing love –*
> *Of quickening grace – and joys above.*
>
> *Lord, write this gospel in my heart*
> *And in its blessings give me part;*
> *Until I see my Saviour's face.*
> *And sing: 'I'm saved by gospel grace'.*

But what, in particular, do believers have to preach about Christ?
Well, I've said it: 'Christ crucified'. Yes, but observe the apostle's way of putting it in our passage: 'We preach... Jesus Christ as Lord' (2 Cor. 4:5). 'We see Jesus, who was made a little lower than the

angels, now crowned with glory and honour because he suffered death' (Heb. 2:9). How vital this is. Christ crucified, yes, but it was the *Lord* Jesus Christ who was crucified, the *Lord* Jesus Christ who was raised, and the *Lord* Jesus Christ who declared:

All authority in heaven and on earth has been given to me. Therefore go and make disciples of all nations, baptising them in the name of the Father and of the Son and of the Holy Spirit, and teaching them to obey everything I have commanded you. And surely I am with you always, to the very end of the age (Matt. 28:18-20).

'Jesus knew that the Father had put all things under his power' (John 13:3). 'God [has] placed all things under his [Christ's] feet and appointed him to be head over everything for the church' (Eph. 1:22). 'In Christ all the fullness of the Deity lives in bodily form, and you have been given fullness in Christ, who is the head over every power and authority' (Col. 2:9-10).

Christ is King (Luke 1:31-33; John 18:36-37; 19:19-22): that's the root of it; 'therefore' – that's the consequence: 'All authority in heaven and on earth has been given to me. Therefore go and...'. We have to go and preach Christ, looking to God to make converts, teaching them to observe everything Christ commanded – and all in Christ's name. Here, once again, we come across a vital principle, one which needs to be emphasised today. We must preach the Lordship of Christ. There is no such thing as 'the carnal Christian' (one who knows Christ as Saviour, but not as Lord) – in the sense that this is something quite normal and acceptable.[9] When Paul used this terminology (1 Cor. 3:1-4), he was doing so in order to *rebuke* the Corinthians. It is no part of the new covenant to allow professed believers to settle into a carnal security, a once-saved-always-saved mentality. The proper New Testament doctrine is that the elect of God, once called, will persevere in holiness and grow in grace and the knowledge of Christ, submitting to Christ as Lord; otherwise, their profession is false (Heb. 12:14; 2 Pet. 3:18). The Lord Jesus made it clear: 'By their fruit you will recognise them.

---

[9] Contrary to this: 'You don't need to make Jesus the Lord of your life to be saved; but rather, just believe that Christ died for your sins and has risen from the dead' (David J. Stewart: 'Lordship Salvation Exposed' on jesus-is-savior.com).

Not everyone who says to me: "Lord, Lord", will enter the kingdom of heaven, but only he who does the will of my Father who is in heaven' (Matt. 7:20-21). Salvation is justification leading to sanctification which leads to everlasting glory. No link in the chain must be missing: no sanctification, no glorification! If there is justification, salvation is assured; but without sanctification, it will be salvation as by fire (1 Cor. 3:10-15). The warning passages of Hebrews (Heb. 3:12 – 4:11; 6:4-12; 10:35-39; 12:15-17,25) are real, not hypothetical. All this must be made perfectly clear to sinners, in essence right from the outset, and consistently and constantly as sinners grow in the grace of Christ. And it will be clear – if we preach Christ Jesus *as Lord* to them. That Christ is *Lord*, that Christ is *King*, is the distinct impression the Jews of Thessalonica drew from the preaching of Paul and Silas: 'These men who have caused trouble all over the world have now come here... They are all defying Caesar's decrees, saying that there is another king, one called Jesus' (Acts 17:6-7). We know the kind of preaching the Colossians had been converted under since they had 'received Christ Jesus as Lord' (Col. 2:6).

Peter certainly exemplified this kind of preaching on the day of Pentecost:

'God has raised this Jesus to life... Exalted to the right hand of God, he has received from the Father the promised Holy Spirit and has poured out what you now see and hear... Therefore let all Israel be assured of this: God has made this Jesus, whom you crucified, both Lord and Christ'. When the people heard this, they were cut to the heart and said to Peter and the other apostles: 'Brothers, what shall we do?' (Acts 2:32-37).

Then, preaching to the crowd that gathered at the healing of the man at the entrance to the temple: 'The God of Abraham, Isaac and Jacob, the God of our fathers, has glorified his servant Jesus' (Acts 3:13). Again, writing his letter, Peter declared: 'God... raised him from the dead and glorified him' (1 Pet. 1:21).

If Christ is Lord – and he is – then sinners, in conversion, must and will submit to him in obedience. Obedience and trust, trust and obedience, are inextricably linked in the New Testament. Note how Paul opened and closed his letter to the Romans: 'Through him [Christ] and for his name's sake, we received grace and apostleship to call people from among all the Gentiles to the *obedience* that comes from faith' (Rom. 1:5). The 'gospel and the proclamation of Jesus Christ... now revealed and made known through the prophetic writings by the command of the eternal God, so that all nations might believe and *obey* him' (Rom. 16:25-26). Obedience is not only a key 'word'; without obedience to Christ, we are yet in our sins, under the lordship of Satan. Either Christ rules or Satan. Believers are those who are '*obedient* to the faith' (Acts 6:7); that is, 'though [they] used to be slaves to sin, [they have] wholeheartedly *obeyed* the form of teaching to which [they] were entrusted. [They] have been set free from sin and have become slaves to righteousness' (Rom. 6:17-18). God's elect are sanctified 'for *obedience*' to Jesus Christ (1 Pet. 1:1-2) who is 'the source [author, NKJV] of eternal salvation to all who *obey* him' (Heb. 5:9), having 'purified [themselves] by *obeying* the truth' (1 Pet. 1:22). Unbelievers, on the other hand, are disobedient (Heb. 3:18; 4:6). They 'do not know God, and do not *obey* the gospel of our Lord Jesus' (2 Thess. 1:8; 1 Pet. 2:7-8; 4:17-18; see also Acts 5:29,32; 26:19; Rom. 2:8; 6:16; 10:16,21; 15:18; 16:19; 2 Cor. 2:9; 7:15; 10:5-6; Eph. 2:2; 5:6; Phil. 2:12; Col. 3:6 (footnote); 2 Thess. 3:14; Tit. 1:16; 3:3; Heb. 4:11; 11:8; 1 Pet. 1:14,22).

During that final Passover celebration, 'supper being ended' (John 13:2), Jesus, having washed his disciples' feet, gave them an expanded version of his law. Loving obedience to me, said Christ, spelling out his law for his disciples, is the badge of all true believers, the evidence of their spirituality, the *essential* evidence of their spirituality:

You call me 'Teacher' and 'Lord', and rightly so, for that is what I am. Now that I, your Lord and Teacher, have washed your feet, you also should wash one another's feet. I have set you an example that you should do as I have done for you. I tell you the truth, no servant is greater than his master, nor is a messenger greater than the one who sent him. Now that you know these things, you will be blessed if you do them (John 13:13-17). A new command I give you: Love one another. As I have loved you, so you must love one another. By this all men will know that you are my disciples, if you love one another (John 13:34-35). Do not let your hearts be troubled. Trust in God; trust also in me... Believe me (John 14:1,11). If you love me, you will obey what I command (John 14:15). Whoever has my commands and obeys them, he is the one who loves me (John 14:21). He who does not love me will not obey my teaching. These words you hear are not my own; they belong to the Father who sent me (John 14:24). Remain in me (John 15:4). This is to my Father's glory, that you bear much fruit, showing yourselves to be my disciples (John 15:8). My command is this: Love each other as I have loved you (John 15:12). You are my friends if you do what I command (John 15:14). This is my command: Love each other (John 15:17). Remember the words I spoke to you (John 15:20). The kings of the Gentiles lord it over them; and those who exercise authority over them call themselves benefactors. But you are not to be like that. Instead, the greatest among you should be like the youngest, and the one who rules like the one who serves (Luke 22:25-26).

Knowing God in Christ, obeying God, loving God, are all one and the same. Sinners cannot have Christ as Saviour unless they yield to him as Lord. They cannot truly savingly believe unless they submit to him in obedience. Their obedience makes no contribution to their justification, of course, but without it they cannot be saved. To put it another way: this is not salvation by works, but works which must inevitably follow justification, As Paul told the Ephesians:

It is by grace you have been saved, through faith – and this not from yourselves, it is the gift of God – not by works, so that no one can boast. For we are God's workmanship, created in Christ Jesus to do good works, which God prepared in advance for us to do (Eph. 2:8-10).

All this must be made clear in the preaching of the gospel. The new covenant demands nothing less. Preaching Christ as Lord, and backing it by consistent and constant practice, will enforce this.

8. Things to Be Avoided

Paul, in setting out 'this new-covenant ministry', did not let the Corinthians run away with the wrong impression: it isn't all peaches and cream! In addition to the previous point on the necessity of obedience in the converted, Paul went on, pulling no punches, to give us a few negatives, negatives we need to bear in mind – and act on! Never more so than today! Listen to the apostle:

We have renounced secret and shameful ways; we do not use deception, nor do we distort the word of God. On the contrary, by setting forth the truth plainly we commend ourselves to every man's conscience in the sight of God (2 Cor. 4:2).

So declared the apostle. Once again, the context makes it plain what he was saying. As I have already noted, the word he uses is *phanerōsis*, 'manifestation', observing that our work is to tell men the truth, to make the truth known to them, 'to tell it as it is'. I stress the 'to tell it as it is'. 'We have renounced disgraceful, underhanded ways. We refuse to practice cunning or to tamper with God's word, but *by the open statement of the truth* we would commend ourselves to everyone's conscience in the sight of God' (ESV). The Judaisers were prepared to use deceitful tactics, sleight of hand. To get their way, the false teachers were not averse to using flattery: 'For such people are not serving our Lord Christ, but their own appetites. By smooth talk and flattery they deceive the minds of naïve people' (Rom. 16:18). Paul, abhorring this, let the Thessalonians know he would never stoop to such tactics: 'You know we never used flattery, nor did we put on a mask to cover up greed – God is our witness' (1 Thess. 2:5). In saying such things to the Romans and Thessalonians, Paul, of course, was warning them not to be duped by flattery and all the rest!

And since the apostle told us to 'put aside the deeds of darkness and put on the armour of light' (Rom. 13:12), let us make sure we don't adopt the weapons of darkness to try to dispel the world's darkness. As Paul declared:

Though we live in the world, we do not wage war as the world does. The weapons we fight with are not the weapons of the world. On the contrary, they have divine power to demolish strongholds. We demolish arguments and every pretension that sets itself up against the knowledge of God, and we take captive every thought to make it obedient to Christ (2 Cor. 10:3-5).

Incidentally – but it's not incidental; it's central – if we are to see conversions, we have to use the spiritual weapons given us by the Spirit. D.Martyn Lloyd-Jones warned against 'trying to fight Goliath in Saul's armour':

Never! That is never the way. You will only stumble. You will look an impressive figure when you come out of your tent, but you will stumble and you will be defeated. Let David fight in David's way! Let him be a fool, let him be ridiculous, let him just pick up those stones and use his sling. Let him appear to be a lunatic in the sight of the giant, and perhaps of his own people also. That is God's way.[1]

The point I wish to make here is this: if we would be adept and nimble – competent – in using these spiritual weapons, we ourselves must be fully acquainted with them. A man who has built an engine, say, knowing all the parts and how they fit together, will drive that engine with skill – driving it even to its limits – and do so with confidence because he fully comprehends the intricate working of the machine under his hand. If we wish to see growth in the churches – conversions – we have to use the Spirit's weapons, and only them, and only by the Spirit (Zech. 4:6; Eph. 6:10-20).

Pressing the illustration a little further, we need to have spiritual growth ourselves before we can use our spiritual arms to best and full effect. Growth in the churches, therefore, should not be measured primarily by numbers, and certainly not by the size of its 'budget';[2] rather, it should be measured by the increase in spiritual

---

[1] D.Martyn, Lloyd-Jones: 'The Weapons Of Our Warfare' in *Knowing The Times...*, The Banner Of Truth Trust, Edinburgh, 1989, p215.

[2] How that word 'budget' – increasingly common in use – gives the game away! The churches ought not to be global corporations. I urge all who ape the world, and go for expansion into macro-business, to take a good, hard look at 1 Cor. 1:26 – 2:10. I have observed preachers not infrequently move seamlessly from preaching the gospel into what amounts to a share-holders' meeting, with accounts, projects, appeals for cash, and all the rest of it.

maturity made evident among the believers. As I say, this is no 'incidental'!

Moreover, the Judaisers were trying to lord it over their hearers. Paul would have none of their doctrine, nor their practice. In the new covenant, we serve Christ as his bond-servants: we serve sinners to see them saved, and we serve fellow-saints to see them (and ourselves) edified. In the ultimate, justification leading to sanctification leads to everlasting glory. There is no way to short-circuit this. There is no way to glory but *via* the cross and holiness. This, too, must be made very clear when we are addressing would-be converts. We have no excuse; Jesus showed us the way: 'Large crowds were travelling with Jesus, and turning to them he said':

If anyone comes to me and does not hate his father and mother, his wife and children, his brothers and sisters – yes, even his own life – he cannot be my disciple. And anyone who does not carry his cross and follow me cannot be my disciple. Suppose one of you wants to build a tower. Will he not first sit down and estimate the cost to see if he has enough money to complete it? For if he lays the foundation and is not able to finish it, everyone who sees it will ridicule him, saying: 'This fellow began to build and was not able to finish'. Or suppose a king is about to go to war against another king. Will he not first sit down and consider whether he is able with ten thousand men to oppose the one coming against him with twenty thousand? If he is not able, he will send a delegation while the other is still a long way off and will ask for terms of peace. In the same way, any of you who does not give up everything he has cannot be my disciple. Salt is good, but if it loses its saltiness, how can it be made salty again? It is fit neither for the soil nor for the manure pile; it is thrown out. He who has ears to hear, let him hear (Luke 14:25-35).

Thus its must be with us: at all times we are to be open and honest about our agenda and method. It is not always so.[3] When we preach, how often do we say it all, how often do we pull punches, how often do we fudge the difficult bits? Do we carry a supply of soft soap? What's behind it? We want to be well thought of! But Paul had his eye on Christ, and he knew Christ had his eye on him. The same should go for us. The man who has his eye on himself, will cut corners – especially awkward corners. Are we trying to

---

[3] I will look at John 6 in this regard.

make a name for ourselves, or attract attention to ourselves? Let's have done with it! We must preach – literally, placard before men (Gal. 3:1) – Christ. We dare not seek mere numbers, courting popularity. Paul's attitude must be ours:

Am I now trying to win the approval of men, or of God? Or am I trying to please men? If I were still trying to please men, I would not be a servant of Christ (Gal. 1:10).

Gill on 2 Corinthians 4:2, stated that the apostles:

Used no sly and artful methods to please men, to gain applause from them, or make merchandise of them. They did not lie in wait to deceive, watching an opportunity to work upon credulous and incautious minds. They did not, by good words and fair speeches, deceive the hearts of the simple, nor put on different forms, or make different appearances, in order to suit themselves to the different tempers and tastes of men, as did the false apostles.[4]

He went on:

They did not corrupt [Scripture] with human doctrines, or mix and blend it with philosophy, and vain deceit; they did not wrest the Scriptures to serve any carnal or worldly purpose; nor did they accommodate them to the lusts and passions of men, or conceal any part of truth, or keep back anything which might be profitable to the churches.

Again:

They with all plainness and evidence clearly preached the truth as it is in Jesus, presenting it to, and pressing it upon the consciences of men – where they left it, and to which they could appeal. And all this they did, in the sight and presence of the omniscient God, to whom they knew they must give an account of themselves and their ministry.

Calvin on 2 Corinthians 4:2-3:

As to himself, [Paul] says that he rejects or disdains disguises, because Christ's face, the more that it is seen opened up to view in his preaching, shines forth so much the more gloriously. I do not, however, deny, that he alludes at the same time to the veil of Moses,

---

[4] There is a world of difference between being flexible and using flattery, being two-faced and playing to the gallery.

(Ex. 34:33) of which he had made mention, but he ascribes a quite different veil to the false apostles. For Moses covered his face, because the excessive brightness of the glory of the law could not be endured by tender and bleared eyes. They, on the other hand, put on a veil by way of ornament. Besides, as they would be despicable, indeed, infamous, if the simplicity of the gospel shone forth, they, on this account, hide their shame under ever so many cloaks and masks.

As to 'not walking in craftiness': there can be no doubt that the false apostles delighted themselves greatly in the craftiness that Paul reproves, as though it had been a distinguished excellence, as we see even at this day some, even of those who profess the gospel, who would rather be esteemed subtle than sincere, and sublime rather than solid, while in the meantime all their refinement is mere childishness. But what would you do? It delights them to have a name for acuteness, and they have, under that pretext, applause among the ignorant. We learn, however, in what estimation Paul holds this appearance of excellence. Craftiness he declares to be unworthy of Christ's servants... Let the servants of Christ... reckon it enough to have approved their integrity to the consciences of men in the sight of God, and pay no regard to the corrupt inclinations of men, or to popular applause.

Take the law: these law mongers well knew the knotty points in the law, of course, especially when it came to actual performance. But the Judaisers certainly wouldn't have told Gentiles about all that! See 2 Corinthians 11:12-15. Indeed, the agitators would have acted much as the false teachers Peter wrote against – promising others liberty while they themselves were slaves (2 Pet. 2:19). Satan was in all this, of course, and the apostles constantly and repeatedly encouraged and warned believers to be on their guard. Paul was anxious that the Ephesians should 'no longer be infants, tossed back and forth by the waves, and blown here and there by every wind of teaching and by the cunning and craftiness of men in their deceitful scheming' (Eph. 4:14).

The new-covenant minister plays no such game! He knows his ministry must be carried out as 'in the sight of God' (2 Cor. 4:2), or 'before God'. How often Scripture reminds us of it (Luke 16:15; Acts 4:19; 8:21; 2 Cor. 2:17; 7:12; Gal. 3:11; 1 Tim. 6:13; 1 Pet. 3:4). This is, on the one hand, a comfort and encouragement, but – especially here in the context – a conscience-pricking challenge. I'm sure the apostle had God's warning to Ezekiel in mind:

When I bring the sword against a land, and... their watchman... sees the sword coming against the land and blows the trumpet to warn the people, then if anyone hears the trumpet but does not take warning and the sword comes and takes his life, his blood will be on his own head. Since he heard the sound of the trumpet but did not take warning, his blood will be on his own head. If he had taken warning, he would have saved himself. But if the watchman sees the sword coming and does not blow the trumpet to warn the people and the sword comes and takes the life of one of them, that man will be taken away because of his sin, but I will hold the watchman accountable for his blood. Son of man, I have made you a watchman for the house of Israel; so hear the word I speak and give them warning from me. When I say to the wicked: 'O wicked man, you will surely die', and you do not speak out to dissuade him from his ways, that wicked man will die for his sin, and I will hold you accountable for his blood. But if you do warn the wicked man to turn from his ways and he does not do so, he will die for his sin, but you will have saved yourself (Ezek. 33:2-9).

Just as the prophets had a duty to proclaim precisely what God had stipulated, so have we under the new covenant. I know we are not prophets: we have not been given a specific message for specific men. The general point stands, however: sinners are perishing; we have the answer; we must bear a responsibility to try to point them to the Redeemer. And in so doing, we must not peddle the word of God. Paul certainly didn't do it:

Thanks be to God, who always leads us in triumphal procession in Christ and through us spreads everywhere the fragrance of the knowledge of him. For we are to God the aroma of Christ among those who are being saved and those who are perishing. To the one we are the smell of death; to the other, the fragrance of life. And who is equal to such a task? Unlike so many, we do not peddle the word of God for profit. On the contrary, in Christ we speak before God with sincerity, like men sent from God (2 Cor. 2:14-17).

In saying this, the apostle was warning his readers, telling them to be on their guard against all flattery, all tampering with Scripture, all clever tricks. Just like the conjurer, these false teachers knew how to mislead and misdirect by clever patter. Christ wants his followers to 'be as shrewd as snakes' (Matt. 10:16). There was need in his day, and there is in ours! Be awake!

Moreover, 'as for us', said the apostle, 'we have renounced secret and shameful ways'. In telling the Corinthians this, Paul, of course, was laying down a marker for them – and for us! – to follow. Such methods certainly offer themselves to us, and very tempting they can be – for the best of motives. Nevertheless, as Paul was determined to renounce deceitful ways and practices, so must we. We have to follow his pattern, a pattern he laid down for all the churches *for all time*. As he told the Thessalonians:

The appeal we make does not spring from error or impure motives, nor are we trying to trick you. On the contrary, we speak as men approved by God to be entrusted with the gospel. We are not trying to please men but God, who tests our hearts. You know we never used flattery, nor did we put on a mask to cover up greed – God is our witness. We were not looking for praise from men, not from you or anyone else (1 Thess. 2:3-6).

Too often today, however, churches fail to stick to the apostle's dictum. Rather, they resort to bribery and misrepresentation, deliberately, as a matter of policy, using the very weapons and techniques rejected by Paul. In so doing, they forsake the way of the new covenant, and adopt the techniques of the world and false teachers. Let me flesh this out by giving some examples of what I am talking about.

The church advertises a free supper, say[5] – but its real purpose is to get sinners under the preaching of the gospel. Well, if that's really what it's about, say so! Of course, for an increasing number, perhaps, what's on offer *is* hedonistic satisfaction, and that's all it amounts to – the goings-on tinged with enough of 'Jesus' to make it 'acceptable'! In which case, they are not dissembling. But if they really do want to preach the gospel, let them say so! That's just one example of what I'm talking about.

How careful we need to be! Of course! Why should we think otherwise? Take the physician. How careful he must be in the administration of drugs, and how careful and honest he must be in dealing with the patient. So it is with us in the preaching of Christ. How much more so! We must be careful, thoughtful, honest, open. It is a matter of 'conscience' (2 Cor. 4:2). Paul could appeal to the Corinthians' conscience: he had not played fast and loose with the

---

[5] Why? As before, I will look at John 6. There is no more relevant passage in all Scripture.

gospel, he had not distorted it, he had spoken as in the sight of God, and their conscience would testify to it. Moreover, Paul had his own conscience to deal with – which he did (Acts 23:1; 24:16; Rom. 9:1; 2 Cor. 1:12; 2 Tim. 1:3). A tender conscience is a vital mark of every new-covenant minister. Let me quote just one of those verses:

Now this is our boast: our conscience testifies that we have conducted ourselves in the world, and especially in our relations with you, in the holiness and sincerity that are from God. We have done so not according to worldly wisdom but according to God's grace (2 Cor. 1:12).

Let me state the problem. We want unbelievers to attend our services, hear the preaching, and be converted. Yes. There's no question of it. But... and here's the rub, the very act of unbelievers sitting among us, and joining in our services, compromises at once what we are trying to do. Let me explain. We welcome unbelievers to our meetings. We do so at the door, in the 'notices', and, increasingly, on a sheet of paper which we hand them. We include them in our prayers: 'O God, *we* worship you, *we* praise you'. We include them in our hymns: 'Amazing grace, how sweet the sound, that saved a wretch like *me*'. We include them in our readings: 'I consider that *our* present sufferings are not worth comparing with the glory that will be revealed in *us*'. We cannot help it. However carefully we preface these exercises, the unbelievers present are part of it. They mouth the words, they are made to feel included. Indeed, they are included. *But until they are converted, they are **not** part of it, and they should know and feel they are not part of it!*

I have wrestled with this dilemma, as I know others have, and I recognise that good men have differed over the way to deal with it. While we need to be friendly and welcoming – we should want to be friendly and welcoming – the gospel has its own in-built offence to the natural man. And in our eagerness and desire to make sinners welcome, we must do nothing to take away that offence of the gospel. Even so, we must distinguish the offence of the gospel and the offence of our traditions!

But there has been a sea change in recent years. Today, most churches seem blissfully unaware that there is any such problem at all! The predicament most contemporary churches wrestle with is not how to deal with unbelievers so as to avoid deceiving (and eternally ruining) them, but how to attract and hold them, how to make them feel part of what we do. Indeed, it sometimes seems as though this constitutes our *raison d'être*. So much so, inclusivism now seems to be the determining *policy* of most evangelical churches. Everything has to bow down at its altar. Carnal means are used to get unbelievers to attend. The music is deliberately chosen to appeal to them – especially the young. Having struggled to get the unregenerate to come, we must say or do nothing to cause them the slightest offence. Quite the opposite! The over-arching mood is friendliness at all costs. Unbelievers must be made to feel comfortable, at home; nothing must be allowed to disturb them. Services are carefully structured to avoid upsetting them. Anything and everything which might embarrass or disturb is studiously avoided. Any hint of controversy, anything pointed, anything which might scratch – let alone, pierce – the conscience, everything 'negative' is taboo. The offence of the cross is muted – if not eradicated. Softly, softly is the mantra. What used to be called 'divine service' has been reduced, in many cases, to little more than 'man service', a cheery social gathering tinged with religion, 'needs-oriented' – by which I mean the promise to satisfy human desire for a pain-free, happy, fulfilled, successful life – with every relationship guaranteed as much bliss and sparkle as the most optimistic yellow-back romance, complete with its Mills and Boon conclusion.

In churches where inclusivism has gained firmest hold – from the opening bright and breezy remarks after the 'leader' has bounced into view, to the closing chat over a cup of tea (a chat often about yesterday's football, the latest shopping bargain, or last week's holiday; rarely over spiritual matters) – everybody is treated and addressed as a believer. The Alpha course sums it up. According to press releases: 'It is relaxed, non-threatening, low-key, friendly and fun. It is supported by all the main Christian denominations, particularly Roman Catholics'.[6] The current climate of user-friendly, anti-confrontational, 'non-directive' psychological counselling, which sets out to build up self-esteem in man and,

---

[6] uk.alpha.org

consequently, reduces God – with its promise of the penny and the bun – live as you like now and heaven hereafter – has much to answer for. Names, places and ideas such as Carl Rogers, Abraham Maslow, Larry Crabb, Bill Hybels and Willow Creek, Rick Warren and Saddleback, *The Purpose-Driven Church*, the emerging church movement, come to mind.[7]

Grievously, even in not a few churches which still retain a vestige of solemnity, and take some thought about these issues, things have reached a parlous state. I am afraid that many who would throw up their hands in horror at any thought of such things as I have mentioned, have, nevertheless, been influenced – subtly – by the underlying ethos. I fear that most contemporary churches are affected to a lesser or greater degree.

As I see it, this, or something very like it, sums up what goes on in many churches. Any other approach is considered 'unhelpful', a threat, which 'drives the fish away', and works against what the present-day church is looking for.[8] Many contemporary churches, contemporary in more ways than one, design their 'programme' with the attraction of unbelievers uppermost in their thoughts. The days of Acts 2:43; 5:5,11-13; 1 Corinthians 14:24 are long gone.

I know the motive is good. It is to get unbelievers to attend services so as to 'evangelise' them. But the cost is prohibitive. Cost? *Prohibitive* cost? Yes, indeed! Carnal means used to attract sinners, and carnal means used to make them feel at home among us, actually ruin the gospel we should be preaching to them, and runs directly counter to the experience they desperately need – to be convicted of sin, and converted to Christ; to leave their idols and

---

[7] See E.S. Williams: *The Dark Side of Christian Counselling*, The Wakeman Trust & Belmont House Publishing, London and Sutton, 2009; Jay E. Adams: *The Biblical View of Self-Esteem, Self-Love, Self-Image*, Harvest House Publishers, Eugene, 1986. See also the Engel Scale and the Gray Matrix (internetevangelismday.com/engel-scale.php).

[8] I have been accused of it. It is, of course, based on a misunderstanding of Matt. 4:18-22. The fishing Christ was talking about was not with fly or float – but, rather, with the dragnet, scooping up as many as possible. I am not saying skill is not required in the use of the dragnet, but the notion of out-smarting the fish with lure, bait, deception and stealth is far removed from the illustration.

turn to Christ in repentance and faith (1 Thess. 1:4-10, for instance). This ruination is the cost of inclusivism.

Inclusivism. Take the children. Children today are often allocated a principal part – a prominent part – in the service, making them feel important. In the 'children's talk', they are frequently addressed as virtual believers. How often a biblical passage, written to believers, is directly applied to children who, addressed as 'little Christians', are encouraged to produce Christian graces.

Inclusivism. Take the preaching. Above all, take the preaching for (and usually it is 'for' and not 'to' – there is a *big* difference between the two) those who remain after the children have gone out. The preacher, treating the congregation almost from start to finish as believers, often avoids all eye-contact, asks few if any open-ended questions, makes little or no *pointed* application, and rarely if ever uses 'you', but nearly always talks in terms of 'us', 'we' and 'them'. Inclusivism through and through. Of course, there is a place for the inclusive plural, but when it is all – or mostly – such, then inclusivism is the result – often, designedly so. 'User-friendly' is the watchword! Be genial! Polished professionalism is what is wanted, a jokey and anecdotal style of service and preaching, gentle and non-threatening, platitudinous, a 'light touch'. There might be a phrase or two at the end of the sermon, such as 'if you are not trusting Christ' – or some reference to it in the prayer – but the sermon has been so heavily inclusive, that such token gestures count for little. Hymns, prayers, readings – above all, the preaching – the whole shooting match, the complete ambience of the meeting, the very institution (what a word!) – has been telling all and sundry that they are Christians. And, never forget, the message and the method are inextricably linked. Indeed, the method dominates what the hearers perceive as the message. *How* the message is presented almost certainly has a greater effect upon them than *what* is presented. (If 1 Corinthians 9:19-23 is called on to justify such an approach, it can only be done at the expense of misunderstanding the passage). A word of hope delivered in a monotone, a boring address on the sublime... The people will take in and remember the *manner* long after they have forgotten – if they ever heard – the *message*.

After writing this, I happened to listen to a paper on 2 Peter 2 given by Dick Lucas to a ministers' conference.[9] Lucas explained 2 Peter 2:1 by saying that the apostle was addressing his readers as elect when, in fact, some of them were not. He then likened this to the ministers sitting before him. I paraphrase: 'This is what you do, isn't it? You address your congregations as elect – when you know that some of them are not'. Let me comment. There's a vast difference between an apostle, in pre-Christendom days, writing a letter to believers – among whom some false teachers had sneaked in (Gal. 2:4; Jude 4), as Peter made clear (2 Pet. 2:1) – believers who knew only of gatherings where the presence of unbelievers was a rarity (1 Cor. 14:23), and a preacher today, addressing a mixed congregation, meeting in the ambience of a Christendom which has ruined the assemblies of God's people for well over 1500 years. Surely it is simplicity itself – *if he wishes* – for the preacher to divide his congregation by making it clear to his hearers that the text he is preaching is addressed to believers, and, while he wants the unbelievers present to listen to him and long for the glories he describes, until they come to Christ in repentance and faith, none of this actually does belong to them! I have stressed the sticking point, of course.

Inclusivism. The Lord's supper is increasingly being observed as the central part of the 'family service', with insufficient, if any, safeguards put in place against participation by children and unbelievers. Indeed, as for the former, more and more are children being welcomed at the table.

Inclusivism. Take marriages and funerals. Churches are becoming liberal – and increasingly so – in their terms upon which and for whom they will offer such services – and about what they will say and do at such services. And I am talking about marriages and funerals for unbelievers! I speak of what I know! Above all, bear in mind that it is not what the 'ministers' *say* about what is going on in such services; it is what 'ordinary' people *think* is going on that counts!

As a consequence of all this inclusivism, many churches have in their congregation old people who have attended for years, been

---

[9] Found under: AJM11, Nov. 2011, Proclamation Trust Autumn Ministers' Conference, Session 2 (vimeo.com).

treated as virtual believers, addressed as such, feel totally at ease and comfortable in a semi-detached sort of way, and who know they will, after death, be treated as though they had been believers – and are yet unconverted! And not only old people! It is an utter disaster, Christendom with a vengeance. But... if anybody dares to question this contemporary inclusivism...!!! 'Don't you believe in evangelism?'! 'Evangelism' – a word not found in the Bible! – has become one of the chief gods of the age (I am well aware that I am punching an entire battery of red buttons in what I say).

Lloyd-Jones opened his ministry in South Wales in February 1927. Although some of the following is obviously dated, its thrust is relevant still. On March 20th, his preaching must have startled the congregation:

Our Christianity has the appearance of being an adjunct or an appendix to the rest of our lives, instead of being the main theme and the moving force in our existence... We seem to have a real horror of being different. Hence all our attempts and endeavours to popularise the church and make it appeal to people. We seem to be trying to tell people that their joining a church will not make them so very different after all. 'We are no longer Puritans', we say, 'we believe that they over-did things and made Christianity too difficult for people. They frightened people with their strictness and their unnecessarily high standards. We are not so foolish as to do that', we say, and indeed we do not do so. Instead, however, we provide so-called 'sporting parsons', men of whom the world can say that they are 'good sports' – whatever that may mean. And what it does so often mean is that they are men who believe that you can get men to come to chapel and church by playing football and other games with them. 'I'll fraternise with these men', says such a minister. 'I'll get them to like me and to see that I'm not so different from them after all, and then they'll come to listen to my sermons'. And he tries it, but thank God, he almost invariably fails, as he richly deserves. The man who only comes to church or chapel because he likes the minister as a man is of no value at all, and the minister who attempts to get men there by means of that subterfuge is for the time being guilty of lowering the standard of the truth which he claims to believe. For this gospel is the gospel of salvation propounded by the Son of God himself. We must not hawk it about in the world, or offer special inducements and attractions, as if we were shopkeepers announcing an exceptional bargain sale... The world expects the Christian to be different and looks to him for something different, and therein it often shows an insight into life that regular church-goers often lack. The church organises whist-drives, fêtes, dramas, bazaars and things of that sort, so as to attract people. We are becoming almost as wily as the devil himself, but we are really very bad at it; all our attempts are hopeless failures, and the world laughs at us. Now, when the world persecutes the church, she is performing her real mission, but when the world laughs at her she has lost her soul. And the world today is laughing at the church, laughing at her attempts to be nice and to make people feel at home. My friends, if you feel at home in any church without believing in Christ as your personal Saviour, then that church is no church at all, but a place of entertainment or a social club. For the truth of Christianity, and the preaching of the gospel, should make a church intolerable and uncomfortable to all except those who believe, and even they should go away chastened and humble.[10]

Some of the above is, as I say, old hat. Things have moved on. And how! Whist-drives, musical concerts, fish-and-chip suppers are far too tame these days. Many churches have moved up market with a vengeance. We can, we vainly think, out-world the world! Banquets, with a glitzy after-dinner speaker, are commonplace. Clay-pigeon shooting, jousting tournaments, boule contests, cricket matches, Victorian evenings, river trips, barbecues, theatre trips, pub breakfasts... I could go on. And on. I know – I know, I say – where a prospective pastor was thought to be 'the man for us' because of his ability to organise such events. And in the church which did secure him, he and his wife have lost no time in confirming their catering credentials. When I recently asked an (unsympathetic) observer how things are going, I was told that there would be little fear of numbers dropping as long as the standard of the food is kept up. I'm afraid there is more than a grain of truth in such sarcasm.

While there is nothing wrong in providing simple refreshments to cater for those who have travelled a distance, or even to facilitate a time of spiritual conversation, there are inherent dangers. For one thing, the balance can easily shift.[11] The refreshments, instead of

---

[10] Iain H. Murray: *David Martyn Lloyd-Jones: The First Forty Years 1899-1939*, The Banner of Truth Trust, Edinburgh, 1982, pp141-142; see also pp131-151,215.
[11] I know of a funeral service in a Particular Baptist church, where, as the congregation was gathering, the man taking the service was openly joking

being a handmaid to facilitate the spiritual, become the main event. It is surprising just how big an empire can be forged from a tea bag or two. A spoonful of horseradish with a plate of beef is not the same as a smidgeon of beef with a plate of horseradish. Again, discussing football and recipes over a cup of coffee is not spiritual fellowship! 'Fellowship' must be a candidate for the most debased word in the evangelical canon.

I feel so strongly about this, let me drive it home by reference to John 6. In that chapter, Jesus preached what is, perhaps, the most searching sermon he ever preached. Why? Because thousands were flocking to hear him! Really? Yes. And Jesus knew what their motive was. And he would have none of it. So he preached a sermon, he deliberately preached a sermon, that he knew – that he designed – to separate the wheat from the chaff. And he gained his end: 'From this time many of his disciples turned back and no longer followed him' (John 6:66). So what was the motive that so offended Christ? He knew that they had come in their droves because they liked the healings (John 6:2). They liked the miraculous signs (John 6:14). They had a political agenda (John 6:15). And they also liked it when Jesus provided bread for them (John 6:26). My point is this: seeing Christ would have none of it in his day, surely it must be utterly wrong for us to use methods which encourage such carnal motives? In particular, those who major on food (and that, today, is the vast majority), ought to take full account of John 6.

I'm afraid my words will fall on deaf ears. The buzz-word is 'community'. The church must be a 'community church'. The pastor must be the leading light in the 'community'. We must reach out to and be part of the 'community'. Of course, as private individuals, we should use our social contacts to seek to spread the gospel. I am not forgetting the 'salt' and 'light' aspect (Matt. 5:13-16), but I am talking about the church – the church of *Christ*, after all; the church of *Christ* – he who has made his mind known in Scripture. Too often the one word to describe a modern church is

---

with a lady about her 'delicious cakes' – which she regularly provided for the refreshments at the end of the normal evening service. I ask you! Such a topic and at such a time! By the way, I'm not sure that the lady in question has a saving experience!

'social'. In the New Testament it is 'spiritual'. I challenge the churches and their elders – get rid of the social crust, and replace it with the spiritual (Acts 2:42, for example), and see what happens to the attendance.[12] Would to God that churches today obeyed Artaxerxes' positive stipulation for the returning Jews (Ezra 7:23), and, on the negative side, followed their Master himself when he cleansed the temple of all its worldly clutter (Matt. 21:12-13; Mark 11:15-17; Luke 19:45-46; John 2:14-17; see also Mal. 3:1 – 4:6)! As I have said, before a church can expect to grow in terms of conversions, it must grow spirituality – both the members individually and the church corporately. A good job too! I say this because converts must have spiritually mature people to care for them and nurture them. Oh, without spiritual growth, a church *can* grow numerically, but the 'converts' are likely to be Ishmaels and not Isaacs.

Furthermore, we must not forget Acts 6:1-7. While the circumstances, and the personnel involved, are unique, nevertheless the principle stands clear: the overriding business of 'this ministry' is not charitable acts; it is the saving of sinners. There is a balance to be struck, granted, but there is no doubt as to where the weight must fall. We forget this at our peril. Sadly, too often these days, it is being forgotten.

Finally, I am reminded of my youth. 'Separation' was a word and notion much in vogue in those days; rightly so. Nowadays it is hardly ever heard. In fact, as I have just indicated, apparently it is in vogue to show the world that, when all is said and done, we are all the same! In such an atmosphere, is separation thought about? Is it practiced? To 'encourage' us young people to stay clear of the world, our mentors told us the salutary tale of the earnest young man, recently converted, who thought he would go to the dance hall and witness for Christ. Taking the girl in his arms and waltzing out onto the floor, he addressed her thus: 'I'm a Christian'. 'What are you doing here, then?', came the immediate rebuff.

And in the 18th century, dissenters used to speak of the church as 'a garden inclosed' (Song 4:12, AV). Isaac Watts' hymn:

---

[12] See my *Battle*.

8. *Things to Be Avoided*

Zion's a garden walled around,
Chosen and made peculiar ground;
A little spot, inclosed by grace
Out of the world's wide wilderness.

encapsulated the idea.[13] Thus it used to be said that the church is in the world. Nowadays, the world is in the church. Indeed, like the closing page of *Animal Farm*, it is getting increasingly difficult to sort out the Orwellian which is which – the church and the world act so much alike, they merge one into the other. The great day (1 Cor. 3:9-15) will mark the reckoning. 2 Corinthians 6:14 – 7:1 still stands.

Two American correspondents (Nov. 14th 2010) told me of their experience of Reformed Baptist churches in the States. They spoke of:

A shallow belief... younger people who are beginning to come to the doctrines of grace, but really don't know exactly what they believe... Their testimony... is very shallow. Their lack of knowledge of Scripture, their love of contemporary religious music, casual dress, casual attitude towards worship is something they bring with them, and it is a big influence on the church as a whole. Compromise in one area affects all areas of the worship. If these concerns are mentioned to the [leaders], those who have the concerns are seen as old-fashioned, unloving and judgemental. Pressure is put on by these newcomers and new members to compromise the music, and worship in general. Many of the professing non-members are included in various programmes of the church – outreach ministries that represent the church, *etc*. And when new visitors come to the church, these non-members are often seen greeting the visitors, and assuming a position the same as the members, and they are often very forward. The true meaning of membership has been downgraded. It is in these things that we see inclusivism as a dangerous trend and a threat to the stability and health of Christ's true church.

My brothers and sisters, I am sure that we need to return to Paul's spirit and practice in 2 Corinthians 4:1-6. And do so as a matter of urgency. Let us be consistent in our carrying out of our new-covenant ministry.

---

[13] See also Thomas Kelly's hymn : 'Lord, behold us in thy grace'. See also Spurgeon's sermon: 'Supposing Him To Be The Gardener' (number 1699, 1882).

Now for another negative: 'We do not preach ourselves, but Jesus Christ as Lord, and ourselves as your servants for Jesus' sake' (2 Cor. 4:5). Here we have the negative: 'We do not preach ourselves'. Paul immediately followed this with two positives: 'We... preach... Jesus Christ as Lord, and ourselves as your servants for Jesus' sake'. Take the second of the two positives: 'We... preach... ourselves as your servants for Jesus' sake'. This needs very careful nuancing. As I have explained elsewhere,[14] it is altogether too easy for a 'minister' or 'pastor' or whatever to come between the sinner (or the saint) and Christ. This can be done for the best of intentions, but wherever it happens it has a very nasty consequence; namely, priestcraft. This we must avoid at all costs. With this proviso, however, as the apostle says, as believers we are to let it be known that we are the servants of sinners, and that we are willing – we want – to do all we can to bring them to Christ. We are also the servants of believers, to help them in their edification and sanctification. Paul exemplified the way:

Though I am free and belong to no man, I make myself a slave to everyone, to win as many as possible. To the Jews I became like a Jew, to win the Jews. To those under the law I became like one under the law (though I myself am not under the law), so as to win those under the law. To those not having the law I became like one not having the law (though I am not free from God's law but am under Christ's law), so as to win those not having the law. To the weak I became weak, to win the weak. I have become all things to all men so that by all possible means I might save some. I do all this for the sake of the gospel, that I may share in its blessings (1 Cor. 9:19-23).

Or, as in our passage: 'We do not preach ourselves, but Jesus Christ as Lord, and ourselves as your servants *for Jesus' sake*' (2 Cor. 4:5). But, I repeat, we must never let this concern for sinners, this deep desire that they might be saved (Rom. 9:1-4; 10:1), degenerate into making sinners and saints think they need some sort of priest to bring them to Christ. They may go directly to Christ for themselves. They *must* go directly to Christ for themselves. As Paul makes clear, 'we do not preach ourselves' – surely, the counter-balance to

---

[14] See my *Pastor* in particular.

preaching 'ourselves as your servants'. We must never allow anything or any man to come between men and Christ.

I recall reading that Spurgeon refused to repeat the way of salvation to a lady who had approached him time and again over the way to become a Christian. Rejecting her appeal, he told her to go and do what she knew she ought to do: trust the Saviour![15]

Having said that, let not the point be missed: as those who have ourselves been saved by God's grace, we cannot help but have the same spirit as the apostle (Rom. 10:1). As Gill so aptly commented on the verse: Paul, 'as a minister of the gospel... cannot but wish that all that hear him might be converted and saved; and as a believer in Christ he might pray for this in submission to the will of God'. Just so. And this must be our attitude to sinners also. Matthew Henry on the same verse:

Paul here professes his good affection to the Jews... a good wish, a wish that they might be saved – saved from the temporal ruin and destruction that were coming upon them – saved from the wrath to come, eternal wrath, which was hanging over their heads. It is implied in this wish that they might be convinced and converted... Herein he was merciful, as God is, who is not willing that any should perish (2 Pet. 3:9), and desires not the death of sinners. It is our duty truly and earnestly to desire the salvation of our own. This, he says, was his heart's desire and prayer, which intimates... the strength and sincerity of his desire. It was his heart's desire... a real desire... It was his prayer. The soul of prayer is the heart's desire... It was not only his heart's desire, but it was his prayer.

Let me bring this section to a close by speaking of the positive. While the following does not refer to reaching sinners with the gospel, it does indicate the way Paul approached 'the ministry'. Writing to the Corinthians, the apostle let them know the spirit in which he conducted himself – and for what end. He told them of:

The brother who is praised by all the churches for his service to the gospel... He was chosen by the churches to accompany us as we carry the offering, which we administer *in order to honour the Lord himself* and to show our eagerness to help. We want to avoid any criticism of

---

[15] If any reader can supply the reference, I would appreciate it. I think it was in an issue of John Gadsby's *Christian's Monthly Record*, and I think Gadsby was showing disapproval.

the way we administer this liberal gift. *For we are taking pains to do what is right, not only in the eyes of the Lord but also in the eyes of men.* In addition, we are sending with them our brother who has often proved to us in many ways that he is zealous, and now even more so because of his great confidence in you. As for Titus, he is my partner and fellow-worker among you; as for our brothers, they are representatives of the churches and *an honour to Christ* (2 Cor. 8:18-23).

He said this, of course, to encourage the Corinthians in their ministry: 'This service that you perform is not only supplying the needs of God's people but is also overflowing in many expressions of thanks to God. Because of the service by which you have proved yourselves, *men will praise God* for the obedience that accompanies your confession of the gospel of Christ' (2 Cor. 9:12-13).

And, finally, let us hear what the New Testament tells us about this new-covenant ministry. What was true for the apostle, is true for every believer. We preach:

The glorious riches of this mystery, which is Christ in you, the hope of glory. We proclaim him, admonishing and teaching everyone with all wisdom, so that we may present everyone perfect in Christ. To this end I labour, struggling with all his energy, which so powerfully works in me. I want you to know how much I am struggling for you and for those at Laodicea, and for all who have not met me personally. My purpose is that they may be encouraged in heart and united in love, so that they may have the full riches of complete understanding, in order that they may know the mystery of God, namely, Christ, in whom are hidden all the treasures of wisdom and knowledge. I tell you this so that no one may deceive you by fine-sounding arguments. For though I am absent from you in body, I am present with you in spirit and delight to see how orderly you are and how firm your faith in Christ is. So then, just as you received Christ Jesus as Lord, continue to live in him, rooted and built up in him, strengthened in the faith as you were taught, and overflowing with thankfulness. See to it that no one takes you captive through hollow and deceptive philosophy, which depends on human tradition and the basic principles of this world rather than on Christ. For in Christ all the fullness of the Deity lives in bodily form, and you have been given fullness in Christ, who is the Head over every power and authority (Col. 1:27 – 2:10).

8. Things to Be Avoided

I leave the extract there, but Paul carries the argument on, right to the end of the letter to the Colossians. But here it is: we preach Christ as Lord. This will be saving for sinners and sanctifying for saints. Nothing else will be.

9. God's Purpose

This, too, is very clear. Paul puts the fundamental issue in stark terms. Men are sinners, ruined and perishing. More, they are unable to see the glory of the ineffable Christ: 'The god of this age has blinded the minds of unbelievers, so that they cannot see the light of the gospel of the glory of Christ, who is the image of God'. There it is: sinners cannot see 'the glory of Christ... the image of God'. But the apostle takes delight in stating, equally vehemently, right alongside this blunt declaration of the issue facing us, its solution. Through the new-covenant ministry, God brings sinners to 'the knowledge of the glory of God in the face of Christ'. Moreover, Paul has not finished with the theme: he quickly moves on to state that 'grace... is reaching more and more people [causing] thanksgiving to overflow to the glory of God'. No wonder, therefore, that he concludes: 'Therefore we do not lose heart' (2 Cor. 4:6,15-16).

The problem facing us may be massive. It is! Satanic domination of mankind is far beyond man's power to overcome, and the sinner's resistance to the gospel – motivated by Satan – is implacable. The sinner is dead. The sinner will not believe. The sinner cannot believe. Satan has him under his sway. But the solution is equally dramatic, and more so: God shines into sinners' hearts. It is even more than that! God shines into sinners' hearts, and does so in order to bring about his glory through Jesus Christ, his Son. It is nothing less than the age-old battle lines being drawn once again. Immediately after the fall of man, God announced that there would be continual warfare between himself and Satan, a war that would rage until the end of time, but with the victory certain: God will be triumphant through Christ. Addressing Satan, God declared: 'I will put enmity between you and the woman, and between your offspring and hers; he will crush your head, and you will strike his heel' (Gen. 3:15). In other words, right from the fall of Adam, God predicted that he, in Christ, by his Spirit, would triumph over Satan and rescue every last elect sinner from his grasp. Satan himself, right from the start, has been destined for everlasting destruction (Rev. 20:7-10). And, in accomplishing this complete and final overthrow of the devil, God intends his own everlasting glory (Rev. 19:1-6).

Oh, Satan has done all he can to thwart God's plan, even seeking the destruction of the Christ-child at his birth (Matt. 2:3-23; Rev. 12:1-6). Frustrated in that, did Satan give up? He did not. Satan launched another attack on the Lord by tempting Christ in the wilderness (Luke 4:1-13). When this failed, the devil quitted the field – but only 'until an opportune time' presented itself. How many attacks went unrecorded, we have no way of knowing, of course, but we are told that, just before the Saviour's crucifixion, Satan entered Judas (John 13:27) and wanted to sift Peter like wheat (Luke 22:31). And we have John's vision:

There was war in heaven. Michael and his angels fought against the dragon, and the dragon and his angels fought back. But he was not strong enough, and they lost their place in heaven. The great dragon was hurled down – that ancient serpent called the devil, or Satan, who leads the whole world astray. He was hurled to the earth, and his angels with him. Then I heard a loud voice in heaven say: 'Now have come the salvation and the power and the kingdom of our God, and the authority of his Christ. For the accuser of our brothers, who accuses them before our God day and night, has been hurled down. They overcame him by the blood of the Lamb and by the word of their testimony; they did not love their lives so much as to shrink from death. Therefore rejoice, you heavens and you who dwell in them! But woe to the earth and the sea, because the devil has gone down to you! He is filled with fury, because he knows that his time is short'. When the dragon saw that he had been hurled to the earth, he pursued the woman who had given birth to the male child. The woman was given the two wings of a great eagle, so that she might fly to the place prepared for her in the desert, where she would be taken care of for a time, times and half a time, out of the serpent's reach. Then from his mouth the serpent spewed water like a river, to overtake the woman and sweep her away with the torrent. But the earth helped the woman by opening its mouth and swallowing the river that the dragon had spewed out of his mouth. Then the dragon was enraged at the woman and went off to make war against the rest of her offspring – those who obey God's commandments and hold to the testimony of Jesus (Rev. 12:7-17).

Even so, God will triumph in glory. The point here, however, is that this glory is not reserved to the end of the age, or eternity; God gets the glory in every conversion of a sinner here and now, throughout this age: 'Grace... is reaching more and more people [causing] thanksgiving to overflow to the glory of God' (2 Cor. 4:15). In promising the Spirit, Christ was clear: 'When the Counsellor comes, whom I will send to you from the Father, the Spirit of truth who goes out from the Father, he will testify about me. And you also must testify, for you have been with me from the beginning... He will bring glory to me by taking from what is mine and making it known to you' (John 15:26-27; 16:14). As A.W.Tozer put it: 'To glorify Jesus is the business of the church, and to glorify Jesus is the work of the Holy Ghost'.[1] *This* is 'the glorious new-covenant ministry'. The work of the Spirit is to glorify God 'through Christ Jesus' by 'the law of the Spirit of life' setting sinners 'free from the law of sin and death' (Rom. 8:2).

The end or purpose of the gospel ministry, therefore, is not merely the *good* of men – it is that, of course – but it is the glory of God in Christ. *This* is the end of the new covenant, and its ministry; *this* is why God established it. 'To [God] be glory in the church and in Christ Jesus throughout all generations, for ever and ever! Amen' (Eph. 3:21). God will get glory in his judgements, yes, but he also gets glory – greater glory – in the saving of sinners, and in the subsequent transformation of them into the likeness of Christ (Rom. 8:29-30). Paul can tell believers: 'Men will praise God for the obedience that accompanies your confession of *the gospel of Christ*'. And, as he immediately goes on to say, we do not 'live by the standards of this world. For though we live in the world, we do not wage war as the world does. The weapons we fight with are not the weapons of the world. On the contrary, they have divine power to demolish strongholds. We demolish arguments and every pretension that sets itself up against the knowledge of God, and we take captive every thought *to make it obedient to Christ*' (2 Cor. 9:13; 10:2-5).

God has established the new covenant through Christ, and works in sinners' hearts by his Spirit, precisely in order to glorify himself. Do not miss the triune nature of this: the end of the new covenant is the glory of the triune God. (See John 5:19-32; 13:31-

---

[1] Tozer p27.

32; 14:13; 16:14; 17:1,4-5,10,22,24; Eph. 1:3-14; 1 Pet. 1:21; 4:11; 5:1,4,10; 2 Pet. 1:3, for instance). How wonderfully this was exemplified by Jesus making the blind man see:

As [Jesus] went along, he saw a man blind from birth. His disciples asked him: 'Rabbi, who sinned, this man or his parents, that he was born blind?' 'Neither this man nor his parents sinned', said Jesus, 'but this happened so that the work of God might be displayed in his life' (John 9:1-3).

Some of the Jews certainly saw it in that light: 'These are not the sayings [or works] of a man possessed by a demon. Can a demon open the eyes of the blind?' (John 10:21), they retorted, when others accused Jesus of being 'demon-possessed'.

And take the raising of Lazarus:

Now a man named Lazarus was sick. He was from Bethany, the village of Mary and her sister Martha. This Mary, whose brother Lazarus now lay sick, was the same one who poured perfume on the Lord and wiped his feet with her hair. So the sisters sent word to Jesus: 'Lord, the one you love is sick'. When he heard this, Jesus said: 'This sickness will not end in death. No, it is for God's glory so that God's Son may be glorified through it'... Then Jesus said: 'Did I not tell you that if you believed, you would see the glory of God?' (John 11:1-4,40).

True it is that 'the heavens declare the glory of God; the skies proclaim the work of his hands. Day after day they pour forth speech; night after night they display knowledge. There is no speech or language where their voice is not heard. Their voice goes out into all the earth, their words to the ends of the world' (Ps. 19:1-4). Yes! But, in the gospel, God gets a glory that is greater by far than the glory of God in and through nature. Isaac Watts:

> *Now to the Lord, a noble song!*
> *Awake, my soul! awake, my tongue!*
> *Hosanna to th'eternal Name,*
> *And all his boundless love proclaim.*

> *See where it shines in Jesus' face,*
> *The brightest image of his grace;*
> ***God, in the person of his Son,***
> ***Has all his mightiest works outdone.***

9. God's Purpose

The spacious earth and spreading flood
Proclaim the wise and powerful God;
And his rich glories from afar
Sparkle in every rolling star.

But in his looks a glory stands,
The noblest labour of thy hands;
The pleasing lustre of his eyes
Outshines the wonders of the skies.

Grace! 'tis a sweet, a charming theme!
My thoughts rejoice at Jesus' name!
Ye angels, dwell upon the sound!
Ye heavens, reflect it to the ground!

Oh, may I live to reach the place
Where he unveils his lovely face;
There all his beauties to behold,
And sing his name to harps of gold!

Another from the same stable:

Father, how wide thy glory shines!
How high thy wonders rise!
Known through the earth by thousand signs,
By thousands through the skies.

Those mighty orbs proclaim thy power,
Their motions speak thy skill,
And on the wings of every hour
We read thy patience still.

But when we view thy strange design
To save rebellious worms,
Our souls are filled with awe divine
To see what God performs.

Our thoughts are lost in reverent awe;
We love and we adore;
The first archangel never saw
So much of God before.

Here the whole Deity is known,
Nor dares a creature guess
Which of the glories brightest shone,
The justice, or the grace.

9. God's Purpose

William Gadsby:

Oh! what matchless condescension
The eternal God displays,
Claiming our supreme attention
To his boundless works and ways;
His own glory
He reveals in gospel days.

In the person of the Saviour
All his majesty is seen!
Love and justice shine for ever;
And, without a veil between,
We approach him,
And rejoice in his dear name.

Would we view his highest glory?
Here it shines in Jesus' face;
Sing and tell the pleasing story,
O ye sinners saved by grace;
And with pleasure,
Bid the guilty him embrace.

In his highest work, redemption,
See his glory in a blaze;
Nor can angels ever mention
Aught that more of God displays.
Grace and justice
Here unite to endless days.

True, 'tis sweet and solemn pleasure,
God to view in Christ the Lord;
Here he smiles, and smiles for ever;
May my soul his name record,
Praise and bless him,
And his wonders spread abroad.

I leave it there. I can think of no better note on which to bring to a close what I have been trying to say. Gadsby has surely captured the essence and end of this 'glorious new-covenant ministry'. In the gospel, in Jesus' face, God's 'brightest glory' most assuredly does 'blaze'. Notice how John observed that until Jesus had been 'glorified' 'the Spirit' was not given (John 7:39). To what was John referring? The death of Christ, of course, and his subsequent resurrection. What? The *death* of Christ his *glory*? Was such a

205

death not a curse? Indeed, it was (Gal. 3:13; Deut. 21:23). Nevertheless, the crucifixion of Christ is his glory. Let me prove it.

Time and again, Jesus had warned his disciples of his coming crucifixion, but they failed to grasp it (Luke 9:22, 43-45,51; 13:33; 18:31-34, for instance). The same can be said of the way he entered Jerusalem on a donkey: only later 'did they realise that these things had been written about him and that they had done these things to him' (John 12:16). Let me fill in the missing piece: 'Only *after Jesus was glorified* did they realise that these things had been written about him and that they had done these things to him'. So, I ask again: Where shall we discover the glory of Christ? Surely in his death on the cross, his resurrection and the application of his work to sinners in their conversion. As to his 'glory', Jesus explained:

'The hour has come for the Son of Man to be glorified. I tell you the truth, unless a grain of wheat falls to the ground and dies, it remains only a single seed. But if it dies, it produces many seeds. The man who loves his life will lose it, while the man who hates his life in this world will keep it for eternal life. Whoever serves me must follow me; and where I am, my servant also will be. My Father will honour the one who serves me. Now my heart is troubled, and what shall I say? "Father, save me from this hour"? No, it was for this very reason I came to this hour. Father, glorify your name!' Then a voice came from heaven: 'I have glorified it, and will glorify it again'. The crowd that was there and heard it said it had thundered; others said an angel had spoken to him. Jesus said: 'This voice was for your benefit, not mine. Now is the time for judgement on this world; now the prince of this world will be driven out. But I, when I am lifted up from the earth, will draw all men to myself'. He said this to show the kind of death he was going to die (John 12:23-33).

Incidentally, John 12:17-23 captures many of the points raised throughout this book. First, we are told that 'the crowd that was with [Jesus] when he called Lazarus from the tomb and raised him from the dead continued to spread the word. Many people, because they had heard that he had given this miraculous sign, went out to meet him. So the Pharisees said to one another: "See, this is getting us nowhere. Look how the whole world has gone after him!"' (John 12:17-19). Christ worked the miracle; the crowd spread the word, telling all and sundry; this led to many coming to Jesus. In particular, the Greeks specifically asked to see him (John 12:20-22). And this led to Christ's pronouncement about his glory (as above).

To continue with the theme of Christ's glory in the cross: After Judas had left the last supper, 'when he was gone, Jesus said: "Now is the Son of Man glorified and God is glorified in him. If God is glorified in him, God will glorify the Son in himself, and will glorify him at once"' (John 13:31-32). And in his final great prayer, 'Jesus... looked towards heaven and prayed':

Father, the time has come. Glorify your Son, that your Son may glorify you. For you granted him authority over all people that he might give eternal life to all those you have given him. Now this is eternal life: that they may know you, the only true God, and Jesus Christ, whom you have sent. I have brought you glory on earth by completing the work you gave me to do. And now, Father, glorify me in your presence with the glory I had with you before the world began (John 17:1-5).

In creation, God declared: 'Let there be light', and darkness and chaos immediately vanished. In the new creation, God decrees salvation, and sinners are transformed: they are perfectly justified at once, and progressively sanctified throughout the rest of their days on earth, being made increasingly Christ-like – ultimately, after death, in the last day, being united with their resurrected body, to be with Christ, to be like Christ and to be glorified with Christ for ever (Rom. 8:1-39). No wonder the apostle could close his letter to the Galatians (in which he spoke so clearly and dogmatically about the end of the law and the glory of the new covenant) in this way: 'May I never boast except in the cross of our Lord Jesus Christ, through which the world has been crucified to me, and I to the world' (Gal. 6:14). This, I submit, is what the new-covenant ministry is all about: the glory of Christ.

And, of course, we have John's vision of the heavenly host (indeed, of all creation) bringing endless praise and glory to God, not only for creation and for his judgements, but, above all, for salvation:

Day and night they never stop saying: 'Holy, holy, holy is the Lord God Almighty, who was, and is, and is to come'. Whenever the living creatures give glory, honour and thanks to him who sits on the throne and who lives for ever and ever, the twenty-four elders fall down before him who sits on the throne, and worship him who lives for ever and ever. They lay their crowns before the throne and say: 'You are worthy, our Lord and God, to receive glory and honour and power, for you created all things, and by your will they were created and have their being'...

The four living creatures and the twenty-four elders fell down before the Lamb. Each one had a harp and they were holding golden bowls full of incense, which are the prayers of the saints. And they sang a new song: 'You are worthy to take the scroll and to open its seals, because you were slain, and with your blood you purchased men for God from every tribe and language and people and nation. You have made them to be a kingdom and priests to serve our God, and they will reign on the earth'. Then I looked and heard the voice of many angels, numbering thousands upon thousands, and ten thousand times ten thousand. They encircled the throne and the living creatures and the elders. In a loud voice they sang: 'Worthy is the Lamb, who was slain, to receive power and wealth and wisdom and strength and honour and glory and praise!' Then I heard every creature in heaven and on earth and under the earth and on the sea, and all that is in them, singing: 'To him who sits on the throne and to the Lamb be praise and honour and glory and power, for ever and ever!' The four living creatures said: 'Amen', and the elders fell down and worshipped...

I looked and there before me was a great multitude that no one could count, from every nation, tribe, people and language, standing before the throne and in front of the Lamb. They were wearing white robes and were holding palm branches in their hands. And they cried out in a loud voice: 'Salvation belongs to our God, who sits on the throne, and to the Lamb'. All the angels were standing around the throne and around the elders and the four living creatures. They fell down on their faces before the throne and worshipped God, saying: 'Amen! Praise and glory and wisdom and thanks and honour and power and strength be to our God for ever and ever. Amen!' Then one of the elders asked me: 'These in white robes – who are they, and where did they come from?' I answered: 'Sir, you know'. And he said: 'These are they who have come out of the great tribulation; they have washed their robes and made them white in the blood of the Lamb. Therefore, they are before the throne of God and serve him day and night in his temple; and he who sits on the throne will spread his tent over them. Never again will they hunger; never again will they thirst. The sun will not beat upon them, nor any scorching heat. For the Lamb at the centre of the throne will be their shepherd; he will lead them to springs of living water. And God will wipe away every tear from their eyes' (Rev. 4:8-11; 5:8-14; 7:9-17; see also Rev. 11:15-19; 12:10-12; 15:3-4; 16:4-7; 18:1-24; 19:1-10).

Conclusion

I remind you, reader, that I have written this book with you as a believer in mind.

Let me start by asking a question: Are you a preacher? Tell me, please, your reaction to that question. If it's: 'No, I'm afraid I'm not a preacher', then I must have gone wrong somewhere – or else you haven't been paying attention! You agree that you are a believer. You are, therefore, as I have shown, a member of that highly-favoured priesthood of the new covenant, the priesthood of all believers. You are, in truth, a minister, a preacher, a priest – in the spiritual sense of the new covenant. So, when I speak of you as a preacher, while I've got the man in the pulpit in mind, I'm also thinking of Mr, Mrs, Master and Miss Everyman-or-woman who is a believer. All of us, as believers, have a 'ministry'. As I have explained, this ministry goes far wider than 'preaching', but, taking the context of 2 Corinthians 4:1-6 as definitive, in this book I am concentrating on this preaching aspect of our ministry. We exercise it – or ought to exercise it – standing in the queue (or line), waiting to see the dentist or the doctor, standing in the school playground (or yard), chatting over the fence, conversing with a relation or friend, talking with our children, commenting on the news, or whatever – whenever we get the opportunity.

So let me begin all over again. Are you a preacher? Of course you are. Indeed, you might well be one in the sense of a man who stands in a pulpit. But if you are a believer, you most certainly are a minister, a preacher, every bit as much as that man.

Now for the next question: Are you a legal preacher? 'Whatever do you mean?' As before, I thought I had made myself clear, but if not, I'll explain, by asking some more questions: Do you try to bring sinners to Christ by preaching the law? Are you hooked on this preparationism-by-the-law business? You are? If so, then read again 2 Corinthians 3 and 4 – the passage we have been going through in this book. Can you find Paul advocating the law when addressing sinners in order to prepare them – especially to *qualify* them – for Christ? Can you imagine it? In light of all that the apostle declared, the notion is utterly risible. 'Ah! But that's just one passage'. So it is, so it is. So here's my suggestion. Go through the entire New Testament, and see if you can find any preacher addressing unbelievers with the gospel – unbelievers who are non-Jews – and doing so by first preaching the law to them. I agree that you will come across the law in addresses to unbelieving *Jews*,[1] but since most of us are dealing with *Gentiles*, the pertinent question is: Where can you find *Gentiles* being addressed with the law? Indeed, where can you find any preacher using the law – even to the Jews – to prepare sinners and make them 'fit' to come to Christ?

The point is, of course, like the apostles, we are to use every new-covenant weapon at our disposal when addressing sinners. As I said, right at the start, we have to be culturally aware, and use language that will reach those we address. It's imperative that we communicate! I would have thought this was a given! Surely we are not so bitten with hyper-Calvinism – fatalism – that we think it doesn't matter what language we use: 'God is sovereign; he can use anything, just as he will'! Of course! Who denies it? I don't! But if that's all there is to it, let's simply repeat: 'The elect have obtained it, and the rest were blinded' (Rom. 11:7, NKJV), and pull up the drawbridge.

Surely not! Romans 11:7 is a truth, yes, but it's not the whole truth! Let us copy the prophets, John the Baptist, Christ and the apostles, and use every spiritual weapon to reach those we wish to help. And that means making a proper assessment of those we address, taking full account of where they are when we find them, being willing – eager – to be flexible in our approach to them with the gospel. I'm afraid some preachers start where they themselves are, and just grind on, reading their notes, or clicking their mouse, irrespective of whether or not the congregation is receiving it. Indeed, I wonder if some of such preachers actually know (or care?) whether or not their hearers are truly listening – let alone *hearing*! A bit hard? I wonder!

Taking it for granted, then, that we really do want to reach our hearers, if we're talking to Jews, then let's use the law and the prophets – not to prepare them, to make them 'fit' for Christ, but to

---

[1] Matt. 19:16-22; Acts 2:10,16-21,25-31,34-35; 3:11-26; 4:11; 7:52-53; 13:39; 22:3,12; 23:3,5; 24:14; 25:7-8; 28:17,23. Paul only used the law when he could say: 'I speak to those who know the law' (Rom. 7:1).

preach the gospel to them. Mind you, many Jews don't have a clue about either the law or the prophets today, I assure you. I've tried it. I recall, fifty years ago, speaking to a group of Jewish young men, and asking them what they made of Isaiah 53. To my utter astonishment, they didn't even know of the existence of Isaiah 53!

But the real point is this: you are a minister of the new covenant. When you want to bring sinners to Christ, therefore, preach – talk to them – in the new-covenant way. Make sure you reach your hearers, and communicate with them, and do so with the gospel. This is 'the glorious ministry' that you have. Exercise it! Come into the new covenant! And that means preaching Christ! Follow the apostle: 'We preach Christ crucified... I resolved to know nothing... except Jesus Christ and him crucified' (1 Cor. 1:23; 2:2). Or in the words of our passage: 'We... preach... Jesus Christ as Lord' (2 Cor. 4:5). And, in the context, we must preach Jesus Christ as Lord to sinners in order to see them converted. Lift up Christ, therefore; he will draw men and women to himself. 'Just as Moses lifted up the snake in the desert, so the Son of Man must be lifted up, that everyone who believes in him may have eternal life' (John 3:14-15). As Jesus declared: 'I, when I am lifted up from the earth, will draw all men to myself' (John 12:32). As I have explained, this cannot be confined to the manner of his death; Christ must be 'lifted up' in our preaching. Notice how often we meet the phrase 'preach Christ' or the equivalent (Acts 3:20; 5:42; 8:5,35; 9:20; 17:3; Rom. 16:25; 1 Cor. 1:23; 2:2; 15:12; 2 Cor. 1:19; 4:5; Phil. 1:15-18; Col. 1:28; 1 Tim. 3:16, for instance). This is new-covenant ministry. Do it! Do as Christ did! Which was? Did he preach the law in John 3? Did he not preach the love of God for sinners? Did he not preach that the highest sin is refusal of Christ and his offer of salvation?

Just as Moses lifted up the snake in the desert, so the Son of Man must be lifted up, that everyone who believes in him may have eternal life. For God so loved the world that he gave his one and only Son, that whoever believes in him shall not perish but have eternal life. For God did not send his Son into the world to condemn the world, but to save the world through him. Whoever believes in him is not condemned, but whoever does not believe stands condemned already because he has not believed in the name of God's one and only Son (John 3:14-18).

This, I say, is new-covenant preaching to sinners. Let us make sure we do it!

I ask again: Are you a legal preacher? No! It may be the same words, but it's a different question. This time I'm speaking about your desire to see fellow-believers, as well as yourself, sanctified. I am sure you want this. But do you go about it by preaching the law to them (and to yourself)? Well, how does that fit with the passage we have been looking at? How can the ministry of the law, as set out by Paul in 2 Corinthians 3, possibly be the sanctifying ministry for believers? I fail to see how the apostle's words can be made to fit with the idea that saints are to grow in grace and godliness by the law. So I appeal to you: come into the new covenant!

'Ah! But that's just one passage'. So it is, so it is. But I repeat my previous suggestion. Go through the entire New Testament, noting the apostolic way, the apostolic motive, the apostolic spur and the apostolic means of sanctification. True, there are a few – a very few – places where the law is used as a model or paradigm – but I know of no place where the apostles made the law the way of sanctification, or the motive for it. As far as I can judge, they always used the new covenant.[2]

Listen to John telling us what he preached to believers when he wanted to see them sanctified. I refer to this: 'My dear children, I write this to you so that you will not sin' (1 John 2:1). Write what? The context makes everything perfectly clear:

This is the message we have heard from him and declare to you: God is light; in him there is no darkness at all. If we claim to have fellowship with him yet walk in the darkness, we lie and do not live by the truth. But if we walk in the light, as he is in the light, we have fellowship with one another, and the blood of Jesus, his Son, purifies us from all sin. If we claim to be without sin, we deceive ourselves and the truth is not in us. If we confess our sins, he is faithful and just and will forgive us our sins and purify us from all unrighteousness. If we claim we have not sinned, we make him out to be a liar and his word has no place in our lives. My dear children, I write this to you so that you will not sin. But if anybody does sin, we have one who speaks to the Father in our defence – Jesus Christ, the Righteous One. He is the [propitiation] for

---

[2] Please see my *Christ* p289 for my full argument.

our sins, and not only for ours but also for the sins of the whole world (1 John 1:5 – 2:2).

Oh, I know there's more to be said – about obeying Christ's commands, for instance (1 John 2:3). But I want you to notice two things about that. *First*, the immediate context is what I have just set out – the atonement, the power of the blood to cleanse us from all sin, and the fact that if we sin as believers, the blood of Christ still keeps us faultless before God. Staggering, isn't it? But that's the very thing that John said! This – this – is the motive and spur for sanctification. That's the first thing. He did not want believers to sin; so he told them that if they did sin, forgiveness is waiting! That's what John preached to believers to sanctify them! How staggering it sounds to us in these days – when legal preaching has virtually captured the field.

Now for the *second*. Yes, we have to obey 'his commands' (1 John 2:3) – that is, of course, Christ's commandments! John was talking about the law of Christ, was he not? John was writing to those who 'walk in the light' (1 John 1:7). He immediately explains: God 'is in the light' (1 John 1:7; 1 Tim. 6:16). But what springs to mind? Surely this:

I am the light of the world. Whoever follows me will never walk in darkness, but will have the light of life... I have come into the world as a light, so that no one who believes in me should stay in darkness... I am the light of the world (John 8:12;9:5; 12:46).

In short, John was taking his readers to Christ: walking in the light, Christ, keeping his commands, means keeping Christ's commands. To try to slide from this into the law of Moses is a tragic misrepresentation and falling short of the apostle's words. And to try, further, to confine John's phrase to the ten commandments is utterly out of order, without the slightest scriptural warrant. Oh, I grant that it is has been the dominant approach throughout Christendom ever since Aquinas, and, even more so, since the time of Calvin, but, I say again, it is utterly foreign to Scripture. What is more, it runs directly counter to God's declared mind in Scripture. He allows no such tinkering with his law (Deut. 4:2; 12:32).[3]

---

[3] Please see the previous note.

So, believer, if you want to be sanctified, and if you want to help others to be sanctified – and as a believer the answer to both must be 'yes' – don't go back to the old covenant; be a new-covenant man or woman: preach Christ! Preach Christ to yourself, first of all, and then to others; individually and then corporately. In all this, look to Christ! Think of the love of God for you in Christ, the power and fullness and freeness of grace in redemption. Think of Christ's shed blood, shed for you. Think of what God in Christ has done for you and in you and to you – and what he has in store for you. In short:

Since, then, you have been raised with Christ, set your hearts on things above, where Christ is seated at the right hand of God. Set your minds on things above, not on earthly things. For you died, and your life is now hidden with Christ in God. When Christ, who is your life, appears, then you also will appear with him in glory. Put to death, therefore, whatever belongs to your earthly nature: sexual immorality, impurity, lust, evil desires and greed, which is idolatry. Because of these, the wrath of God is coming. You used to walk in these ways, in the life you once lived. But now you must rid yourselves of all such things as these: anger, rage, malice, slander, and filthy language from your lips. Do not lie to each other, since you have taken off your old self with its practices and have put on the new self, which is being renewed in knowledge in the image of its Creator. Here there is no Greek or Jew, circumcised or uncircumcised, barbarian, Scythian, slave or free, but Christ is all, and is in all. Therefore, as God's chosen people, holy and dearly loved, clothe yourselves with compassion, kindness, humility, gentleness and patience. Bear with each other and forgive whatever grievances you may have against one another. Forgive as the Lord forgave you. And over all these virtues put on love, which binds them all together in perfect unity. Let the peace of Christ rule in your hearts, since as members of one body you were called to peace. And be thankful. Let the word of Christ dwell in you richly as you teach and admonish one another with all wisdom, and as you sing psalms, hymns and spiritual songs with gratitude in your hearts to God. And whatever you do, whether in word or deed, do it all in the name of the Lord Jesus, giving thanks to God the Father through him (Col. 3:1-17).

This, this will sanctify. The law won't! Don't forget:

My brothers, you... died to the law through the body of Christ, that you might belong to another, to him who was raised from the dead, in order that we might bear fruit to God. For when we were controlled by the

214

sinful nature, the sinful passions aroused by the law were at work in our bodies, so that we bore fruit for death. But now, by dying to what once bound us, we have been released from the law so that we serve in the new way of the Spirit, and not in the old way of the written code (Rom. 7:4-6).
I died to the law so that I might live for God. I have been crucified with Christ and I no longer live, but Christ lives in me. The life I live in the body, I live by faith in the Son of God, who loved me and gave himself for me (Gal. 2:19-20).

All this is repeated time without number throughout the New Testament. *This* is the glorious new-covenant ministry at work. Prove it!

Just one more example: 'Live a life of love', commanded the apostle. But how? 'Be imitators of God, therefore, as dearly loved children and live a life of love, just as Christ loved us and gave himself up for us as a fragrant offering and sacrifice to God' (Eph. 5:1-2). You see the motive and the spur for holiness? Christ! The love of God, in Christ, the blood of Christ... this, this is the motive and the spur for sanctification – not the law!

What is more, the same doctrine that leads sinners to salvation, not only sanctifies saints – it gives doubting saints assurance. Whatever am I talking about? Romans 8, for a start. I have already quoted these verses:

Therefore, there is now no condemnation for those who are in Christ Jesus, because through Christ Jesus the law of the Spirit of life set me free from the law of sin and death. For what the law was powerless to do in that it was weakened by the flesh, God did by sending his own Son in the likeness of sinful man to be a sin offering. And so he condemned sin in sinful man, in order that the righteous requirements of the law might be fully met in us, who do not live according to the flesh but according to the Spirit (Rom. 8:1-4).

Justification is written clearly enough in that paragraph, as is sanctification. And right at the heart of it is this: 'Through Christ Jesus the law of the Spirit of life...'. If a sinner is to be saved, it will be 'through Christ Jesus [in] the law of the Spirit of life'. If a saint is to be sanctified, it will be 'through Christ Jesus [in] the law of the Spirit of life'. 'Ah! But what about assurance? You said this is the way of assurance'. Read on, read on! After several verses dealing with the consequences of justification worked out in practical godliness (sanctification), the apostle comes to this:

Those who are led by the Spirit of God are sons of God. For you did not receive a spirit that makes you a slave again to fear, but you received the Spirit of sonship. And by him we cry: 'Abba, Father'. The Spirit himself testifies with our spirit that we are God's children. Now if we are children, then we are heirs – heirs of God and co-heirs with Christ, if indeed we share in his sufferings in order that we may also share in his glory (Rom. 8:14-17).

You see? 'Through Christ Jesus [in] the law of the Spirit of life' we have been justified, are being sanctified and, now we learn, we are being assured. Not only that, we shall be glorified. It's all here. Nor is that the end of it! The 'new-covenant ministry' truly is a 'glorious ministry'! Listen to these familiar words once again, Paul's words as he drives on in Romans 8:

Our present sufferings are not worth comparing with the glory that will be revealed in us... We..., who have the firstfruits of the Spirit, groan inwardly as we wait eagerly for our adoption as sons, the redemption of our bodies. For in this hope we were saved. But hope that is seen is no hope at all. Who hopes for what he already has? But if we hope for what we do not yet have, we wait for it patiently. In the same way, the Spirit helps us in our weakness. We do not know what we ought to pray for, but the Spirit himself intercedes for us with groans that words cannot express. And he who searches our hearts knows the mind of the Spirit, because the Spirit intercedes for the saints in accordance with God's will. And we know that in all things God works for the good of those who love him, who have been called according to his purpose. For those God foreknew he also predestined to be conformed to the likeness of his Son, that he might be the firstborn among many brothers. And those he predestined, he also called; those he called, he also justified; those he justified, he also glorified. What, then, shall we say in response to this? If God is for us, who can be against us? He who did not spare his own Son, but gave him up for us all – how will he not also, along with him, graciously give us all things? Who will bring any charge against those whom God has chosen? It is God who justifies. Who is he that condemns? Christ Jesus, who died – more than that, who was raised to life – is at the right hand of God and is also interceding for us. Who shall separate us from the love of Christ? Shall trouble or hardship or persecution or famine or nakedness or danger or sword? As it is written: 'For your sake we face death all day long; we are considered as sheep to be slaughtered'. No, in all these things we are more than conquerors through him who loved us. For I am convinced that neither death nor life, neither angels nor demons, neither the present nor the future, nor any powers, neither height nor depth, nor anything else in all creation, will be able to separate us from the love of God that is in Christ Jesus our Lord (Rom. 8:18-39).

Don't forget that these words are the climax of all that Paul has said so far in his letter to the Romans, especially beginning at Romans 5:20-21. A reading of that entire passage (Rom. 5:20 – 8:39) – aloud, and in a different version to your usual preference – will make the point better than any words of mine could. Indeed, for me to say more would be an insult to such a majestic statement!

'Ah! But you are forgetting! You are forgetting – or ignoring – that the Confessions say... the books say... the pastors say... the great men say... they all say that we must preach the law to sinners to bring them to Christ, and we must preach the law to believers to see them sanctified, and as we measure our law-keeping so we best grow in assurance'.

No! I'm not forgetting or ignoring those facts. And facts they are, I agree. The Confessions, the books, the pastors, the great men, yes, they all (well, the vast majority of them) say... Let *them* say! What does *Paul* say? 'I resolved to know nothing while I was with you except Jesus Christ and him crucified'; and: 'May I never boast except in the cross of our Lord Jesus Christ, through which the world has been crucified to me, and I to the world' (1 Cor. 2:2; Gal. 6:14).

'Very well! But if I go down your route,[4] they will call me an antinomian'. So they will, so they will. But remember that they called Jesus a Samaritan (John 8:48), stigmatising him as much as they could. And to get the full sting in the word, bear in mind that the 'expert in the law' could not bring himself even to pronounce it (Luke 10:25-37, especially verse 37). Clearly, the thought that both a priest and a Levite had failed – where a Samaritan had succeeded – was too much for him to stomach. Jesus, of course, deliberately chose 'Samaritan' (see also Luke 17:16; John 4:9,39-40), to make his point. Indeed, not content with calling Christ a Samaritan, the

---

[4] *My* route? I have been putting before you God's route, made known in Scripture.

Jews wrote him off as 'raving mad' (John 8:48; 10:20), and 'demon-possessed' (John 7:20; 8:52; 10:20) – as they did John the Baptist (Matt. 11:18). The fact is, they heaped a catalogue of invective on Christ (Matt. 11:19). So, you see, to be given a pejorative nickname puts you in the same class as your Saviour!

Paul was similarly accused of madness (Acts 26:24). And they also called him the equivalent of an antinomian! In fact, a good case can be made for saying that the real fault is *not* to be called by some-such negative nickname. Let me explain.

The apostles repeatedly had to answer the charge of lawlessness, rebut its danger, and argue against it. Why? Paul (Rom. 3:5,7-9; 6:1 – 7:6; 1 Cor. 8:9; Gal. 5:13-21), Peter (1 Pet. 2:16; 4:1-6; 2 Pet. 2:19), James (1:21-27; 2:1-26) and Jude (Jude 4,11,13) all met it. Why? If the apostles had been arguing that sanctification comes by the law, they would never have needed to do anything of the sort. There's no danger of lawlessness arising from teaching which states that the law is the believer's rule! It only arises when the gospel is taught with the freeness the New Testament warrants and demands. A charge of antinomianism can only be made against a preacher of free grace. Indeed, the fact that such an accusation can be made, that such an accusation ought to be made, is the acid test for all preachers and teachers, and their doctrine. Let me personalise it: if nobody can accuse me of antinomianism, then I'm not preaching the gospel as it ought to be preached – either to sinners for their justification, or to believers for their sanctification! And the same goes for you, reader!

I say again, it is only the preaching of free grace that gives rise to such a possibility. Preaching the law doesn't! Take Jude:

Dear friends, although I was very eager to write to you about the salvation we share, I felt I had to write and urge you to contend for the faith that was once for all entrusted to the saints. For certain men whose condemnation was written about long ago have secretly slipped in among you. They are godless men, who change the grace of our God into a licence for immorality and deny Jesus Christ our only Sovereign and Lord (Jude 3-5).

You see? These infiltrators worked on 'the grace' that the believers had experienced and now treasured; they turned that 'grace' into 'a licence for immorality'; my point, in a nutshell! Nobody could possibly dream of turning the law into 'a licence for immorality', could they? If you sit under a legal preacher, whatever else you might accuse him of, it would not be for encouraging immorality. His constant theme is: 'Do not... do not...' So, as I say, nobody could possibly imagine he was encouraging sin! It is only gospel preachers, preachers of free grace, who can be accused of encouraging licence. And that is precisely what happened in the New Testament churches! If you want to be apostolic in your practice, therefore, preach grace, preach Christ! But, of course, this opens the door to those who want to accuse us of advocating antinomianism. I admit it! In fact, as I have argued, it proves that I am preaching the gospel. The question is, of course: How can we put a stop to goings-on of this kind? How can we prevent antinomianism? 'Ah, that's easy: preach law!' Yes, it seems obvious. That, of course, was one of the main commissions given to the Westminster Assembly, and they certainly supplied what their masters ordered. The result? They majored on law.[5] *But that is precisely what Jude does **not** do or say.* The fact is, we don't want merely to stop immorality – we want to produce Christ-likeness. Now, how did Jude set about *that*? Well, having explored very fully the nature of the attack, he came to this:

Dear friends, build yourselves up in your most holy faith and pray in the Holy Spirit. Keep yourselves in God's love as you wait for the mercy of our Lord Jesus Christ to bring you to eternal life. Be merciful to those who doubt; snatch others from the fire and save them; to others show mercy, mixed with fear – hating even the clothing stained by corrupted flesh. To him who is able to keep you from falling and to present you before his glorious presence without fault and with great joy – to the only God our Saviour be glory, majesty, power and

---

[5] It more than dealt with antinomianism (real and so-called); it over-reacted to it. And, much as Calvin allowed his reaction against the Anabaptists to grossly distort his view of baptism, with grievous consequences, so the men at Westminster with antinomianism. The upshot was, instead of steering the right course between Scylla and Charybdis, in sheering away from antinomianism, they plunged far too much towards legalism, and ended up producing documents heavy with law. Out of 196 questions, the Larger Catechism has more than 60 on the law, a staggering ratio for the age of the new covenant.

authority, through Jesus Christ our Lord, before all ages, now and forevermore! Amen (Jude 20-25).

Not an ounce of law, but plenty of grace! Above all, plenty of Christ. You see? This is what I mean by 'the new-covenant ministry'. Grace produces the possibility of antinomianism. What is the apostolic way of preventing it? Preach yet more grace! Above all things, look to Christ.

Incidentally, do not miss Jude's sting in the tail in verse 4. Where does all error end up? With the denial of Christ! This, again, shows we are on the right track. Christ is the gospel; the gospel is Christ.

So important is this point, let me go to the spring: 'Where sin abounded, grace abounded all the more' (Rom. 5:20); that's where, as I have explained, Paul opened his tremendous argument on this subject. 'Where sin abounded, grace abounded all the more'. 'That's all very well', says an objector to the apostle's doctrine, 'but surely such teaching spells the end of the law, and inevitably leads to antinomianism, does it not? Have you thought this out, Paul? Haven't you been irresponsible, to say the least? Think, man, think! What safeguards will your teaching raise against sin? What bulwark against antinomianism? How will it produce holiness? Can a believer do what he wants, how he wants, when he wants, live careless of questions of sin and godliness, even saying sin is godliness? Surely you will need to spell out very clearly – and do it now! – that the believer is under the law for sanctification. If you do not, antinomianism must be the result'. In short: 'What shall we say then? Shall we go on sinning that grace may increase?' (Rom. 6:1).

Paul has one dismissive, short reply to all such talk: 'Certainly not!' (Rom. 6:2, NKJV). Perish the thought! God forbid! It is utterly unthinkable. But notice, reader, what Paul does not go on to say. It is his silence which is so important here, so telling. *He does not say that the believer is under the law, after all!* Certainly not! In fact, it is the believer's very freedom from the law of Moses which leads to his deliverance from the dominion of sin, and produces a godly life! And that is precisely – precisely – what the apostle does say.

Even so, *this* is the sort of questions which Paul's doctrine *must* provoke; that is, if this is what Paul was saying. Do we find such questions? We certainly do! A glance through Romans 6 and 7 will prove it. We know, therefore, we are drawing the right conclusions from Romans 5:20, because it is precisely this sort of objections and questions which led to Paul's response in Romans 6 and 7. To get the force of what I am saying, please read the entire section, aloud.

The question in Romans 6:15, though bluntly dismissed by Paul, needs to be asked, and inevitably will be asked of all who teach scripturally on the law, since the biblical teaching on the matter sounds so startling: 'What then? Shall we sin because we are not under law but under grace? 'Legal preaching', of course, would never, could never, can never, provoke such a question. And this is as fatal a mark against it as anybody could wish. Biblical teaching on the law and sanctification *must* provoke such a response, such a question, such an accusation. The New Testament shows that that is the very thing which happened under the preaching of those days. Sadly, those who advocate the biblical position on Romans 6 and 7 are dismissed as antinomians, but the fact is, unless a man can be accused of antinomianism he is not preaching the gospel properly. Truth to tell, advocates of the law are legal preachers, and their doctrine tends to outward conformity, not to say legalism. Nevertheless, Paul met the accusation of antinomianism; many others have. Every man who preaches free grace will. Even so, the unjust accusation hurts! *Not* to get it, however, ought to hurt far more!

Let me quote another writer on the theme:

Furthermore, if you preach this gospel of God's grace, you are likely to be charged with antinomianism. But this charge is nothing new in the history of the church... Paul himself was accused of the same thing (Rom. 3:8). Therefore we need not be too much surprised to meet the same charge today. As a matter of fact, unless you are charged thus sooner or later, you are probably not preaching the good news of God's grace as it ought to be preached. For it has been truly pointed out that only the true doctrine of grace can be caricatured as a form of antinomianism. You may be sure you will never be charged with antinomianism as long as you are willing to compromise the message of grace with the smallest modicum of law. But the charge is false when levelled against the preacher of salvation by grace. For in the gospel of salvation by grace alone in Christ we are honouring the law and establishing the law. By his death, our Lord Jesus Christ satisfied in full all the law's holy and just demands. The real antinomians are the legalists, for they either take only one element of the law, or they strip it of its penalties, or they soften and relax its demands; to this extent they are against (Greek *anti*) the law.[6]

So then, to produce godliness, do not preach law. Preach Christ![7]

I ask another question: We are all agreed that you, as a believer, are a preacher – well, then, are you a 'legal preacher' in the sense of trying to bring sinners to salvation by preaching sacraments? If so, please read again 2 Corinthians 4:1-6. Not a sacrament in sight! Indeed, read the rest of the New Testament to find any example of what you are doing. Moreover, while the ordinances (note my vital change of word) of Christ are important, and Christ instituted them for the strengthening of the faith of believers, and to keep them is a mark of obedience to him, be careful that you don't give them an importance beyond the warrant of the New Testament. While Christ's ordinances nourish a believer, sanctification is far more than regular attendance at the Lord's supper! Take baptism (Mark 16:15-16; Matt. 28:18-20): important, yes, but not all-important; not essential for salvation, but essential for a believer in obedience to his Lord. Do not forget the apostle's declaration about himself. This is how he saw things:

I am thankful that I did not baptise any of you except Crispus and Gaius, so no one can say that you were baptised into my name. (Yes, I also baptised the household of Stephanas; beyond that, I don't remember if I baptised anyone else.) For Christ did not send me to baptise, but to preach the gospel – not with words of human wisdom, lest the cross of Christ be emptied of its power... We preach Christ crucified... I resolved to know nothing... except Jesus Christ and him crucified (1 Cor. 1:14-17,23; 2:2).

---

[6] Alva J. McClain: *Law And Grace: A Study of New Testament Concepts as They Relate to the Christian Life*, Moody Press, Chicago, 1967, pp73-74.

[7] For more on this, see my *Grace Not Law: The Answer To Antinomianism*.

Or in the words of our passage: 'We... preach... Jesus Christ as Lord' (2 Cor. 4:5). I say again, not a sacrament in sight. If you want to see sinners saved, and believers sanctified, take them to Christ. Let us never forget the cry of the Greeks: 'Sir, we would like to see Jesus' (John 12:20-21). Even if our hearers don't say it, and unbelievers (and not a few believers!) certainly don't know it, Christ is the one they need! He is all they need!

When Paul addressed the Colossians, he spoke of:

The mystery that has been kept hidden for ages and generations, but is now disclosed to the saints. To them God has chosen to make known among the Gentiles the glorious riches of this mystery, which is Christ in you, the hope of glory. We proclaim him, admonishing and teaching everyone with all wisdom, so that we may present everyone perfect in Christ (Col. 1:26-28).

Let me underscore the apostle's point that this glorious mystery of 'Christ in you', Christ in his people, has been disclosed to every saint – not just to the apostle, not just to so-called ministers. Of course the apostle had a special task, and of course, stated preachers have their task in the churches today, yes. But when we read Paul's words: 'We proclaim [Christ], admonishing and teaching everyone with all wisdom, so that we may present everyone perfect in Christ', we must not limit this to him. We, too, brother and sister, all believers, we, too, must do all we can to 'present everyone perfect in Christ'; that is, we must do all we can to see sinners saved, and saints edified and further glorified.

Finally, you are a new-covenant minister? Excellent! You are seeking to preach the gospel? You are seeking to lift up Christ to both unbelievers and believers? When addressing sinners, you don't mix Christ with law, works, rites, sacraments? When addressing believers, you want them to see that *Christ is all* (Col. 3:11)? You assure them by pointing them to Christ, not the law? You drive them (and yourself) to holiness, you move them (and yourself) to holiness, by looking to Christ? Excellent! Well, then, do not lose heart. Do not get over-worried by the opposition of the world – and not a few in the church! Expect it. Remember Nehemiah! In fact, if you didn't meet any opposition it would be a sure sign that you were not preaching properly, you were disturbing nobody, and Satan was keeping things nice and quiet, all the while laughing up his sleeve. He will only oppose when he sees his kingdom threatened. Don't court opposition, mind you, but expect it. Do not let the opposition of fellow-believers make you pull your horns in. Take a good dose of that nerve-strengthening tonic handed to you by the apostle:

Therefore, since through God's mercy we have this ministry, we do not lose heart. Rather, we have renounced secret and shameful ways; we do not use deception, nor do we distort the word of God. On the contrary, by setting forth the truth plainly we commend ourselves to every man's conscience in the sight of God. And even if our gospel is veiled, it is veiled to those who are perishing. The god of this age has blinded the minds of unbelievers, so that they cannot see the light of the gospel of the glory of Christ, who is the image of God. For we do not preach ourselves, but Jesus Christ as Lord, and ourselves as your servants for Jesus' sake. For God, who said: 'Let light shine out of darkness', made his light shine in our hearts to give us the light of the knowledge of the glory of God in the face of Christ (2 Cor. 4:1-6).

Believer, you have received this ministry! Serve God, worship God, live your spiritual life to the full, therefore. And that means – in the first instance – enjoy Christ for yourself! Be assured! Keep looking unto him, keep looking into his face. Many know the words of the chorus by Helen Lemmel:

> *Turn your eyes upon Jesus,*
> *Look full in his wonderful face,*
> *And the things of earth will grow strangely dim,*
> *In the light of his glory and grace.*

But I wonder how many know the verses:

> *O soul, are you weary and troubled?*
> *No light in the darkness you see?*
> *There's a light for a look at the Saviour,*
> *And life more abundant and free!*

> *Through death into life everlasting*
> *He passed, and we follow him there;*
> *Over us sin no more hath dominion –*
> *For more than conquerors we are!*

Conclusion

His word shall not fail you – he promised;
Believe him, and all will be well:
Then go to a world that is dying,
His perfect salvation to tell!

The 'face' of Christ, of course, means the person of Christ. It all centres on him. You are fully justified in Christ – made perfect in God's sight. Now seek to live to perfection because of God's love to you, not out of fear that he might punish you, or that others will look down their noses at you. They will; they did to Christ. But live to please God, live in the assurance of his love to you, live a sanctified life, a Christ-like life, and do so out of gratitude for what he has done for you, and done in you, through Christ. You are a royal priest, a kingly priest; live like it! Carry out all your priestly duties and responsibilities, because of his love for you:

Therefore, my dear friends, as you have always obeyed – not only in my presence, but now much more in my absence – continue to work out your salvation with fear and trembling, for it is God who works in you to will and to act according to his good purpose. Do everything without complaining or arguing, so that you may become blameless and pure, children of God without fault in a crooked and depraved generation, in which you shine like stars in the universe as you hold out the word of life (Phil. 2:12-16).

And – but since this will take us beyond our passage, I must be brief – in all your sufferings and trials, though they show that you are only a poor jar of clay, all will serve to prove yet again that you do indeed enjoy the all-surpassing glory of the new covenant. As Paul says:

But we have this treasure in jars of clay to show that this all-surpassing power is from God and not from us. We are hard pressed on every side, but not crushed; perplexed, but not in despair; persecuted, but not abandoned; struck down, but not destroyed. We always carry around in our body the death of Jesus, so that the life of Jesus may also be revealed in our body. For we who are alive are always being given over to death for Jesus' sake, so that his life may be revealed in our mortal body. So then, death is at work in us, but life is at work in you. It is written: 'I believed; therefore I have spoken'. With that same spirit of faith we also believe and therefore speak, because we know that the one who raised the Lord Jesus from the dead will also raise us with Jesus and present us with you in his presence. All this is for your benefit, so that the grace that is reaching more and more people may cause thanksgiving to overflow to the glory of God. Therefore we do not lose heart. Though outwardly we are wasting away, yet inwardly we are being renewed day by day. For our light and momentary troubles are achieving for us an eternal glory that far outweighs them all. So we fix our eyes not on what is seen, but on what is unseen. For what is seen is temporary, but what is unseen is eternal...

Since, then, we know what it is to fear the Lord, we try to persuade men... If we are out of our mind, it is for the sake of God; if we are in our right mind, it is for you. For Christ's love compels us, because we are convinced that one died for all, and therefore all died. And he died for all, that those who live should no longer live for themselves but for him who died for them and was raised again. So from now on we regard no one from a worldly point of view. Though we once regarded Christ in this way, we do so no longer. Therefore, if anyone is in Christ, he is a new creation; the old has gone, the new has come! All this is from God, who reconciled us to himself through Christ and gave us the ministry of reconciliation: that God was reconciling the world to himself in Christ, not counting men's sins against them. And he has committed to us the message of reconciliation. We are therefore Christ's ambassadors, as though God were making his appeal through us. We implore you on Christ's behalf: Be reconciled to God. God made him who had no sin to be sin for us, so that in him we might become the righteousness of God.

As God's fellow-workers we urge you not to receive God's grace in vain. For he says: 'In the time of my favour I heard you, and in the day of salvation I helped you'. I tell you, now is the time of God's favour, now is the day of salvation.

We put no stumbling-block in anyone's path, so that our ministry will not be discredited. Rather, as servants of God we commend ourselves in every way: in great endurance; in troubles, hardships and distresses; in beatings, imprisonments and riots; in hard work, sleepless nights and hunger; in purity, understanding, patience and kindness; in the Holy Spirit and in sincere love; in truthful speech and in the power of God; with weapons of righteousness in the right hand and in the left; through glory and dishonour, bad report and good report; genuine, yet regarded as impostors; known, yet regarded as unknown; dying, and yet we live on; beaten, and yet not killed; sorrowful, yet always rejoicing; poor, yet making many rich; having nothing, and yet possessing everything...

Though we live in the world, we do not wage war as the world does. The weapons we fight with are not the weapons of the world. On the contrary, they have divine power to demolish strongholds. We demolish arguments and every pretension that sets itself up against the knowledge of God, and we take captive every thought to make it obedient to Christ...

May the grace of the Lord Jesus Christ, and the love of God, and the fellowship of the Holy Spirit be with you all (2 Cor. 4:7-16; 5:11-21; 6:1-10; 10:3-5; 13:14).

Whistling in the dark?

'You're whistling in the dark, aren't you?' No! Not at all! As believers, we know that what we have been exploring is Scripture. The system spelled out by Paul is the infallible cure for the world's ills. It is the only cure there is for mankind. Of that there is no doubt!

Consequently, reader, now is the time for faith. Circumstances are bad; prospects are worse. But... let us remind ourselves that the prospects for the first believers were daunting – an understatement, if ever there was one! The power, the venerable tradition, the antiquity of Judaism; the widespread hedonism, paganism and philosophical prowess of Greece; and the political and military might of Rome – all must have seemed tremendous odds to the handful of early believers, most of whom were unschooled non-orators (Acts 4:13). The odds did not only seem overwhelming; they were! That little band of believers knew they had to take the gospel throughout the world (Matt. 28:18-20; Mark 16:15-16; Luke 24:47; Acts 1:8). Yet they had seen what the Jews and Romans had done to their Lord. Everything, surely, was more than enough to make them give up – right at the starting gate!

But they had the promise of Christ to help them obey his command (Luke 24:47; John 14:15-21; 16:5-15; Acts 1:8). They had the Spirit. They had the good news. And so they went forth. Despite severe opposition and persecution, they did not retreat. 'Retreat' and 'retrench' were not in their vocabulary. Rather, even as they were being force-fed with the first sips of opposition, they prayed for boldness to go on (Acts 4:23-30). And God answered their prayers, gave them opportunities to be bold,[8] and blessed their efforts, so that not only was the place shaken as they prayed: they were enabled by God's grace to turn the world upside down by

---

[8] Don't forget the earlier note on praying for patience. God gives us patience by giving us things to make us impatient!

227

their ministry (Acts 17:6, AV). Let me remind you of the actual scriptures:

The priests and the captain of the temple guard and the Sadducees came up to Peter and John while they were speaking to the people. They were greatly disturbed because the apostles were teaching the people and proclaiming in Jesus the resurrection of the dead. They seized Peter and John, and because it was evening, they put them in jail until the next day. But many who heard the message believed, and the number of men grew to about five thousand. The next day the rulers, elders and teachers of the law met in Jerusalem... They had Peter and John brought before them and began to question them: 'By what power or what name did you do this?' Then Peter, filled with the Holy Spirit, said to them: 'Rulers and elders of the people! If we are being called to account today for an act of kindness shown to a cripple and are asked how he was healed, then know this, you and all the people of Israel: It is by the name of Jesus Christ of Nazareth, whom you crucified but whom God raised from the dead, that this man stands before you healed. He is "the stone you builders rejected, which has become the capstone". Salvation is found in no one else, for there is no other name under heaven given to men by which we must be saved'. When they saw the courage of Peter and John and realised that they were unschooled, ordinary men, they were astonished and they took note that these men had been with Jesus. But since they could see the man who had been healed standing there with them, there was nothing they could say. So they ordered them to withdraw from the Sanhedrin and then conferred together. 'What are we going to do with these men?' they asked. 'Everybody living in Jerusalem knows they have done an outstanding miracle, and we cannot deny it. But to stop this thing from spreading any further among the people, we must warn these men to speak no longer to anyone in this name'. Then they called them in again and commanded them not to speak or teach at all in the name of Jesus. But Peter and John replied: 'Judge for yourselves whether it is right in God's sight to obey you rather than God. For we cannot help speaking about what we have seen and heard'. After further threats they let them go. They could not decide how to punish them, because all the people were praising God for what had happened. For the man who was miraculously healed was over forty years old.

On their release, Peter and John went back to their own people and reported all that the chief priests and elders had said to them. When they heard this, they raised their voices together in prayer to God. 'Sovereign Lord', they said, 'you made the heaven and the earth and the sea, and everything in them. You spoke by the Holy Spirit through the mouth of your servant, our father David: "Why do the nations rage and the peoples plot in vain? The kings of the earth take their stand and the rulers gather together against the Lord and against his Anointed One". Indeed, Herod and Pontius Pilate met together with the Gentiles and the people of Israel in this city to conspire against your holy servant Jesus, whom you anointed. They did what your power and will had decided beforehand should happen. Now, Lord, consider their threats and enable your servants to speak your word with great boldness. Stretch out your hand to heal and perform miraculous signs and wonders through the name of your holy servant Jesus'. After they prayed, the place where they were meeting was shaken. And they were all filled with the Holy Spirit and spoke the word of God boldly (Acts 4:1-31).

Centuries before, David had trodden a similar path when faced with a sneering attack:

Many are asking: 'Who can show us any good?' Let the light of your face shine upon us, O LORD. You have filled my heart with greater joy than when their grain and new wine abound (Ps. 4:6-7).

And so the first believers went on and on taking the battle to the enemy. The unbelieving Jews of Thessalonica were incensed when Paul and Silas reached there with the gospel, describing them thus: 'These who have turned the world upside down have come here too' (Acts 17:6, NKJV). Shocking! Do you see the point! In those early days, it wasn't the believers who were afraid and on the defensive! It was the world!

Something similar happened at Ephesus when Paul went there:

Many of those who believed...openly confessed their evil deeds. A number who had practiced sorcery brought their scrolls together and burned them publicly. When they calculated the value of the scrolls, the total came to fifty thousand drachmas. In this way the word of the Lord spread widely and grew in power... About that time there arose a great disturbance about the Way. A silversmith named Demetrius, who made silver shrines of Artemis, brought in no little business for the craftsmen. He called them together, along with the workmen in related trades, and said: 'Men, you know we receive a good income from this business. And you see and hear how this fellow Paul has convinced and led astray large numbers of people here in Ephesus and in practically the whole province of Asia. He says that man-made gods are no gods at all. There is danger not only that our trade will lose its good name, but also that the temple of the great goddess Artemis will be discredited, and the goddess herself, who is worshipped throughout the province of Asia and the world, will be robbed of her divine majesty' (Acts 19:18-27).

Of course, there is much that is extraordinary in these accounts, but leaving that aside, the abiding principles stand out. However powerful the enemies of the gospel might be, however entrenched their position, however firm their grip, however substantial their resources and deep their pocket, nothing – nothing and nobody – not even Satan himself – can withstand the power of God in the gospel. Can I say that again: *nothing – nothing and nobody – not even Satan himself – can withstand the power of God in the gospel.*

Moreover, the new-covenant ministry didn't work simply when Judaism, hedonistic and pagan Greece, and imperial Rome confronted the gospel. It works today, it works for us. Faced as we are with apathy, hedonism, Islam, atheism, false religion of every hue, Rome (ever-changing but ever the same), Christendom and all the rest – the new-covenant ministry is a glorious ministry. It is the *only* ministry that will rescue man. Jesus Christ is still the only Redeemer (John 14:6; Acts 4:12). Let us not cave in to political correctness: Jesus Christ is not a Saviour – he is **THE** Saviour, the *only* Saviour. Sin and sins are still the same as ever; man is still the same. And still it is the gospel and only the gospel that has the answer: it is Christ and only Christ who saves, sanctifies and glorifies.

Islam (in its various forms) may seem to be conquering the world. Christianity may seem to be withering. Institutional churches are largely impotent. Western society may be in the grip of deadening spiritual apathy, and worse may be just over the horizon. Furthermore, false doctrine is raising its head in the churches at an alarming rate. Many believers are turning to the world, turning back to the Fathers, in a vain hope of stemming the tide. The days are dark indeed, and growing darker. Nevertheless, let us learn from 2 Corinthians 4:1-6, and take courage, and renew our efforts. Dark as it was when God brought the gospel into the world, the LORD had begun a new thing. Judaism, Greek philosophy, the might of imperial Rome, would have to fall. And fall they did.

The same applies today! Sabine Baring-Gould:

Conclusion

At the sign of triumph, Satan's host doth flee;
On then, Christian soldiers, on to victory!
Hell's foundations quiver, at the shout of praise;
Brothers lift your voices, loud your anthems raise.

Crowns and thrones may perish, kingdoms rise and wane,
But the church of Jesus constant will remain.
Gates of hell can never 'gainst that church prevail;
We have Christ's own promise, and that cannot fail.

Christ still has all power (Matt. 28:18; John 13:3; Eph. 1:22). God
still reigns. He can yet raise up men and women to do his will, and
bring about better days. We have the categorical assurance: 'Out
of... stones God can raise up children for Abraham' (Matt. 3:9). So
let us trust our Father. Faith is still the means that God uses in his
people to 'subdue kingdoms'. Others before us were those 'who
through faith conquered kingdoms... gained what was promised;
[they] shut the mouths of lions, quenched the fury of the flames,
and escaped the edge of the sword; [their] weakness was turned to
strength' (Heb. 11:33-34). While some experienced remarkable
deliverances, others did not (Heb. 11:35-38), but still they endured
by faith (Heb. 10:32-34). The age of 'these who have turned the
world upside down' (Acts 17:6, NKJV) has not yet come to an end.
Christ still says: 'All authority in heaven and on earth has been
given to me. Therefore go and make disciples of all nations,
baptising them in the name of the Father and of the Son and of the
Holy Spirit, and teaching them to obey everything I have
commanded you. And surely I am with you always, to the very end
of the age' (Matt. 28:18-20). Let us, therefore, 'be men of courage'
(1 Cor. 16:13). Let us have the spirit of the apostle, expressed in his
letter to the Ephesians:

Be strong in the Lord and in his mighty power. Put on the full armour
of God so that you can take your stand against the devil's schemes. For
our struggle is not against flesh and blood, but against the rulers,
against the authorities, against the powers of this dark world and
against the spiritual forces of evil in the heavenly realms. Therefore put
on the full armour of God, so that when the day of evil comes, you
may be able to stand your ground, and after you have done everything,
to stand. Stand firm then, with the belt of truth buckled around your
waist, with the breastplate of righteousness in place, and with your feet
fitted with the readiness that comes from the gospel of peace. In

addition to all this, take up the shield of faith, with which you can extinguish all the flaming arrows of the evil one. Take the helmet of salvation and the sword of the Spirit, which is the word of God. And pray in the Spirit on all occasions with all kinds of prayers and requests. With this in mind, be alert and always keep on praying for all the saints. Pray also for me, that whenever I open my mouth, words may be given me so that I will fearlessly make known the mystery of the gospel, for which I am an ambassador in chains. Pray that I may declare it fearlessly, as I should (Eph. 6:10-20).

I have already quoted the following passage in part. Being close to the final words Paul ever wrote in Scripture, they form a fitting climax to what I have tried to say in writing this book. Do not, I exhort you, confine these words to history, limiting them to Timothy. Above all, do not limit these words to 'professional ministers'. These words apply to you as a believer; yes, you:

In the presence of God and of Christ Jesus, who will judge the living and the dead, and in view of his appearing and his kingdom, I give you this charge: Preach the word; be prepared in season and out of season; correct, rebuke and encourage – with great patience and careful instruction. For the time will come when men will not put up with sound doctrine. Instead, to suit their own desires, they will gather around them a great number of teachers to say what their itching ears want to hear. They will turn their ears away from the truth and turn aside to myths. But you, keep your head in all situations, endure hardship, do the work of an evangelist, discharge all the duties of your ministry. For I am already being poured out like a drink offering, and the time has come for my departure. I have fought the good fight, I have finished the race, I have kept the faith. Now there is in store for me the crown of righteousness, which the Lord, the righteous Judge, will award to me on that day – and not only to me, but also to all who have longed for his appearing... Demas, because he loved this world, has deserted me and has gone to Thessalonica. Crescens has gone to Galatia, and Titus to Dalmatia. Only Luke is with me... Alexander the metalworker did me a great deal of harm. The Lord will repay him for what he has done. You too should be on your guard against him, because he strongly opposed our message. At my first defence, no one came to my support, but everyone deserted me. May it not be held against them. But the Lord stood at my side and gave me strength, so that through me the message might be fully proclaimed and all the Gentiles might hear it. And I was delivered from the lion's mouth. The Lord will rescue me from every evil attack and will bring me safely to his heavenly kingdom. To him be glory for ever and ever. Amen. (2 Tim. 4:1-8,10-18).

Let us then, open our mouths: 'Open wide your mouth and I will fill it' (Ps. 81:10). The verse may be capable of more than one interpretation, but did not the early believers prove it true in the sense in which I am taking it? Let us look to God to give us just the very words to speak. And let us preach Christ without restraint or reservation; let us 'speak the word of God more courageously and fearlessly... contending as one man for the faith of the gospel without being frightened in any way by those who oppose' us (Phil. 1:14,27-28), confident that 'this ministry', 'the mystery of the gospel', 'the glorious new covenant', will prove yet again that it is the power of God to take ruined sinners, blinded, Satan-dominated, dead sinners, and save them; that is justify, assure, sanctify and glorify them. Above all, this – and only this – will set forth 'the knowledge of the glory of God in the face of Christ'. And that, towering above all else, is what we most desire.

'May the God of peace, who through the blood of the eternal covenant brought back from the dead our Lord Jesus, that great Shepherd of the sheep, equip [us] with everything good for doing his will, and may he work in us what is pleasing to him, through Jesus Christ, to whom be glory for ever and ever. Amen' (Heb. 13:20-21).

Let this be the final word – as it will be in the history of the world:

'Christ Jesus... being in very nature God, did not consider equality with God something to be grasped, but made himself nothing, taking the very nature of a servant, being made in human likeness. And being found in appearance as a man, he humbled himself and became obedient to death – even death on a cross! Therefore God exalted him to the highest place and gave him the name that is above every name, that at the name of Jesus every knee should bow, in heaven and on earth and under the earth, and every tongue confess that Jesus Christ is Lord, to the glory of God the Father' (Phil. 2:5-11).

Appendix: Stated Preaching and Teaching[1]

In the body of the book, while I argued that every believer is a 'minister', a priest, a preacher, a teacher, I also made it clear that I am in no way speaking against a stated ministry carried out by capable men. I also indicated that I would say more about it in the Appendix. Here it is.

But I now find myself with the same problem as I had in the body of the book – but in reverse. While I now want to stress the need for a stated ministry, I do not want to give the impression that I limit 'preaching' to formal pulpit work. Indeed, I am most anxious that I should not say anything that might serve to enforce the institutional view of preaching – namely, by a clergyman standing in a pulpit, lecturing a silent audience, often with a physical (and not only physical) gap between the two. This concept owes nothing to the New Testament, but everything to the inventions of the Fathers 1800 years ago. Just because the translators have grossly overworked the word 'preach' in our Bibles, we must not allow ourselves to think instinctively in this Christendom-way every time we meet the word. While the New Testament does speak of a stated teaching ministry, the weight falls overwhelmingly on the 'informal' sort of preaching,[2] and this must not be dismissed as of little or no consequence. Informal conversation, open-air evangelism (as it is commonly called), instruction in a small group, parents instructing their children, spiritual conversation, and so on – all these, and others, come under the umbrella of 'preaching'.

Nevertheless, in this Appendix, I am primarily concerned with what I might call 'pulpit work'. Yet even in this I would not be

---

[1] From now on, to save being cumbersome, when I talk about 'preaching' I also include 'teaching', and *vice-versa*.

[2] For further material, I cannot speak too highly of David C. Norrington: *To Preach Or Not To Preach: The Church's Urgent Question*, Ekklesia Press, Omaha. Note that this edition includes an Introduction by Jon Zens and Norrington's replies to his critics, both invaluable.

misunderstood. I do not pretend that – to coin a phrase – the furniturial (I nearly said 'funereal') arrangements of our meeting houses have New Testament warrant. Personally, I much prefer to stand on a slightly raised platform openly before the people, close to them, virtually surrounded by them. I certainly do not want to be imprisoned in a coffin, cut off behind a massive desk (or worse, a wobbly lectern reaching almost to the throat). Even so, 'pulpit work' is preaching – or should be. Bearing in mind all these caveats, let us go on.

Some might object to my spending so much time on preaching. I am unrepentant. I do it because of the high importance the New Testament attaches to the subject. Indeed, it is hard to see how it could place a higher importance on it. Surely, no one can come to any other conclusion after reading words such as:

'Everyone who calls on the name of the Lord will be saved'. How, then, can they call on the one they have not believed in? And how can they believe in the one of whom they have not heard? And how can they hear without someone preaching to them? (Rom. 10:13-14).
For Christ did not send me to baptise, but to preach the gospel... For the message of the cross is foolishness to those who are perishing, but to us who are being saved it is the power of God... God was pleased through the foolishness of what was preached to save those who believe. Jews demand... and Greeks look... but we preach Christ crucified... but to those whom God has called... Christ the power of God and the wisdom of God... When I came to you, brothers, I did not come with eloquence or superior wisdom as I proclaimed to you the testimony about God. For I resolved to know nothing while I was with you except Jesus Christ and him crucified... My message and my preaching were not with wise and persuasive words, but with a demonstration of the Spirit's power, so that your faith might not rest on men's wisdom, but on God's power (1 Cor. 1:17 – 2:5).
In the presence of God and of Christ Jesus, who will judge the living and the dead, and in view of his appearing and his kingdom, I give you this charge: preach the word; be prepared in season and out of season; correct, rebuke and encourage – with great patience and careful instruction... Discharge all the duties of your ministry (2 Tim. 4:1-5).

'Christ Jesus came into the world to save sinners' (1 Tim. 1:15), and he accomplished this redemption by his cross. But that redemption is usually applied to sinners by the Holy Spirit working in and through the preaching of the gospel. Indeed, it was predicted of Christ – and he himself claimed it: 'The Spirit of the Sovereign LORD is on me, because the LORD has anointed me to preach good news to the poor. He has sent me to bind up the broken-hearted, to proclaim freedom for the captives and release from darkness for the prisoners, to proclaim the year of the LORD's favour' (Isa. 61:1-2; Luke 4:16-21). And how did Mark open his account of Christ's ministry? 'After John was put in prison, Jesus went into Galilee, proclaiming the good news of God: "The time has come", he said. "The kingdom of God is near. Repent and believe the good news!"' (Mark 1:14-15; see also Matt. 4:23; 11:5; Luke 7:22). And it is not long before Mark is recording Christ's words: 'Let us go somewhere else – to the nearby villages – so I can preach there also. That is why I have come' (Mark 1:38; see also Luke 4:43). It is this which makes it difficult to over-estimate the place of preaching in the economy of God.

J.A.James:

The end and aim of the ministry are to be gathered from the apostle's solemn and comprehensive language: 'THEY WATCH FOR YOUR SOULS AS THEY THAT MUST GIVE ACCOUNT'. There, in that short, but sublime and awful sentence, *the* end of the [ministry] is set before us. The design of the pulpit is identical with that of the cross; and the preacher is to carry out the design of the Saviour in coming to seek and to save that which was lost. Preaching and teaching are the very agency which Jesus Christ employs to save those souls for which he died on Calvary. If souls are not saved, whatever other designs are accomplished, the great purpose of the ministry is defeated.[3]

Consider the New Testament words for preaching and teaching. There are two aspects which I want to underline: the *quality* of the words which are used, and their *quantity*. In drawing attention to both the quality and the quantity, I want to show that the New Testament places a very large emphasis upon preaching, and it means something very substantial by it.

First, the *quality* of the words used for what I am referring to. The New Testament has a very rich and wide vocabulary for this

---

[3] John Angell James: *An Earnest Ministry the Want of the Times*, Hamilton, Adams & Co., London, 1848, pp18-19, emphasis his.

work – 'preaching, declaring, asserting, commanding, imploring, instructing, reasoning, proclaiming, publishing, discoursing, persuading, announcing, showing', and so on. And sometimes several Greek words are used for the one English word; that is, the original vocabulary is subdivided, in addition to having meanings which overlap each other, and so reinforce and enrich the concept.

Take 'preaching' as a case in point. There are at least eleven Greek verbs which are translated as 'preaching' or similar. Eleven! One means 'to proclaim the good news'; another, 'to be a herald, to proclaim or publish'; another, 'to be bold in speech'. In addition, some of these words mean virtually the same thing – *but not quite*. Hence the New Testament has more than one word for 'proclaiming as a herald', for instance. This, in itself, is a remarkable fact. Think of it: more than one word to describe the work of 'the town crier'! The Holy Spirit, it seems, chose to make the language, describing this great work, as rich as could be, and surely he had a purpose in so doing.

Take 'testify'. Peter, at Pentecost, preached publicly to the gathered masses; that is, 'he testified and exhorted them' (Acts 2:40, NKJV).[4] Paul, addressing the Ephesian elders for the last time, reminded them that he had 'kept back nothing that was helpful, but proclaimed it to you, and taught you publicly and from house to house' (that is, I take it, both publicly and privately) 'testifying... repentance towards God and faith towards our Lord Jesus Christ'.[5] He called this his 'ministry which [he] received from the Lord Jesus, to testify solemnly of the gospel of the grace of God'. He was able to speak of 'you all, among whom I have gone preaching the kingdom of God'. He could say he had 'not shunned to declare... the whole counsel of God' to them (Acts 20:17-27, NKJV). This shows us that 'to testify' means 'to preach the gospel to sinners', yes. But it includes far more. Look again at Paul's statements in the Acts 20 passage. And both Peter (Acts 2) and Paul (Acts 20) were clearly engaged in an activity which was public. It

---

[4] 'He warned them; and he pleaded with them' (NIV).
[5] 'I have declared... that they must turn to God in repentance and have faith in our Lord Jesus' (NIV).

was, as Paul said, 'preaching'. In Acts 8:25 (NKJV) the word 'testify' is linked with 'preach'.[6]

And in itself, 'testify' is another example of the rich vocabulary the Holy Spirit adopted – there are five or six Greek words for it. I realise that these are compounds. I further acknowledge that sometimes the word is used to mean something other than 'preaching'. Even so, there is a richness, a variety of language, based on 'testify', which *is* used for preaching, which shows that the Holy Spirit was making an important point (something the early church grasped) about this public work.

Take 'declare' as a further example. In the New Testament, there are at least eleven Greek verbs for this one English verb. Some of these overlap with some which are used for 'preaching', of course – there are not twenty-two different verbs for the two words – but there are well over a dozen. The Greek words for 'declare' are very rich indeed. They include 'to announce tidings, to announce a report, to declare fully, to signify, to report down, to conduct a narration through to the end, to relate in full, to lead out, to unfold in teaching, to declare, to make known, to declare plainly', and so on. What a vocabulary!

Teaching is linked with preaching in the New Testament (Matt. 4:23; 9:35; Acts 1:1; 5:42; 14:21; 15:35; 2 Tim. 4:2). While it can be a private business, teaching is thought of in Scripture largely as a public work, and can involve a loud voice (John 7:28, for instance). Now there are about half a dozen words for 'teaching'. Their combined meanings include 'to train, to give instruction, to instruct and train, to sound down, instruct orally, to tell down or thoroughly'. The main verb is the Greek word from which we derive 'didactic'. Teaching is linked with 'admonishing' (or with the verb 'to admonish') (Col. 1:28; 3:16), 'command' (1 Tim. 4:11).

As for the rich vocabulary the New Testament uses when speaking of preaching, 'time would fail me' to speak of 'manifest, communicate, announce, show, tell, rehearse, report, persuade, entreat, exhort, proclaim, urge, reason, explain, prove, call out, beseech' and all the rest. But just one comment on 'beseech'. The

---

[6] NIV has 'proclaimed'.

verb which is used most often in the New Testament means 'to call to one's side'. 'It is used for every kind of calling addressed to a person which is meant to produce a particular effect', whether it be to sinners for salvation, or to saints for comfort or conviction or whatever. What a rich word it is!

All this speaks of a weighty, multi-nuanced, public and authoritative work. One can understand – not, as I have explained, that I agree with them – why so many believers in the past have erected large, imposing pulpits, and used other such props for their preachers and teachers. They, perhaps, wanting to capture the biblical nuances of preaching, have resorted to carnal methods to get it. A commendable purpose but, even so, a grave mistake. As Henry Jacob, the first Independent, said in 1611 when dismissing ordination by apostolic succession: 'Christ's true ministers... have a better original'. I am not appealing for the props. As I have made clear, in my opinion they get in the way of real preaching.

But I am saying that the *quality* of the language for the work we call 'preaching' speaks of its importance. I do not deny that there is such a thing as person-to-person witnessing, conversational testimony and instruction, and so on, nor do I for a moment denigrate such. Indeed, one of the great ends of the preaching and teaching ministry is to produce a church which can, under God, nurture itself, grow spiritually and mature – and see converts. And that involves person-to-person preaching, teaching and witnessing. But there is no doubt that the New Testament does also speak of the *public* work of preaching. Heralds, announcers, declarers are in effect town criers. There is even an element of loudness, 'a lifting up of the voice' about it which is well-illustrated by the ministry of the Old Testament prophets when predicting the gospel – and which is carried over into the New Testament: 'You who bring good tidings to Zion, go up on a high mountain. You who bring good tidings to Jerusalem, lift up your voice with a shout, lift it up, do not be afraid; say to the towns of Judah: "Here is your God!"' (Isa. 40:9; 52:7-8; Nah. 1:15; Rom. 10:15; see also Isa. 41:26-27). While the Puritans did not have it all right, they were generally known as loud preachers. In other words, they announced, declared, published, proclaimed as town criers. That is, they preached![7]

So much for the quality of the New Testament words for 'preaching'. It is a rich, an abundant, vocabulary.

Now for the *quantity*, or the frequency of usage, in the New Testament, of words which speak of preaching. A glance at a concordance will quickly show how common they are. For instance, 'preaching', in its various forms, appears well over one hundred times; 'teaching' about the same. And when this is combined with the use of linked words, the conclusion is inescapable. Preaching and teaching, while not the be-all-and-end-all of church life, is a vital aspect of it. It comes first in the list in Acts 2:42 – the manifesto (apart from discipline, which was not needed at that stage) of church life until Christ shall come. It comes first in Paul's manifesto (2 Tim. 3:10). As he said: Christ had sent him 'to preach the gospel' (1 Cor. 1:17). And this was his conviction: 'God was pleased through the foolishness of what was preached to save those who believe' (1 Cor. 1:21). It pleases God still to edify saints and convert sinners by it.

Let me gather all this together. A large part of three New Testament books is taken up with public preaching and teaching; I refer to 1 and 2 Timothy and Titus. A glance through these books will show how Paul used terms like 'teach, the ministry, instruct, doctrine, command and teach, give attention to reading,[8] to exhortation, to doctrine or teaching, exhort, remind, charging, rightly dividing the word of truth, correcting, affirm constantly'. Timothy was told to

---

[7] It would be foolish in the extreme, besides being counter-productive, to use the technique of a town crier when talking to a friend. Witness Queen Victoria's complaint about Gladstone, to which I referred in the body of the book.

[8] Not the reading of sermons, of course! I know it will get me into hot water for saying it, but paper (or laptop) puts a dreadful damper on preaching. No! It is probable that Paul was referring to the public reading of such Scriptures as were available at that time. The dates of 1 and 2 Timothy and Titus – 2 Timothy was the last of Paul's letters – are significant in light of 2 Pet. 3:15-16.

'give [himself] wholly to' 'these matters', with consequent blessing promised to him and his hearers (1 Tim. 4:15-16).

When Paul explained that he was 'writing... these instructions so that... [he, Timothy] will know how people ought to conduct themselves in God's household, which is the church of the living God' (1 Tim. 3:14-15), the Spirit was recording these things so that *all the saints in all the churches for all time* should know how to behave. The alternative – that the letters to Timothy and Titus referred only to them and their particular times – is unthinkable. Such a principle would virtually negate contemporary application of any and every doctrine or practice found in Scripture.

One of the qualifications of an elder is that he must be 'able to teach' (1 Tim. 3:2). 'He must hold firmly to the trustworthy message as it has been taught, so that he can encourage others by sound doctrine and refute those who oppose it' (Tit. 1:9). Christ gives elders to his church, men 'whose work is preaching and teaching' (1 Tim. 5:17). As I have just explained, Paul wrote about these things to Timothy so that he might 'know how people ought to conduct themselves in God's household, which is the church of the living God' (1 Tim. 3:15). And what was Paul's great call to Timothy? Just this: 'All Scripture is God-breathed and is useful for teaching, rebuking, correcting and training in righteousness, so that the man of God may be thoroughly equipped for every good work' (2 Tim. 3:16-17). Having stated this, Paul thundered:

In the presence of God and of Christ Jesus, who will judge the living and the dead, and in view of his appearing and his kingdom, I give you this charge: preach the word; be prepared in season and out of season; correct, rebuke and encourage – with great patience and careful instruction. For the time will come when men will not put up with sound doctrine. Instead, to suit their own desires, they will gather around them a great number of teachers to say what their itching ears want to hear. They will turn their ears away from the truth and turn aside to myths. But you, keep your head in all situations, endure hardship, do the work of an evangelist, discharge all the duties of your ministry (2 Tim. 4:1-5).

Yes, the words applied particularly to Timothy at Ephesus. But, as I have already remarked, Paul wrote these letters – these Scriptures – for the church for all time. His words, therefore, apply to us today. To us! Especially relevant are they, please note, in days of apostasy

– who can deny that we live in such times? Above all, observe how Paul emphasises his command by reference to Christ's return. What more penetrating motive could we need, or could we have, for doing all we can to improve gospel preaching today, than the searching light of that day soon to come? In the main body of this work, I referred to Ezekiel and his sense of discharging his ministry in the sight of God and of being accountable to him.

I have written this book because I want to do what I can to provoke a better and more successful gospel preaching – both informal and formal – than we know at present, and than we have known for many years. The preaching of the gospel lies close to the cross of Christ, and is a vital part in God's way of bringing sinners to everlasting salvation. Nothing must be allowed to hinder us being the best gospel preachers we can be, whether statedly, as recognised in the local assembly, or informally as a member of the new covenant, and thus belonging to that most privileged of all select companies: the priesthood of all believers.

Printed in Great Britain
by Amazon.co.uk, Ltd.,
Marston Gate.

5917901R00144